THE MARKET: PRACTICE AND POLICY

British Association for the Advancement of Science books published by Macmillan

THE MARKET

Practice and Policy

Proceedings of Section F (Economics) of the British
Association for the Advancement of Science,
Swansea, 1990

Edited by Frank Hahn

Professor of Economics
University of Cambridge

First published 1992 by
THE MACMILLAN PRESS LTD
Houndmills, Basingstoke, Hampshire RG21 2XS
and London
Companies and representatives
throughout the world

ISBN 0–333–55651–8

A catalogue record for this book is available
from the British Library

Printed in Great Britain by
Billing and Sons Ltd
Worcester

Contents

Acknowledgement

I should like to acknowledge the contribution to the preparation of this book of Peter Simpson, Recorder of Section F, and David Reisman, Editor of the Section F Series. I should also like to thank the authors of the chapters for their contributions.

F. H.

Notes on the Contributors

Ken George is Professor of Economics and Head of Department at the University College of Swansea. He is the author of several books and articles on industrial economics.

Charles A. E. Goodhart is the Norman Sosnow Professor of Banking and Finance at the London School of Economics. Before joining LSE in 1985, he worked at the Bank of England for seventeen years as a monetary adviser, becoming a chief adviser in 1980. Earlier he had taught at the University of Cambridge. He has written a number of books on monetary economics, including *Money, Information and Uncertainty* (1989), *Monetary Theory and Practice* (1984) and *The Evolution of Central Banks* (1988).

Frank Hahn is Professor of Economics at the University of Cambridge. His many publications deal with a range of topics in economic theory, including stability, employment, growth, equilibrium and transactions costs.

Graham Loomes is currently Director of the Centre for Experimental Economics at the University of York. Previously he was Director of the Graduate Programme in Health Economics at the University of York.

Edward Lynk is Lecturer in Economics at the University College of Swansea. His recent research work has included several studies of privatised industries.

Marcus Miller is Professor of Economics at the University of Warwick and co-director of the International Macroeconomic Programme at the Centre for Economic Policy Research, London. He is co-author, with John Williamson, of *Targets and Indicators: A Blueprint for the International Co-ordination of Economic Policy* (1987) and is editing *Exchange Rate Targets and Currency Bands* with Paul Krugman.

Stephen Nickell is Professor of Economics and Director of the Institute of Economics and Statistics at the University of Oxford. He is the author of *Investment Decisions of Firms* (1978) and of numerous papers in learned journals. He is a member of the Councils of both the Econometric Society and the Royal Economic Society as well as being an associate editor of the *Economic Journal*.

Martin Weale is Lecturer in Economics at the University of Cambridge and a Fellow of Clare College, Cambridge. He is author of *Macroeconomic Policy: Inflation, Wealth and the Exchange Rate* (1989) and *British Banking: 1960–85* (1986). He is also known for his work on economic policy and economic statistics.

Paul Weller is an Associate Professor of Economics in the Finance Department, University of Iowa, and a Research Fellow at the Centre for Economic Policy Research, London. Before specialising in exchange rates and in finance theory his principal publications were in general equilibrium and in the theory of futures markets.

Introduction

FRANK HAHN

There is much debate concerning the vices and virtues of Market Economies. Recent events in Eastern Europe have re-emphasised the need for clear thinking on this matter. Not surprisingly the subject is central for economists, and has been so since Adam Smith. Yet our understanding, while not negligible, is still incomplete and studies, both theoretical and empirical, are continuing all over the world. I thought that this was a good time to disseminate both what economists know about markets and what they know that they do not know. After all, much of the public debate in the UK has been conducted between Government and Opposition, neither of which are conspicuous for a dispassionate study of the theory or of the facts. This explains the choice of general topic for the British Association meeting in Swansea.

There seem good reasons for not attempting a précis of the individual contributions which follow, here. One of these is that it would be nice to have them read. Another is that they all develop arguments and adduce evidence, to which a summary would do scant justice. I shall therefore ask the reader to be satisfied with a more general account of what is to be found in the following pages.

It was felt necessary to set the scene for the more concrete investigation into particular markets or policies. Adam Smith laid the foundation to the view that an economy where economic decisions were taken by self-regarding individuals would behave 'as if' it were co-ordinated by an 'invisible hand' – the price mechanism. No superior co-ordinating authority is required and indeed such an authority if it existed would do 'worse' than the hand. Economists have investigated the precise conditions required to hold for the Smithian claims to be fulfilled. Very many of them are not met in actual economies. One of these is the absence of 'externalities', that is, direct consequences for one (or a group of) agent resulting from the action of another. Martin Weale argues that in the case of education this condition is not met. Another requirement (noted by Smith himself) is that self-interested agents should not join together to manipulate markets – in other words to form monopolies or pseudo-monopolies. This is of particular relevance to privatisation in the UK (see Chapter 2) where private monopolies have been created. This has the required regulations to counter monopoly power and to induce more Smithian market conditions.

Yet a third requirement for prices to induce order turns on the role the future has for the present. Decisions taken today are taken in the light of beliefs of their future consequences and so on the belief of future circumstances including future prices. Goodhart discusses these matters in the context of financial markets (Chapter 3). It also is a prominent issue in foreign exchange markets (Chapter 4). Here the beliefs generated by currency bands (e.g. in ERM) and so their viability is of particular current importance. Indeed beliefs are bound to play a very important role in the functioning of markets. An important question here is whether there are mechanisms which (e.g. by learning) will lead to people having 'correct' beliefs and if so whether 'correct' beliefs which come to be held are consistent with the efficiency promised by a market economy. (There is some discussion in Chapter 1.)

But there are many other requirements which need to be met by actual market economies if they are to yield Smithian fruits. A crucial requirement turns on the information possessed by agents. How do you know whether the doctor you consult is competent or not? How do you choose the hospital which can best treat your ailments? How do you know the quality of a secondhand car? When there are information gaps institutional arrangements sometimes fill them. For instance the BMA certifies doctors and the AA cars. But this means that something more than simple markets is needed. Some of these matters are discussed by Loomes in the context of health care. (He also examines the attempt to create an internal market in the National Health Service.)

One of the difficulties faced by economic analysis of markets is to produce sufficiently simple theories which can be brought to bear on some important problems of policy. As long as one is dealing with a single sector – or very few sectors – one can hope to get the data and to solve equations. But for problems concerning the economy as a whole – say inflation or unemployment – we cannot hope to take account of the vast variety of goods and agents in any actual economy. Hence the need for macroeconomic models. Nickell (Chapter 7) provides an example of such a model and of its empirical implementation.

One needs, however, to understand that the occasion for macroeconomic policy (e.g. fiscal or monetary policy) arises if it does at all only because the market system has not delivered what Smith and his successors promised. This has caused difficulties for macroeconomists who hold the view that markets more or less fulfil the promise of the introductory text. Inevitably they conclude that macro-policy is not needed and, if employed, useless.

However it is then quite unclear why their theories are couched in the coarse form of macro-analysis. The latter for reasons of policy usefulness are formulated 'as if' there were only one ('representative') agent, labour and good. If policy is unnecessary because the elementary text says it all, then there is nothing to be said beyond the text except possibly to verify its truth empirically. But that has not been possible even with the macro-models – at least all the evidence so far produced can be disbelieved by reasonable people. I hope this paragraph makes it clear how important practical problems depend for their understanding and answer on an understanding of what market economies can deliver.

Unemployment problems (Chapter 7) provide excellent material for concrete thinking concerning markets. The market for labour is not like the market for fish – what are its special features? (One of them will turn on imperfect information on available jobs and wages by the unemployed and of the quality of a particular applicant by the firm.) Why is it possible that large unemployment and high inflation can co-exist? Is it government policies rather than market failures which are to blame? Some of the power (as well as the failings) of economics are here illustrated. The power comes from asking the right questions. For instance, if an unemployed worker prefers employment at the current wage to idleness he should be willing (so one might think) to work below the current wage. The employers surely would prefer to pay less. A mutually advantageous bargain beckons. Why is the evidence so strong that often it is not made? Asking this question has led to a vastly increased understanding of the labour market.

Everything I have discussed so far is largely concerned with understanding things as they are. This is not quite true since the economist's definition of efficiency involves some judgement of value, but not a terribly controversial one. But one now asks even if the market system works perfectly and is efficient can we judge it also to be 'good'? I need hardly remind the reader that this question is unlikely to have an answer which appears right to all reasonable men or women. However, what matters is to provide a language in which the question can be discussed without contradiction and with clarity. It is important to think hard on these matters. There are some (I do not think too much of them) who seem to believe that the 'efficient' and the 'good' are identical. Probably, if pressed, it would emerge that they do not 'really' believe this and only write as if they did. If so at the very least it is sloppy, but at the worst it is dishonest and dangerous. Those who read carefully in the literature of economics are unlikely to fall into these unlovely habits.

I end with a warning. Economics has nothing to match even Newtonian physics. It has only trivial 'laws' amongst which 'the law of demand and supply' is not one. What it does do is to separate nonsense from sense and to provide rather powerful restrictions on what is possible. This still leaves a lot of uncertainty. It may always be so. None the less even with these limitations it is of great use. It is also an invitation to think hard and clearly about a messy and complex set of phenomena. I hope the reader will do so.

1 What Markets Can and Cannot Do

FRANK HAHN

I

Marshall, who presided over this section just one hundred years ago, wrote of economics that 'it was not a body of concrete truth but an engine for the discovery of concrete truth' (p. 159). Though the engine is imperfect and still being improved, Marshall got it exactly right. Economics does provide a method by which complicated, indeed messy, phenomena may be reduced to their essentials and so, at least partly, understood. This claim which I consider to be correct should however not be misinterpreted. Understanding may, but need not, entail power of prediction nor indeed knowledge of remedies. There is, for instance, much greater understanding of cancer than there is knowledge of cures. We understand the evolution of species but would be hard put to predict the next one to emerge.

In this chapter and in those which follow our intention is to discuss economists' understanding of market economies and of particular markets. My task is confined to the first of these.

Market economies have been studied for at least two hundred years and it will not be possible to do justice to more than a fraction of what we have learned. I shall also have to do without the technical apparatus which makes for precision and economy. But my concern is not with an exposition of a large body of theory but rather with a general overview. While I shall occasionally appeal to certain results without proof, the latter will always be readily found in the literature.

II

It will be necessary to say what I mean by market economies although it is a mistake to be too much confined by definitions. Definitions often lead to tiresome disputes concerning the meaning of words. Accordingly I shall not be at all precise here. By a market economy I shall mean an economy where economic decisions, such as what and where to produce or consume, are

1

'predominantly' taken by private agents. This of course means that in considering any particular economy we may wish to argue about the scope of 'predominantly'. But nothing turns on the answer. Someone may consider central intervention weak enough so that the economy qualifies as a market economy while someone else might regard it as sufficiently extensive to want to call it 'mixed' or even planned. Nothing of substance lies behind such disagreements.

However the belief that market economies can be given precise meaning can be harmful. Thus debates, particularly political debates, are often conducted as if only two pure types of economic arrangements are possible – a pure market economy or a completely planned one. But in any actual economy there are always decisions which have to be left to private agents, and governments are always involved in economic matters. Quite evidently there is a continuum between two idealised extremes. It does not matter where on this continuum we choose to locate any actual economy provided we understand that we have more choice than is given by the two extremes.

Our topic – like indeed most topics in the social sciences – can be discussed under two broad headings: positive and normative. Roughly speaking the first of these is concerned with how market economies behave while the second evaluates that behaviour. Under neither heading can we expect definiteness. Positive analysis is incomplete both as to theory and facts. Normative analysis depends on disputable values. It is also not clear that a very strict separation between these two types of questions and their answers is possible. None the less it will be useful to keep them as separate as we can. I shall now start with the positive part of the analysis.

III

Economists have always had a lively sense of original sin. They postulate that on the whole individuals, if they are able to do so, act in their own self-interest. The latter of course may encompass their family etc. But one thing we cannot expect in the ordinary course of life is that individuals will act in 'the common interest'. The most important reason for this is that except in exceptional circumstances no one knows what this 'common interest' is and, even if known, would not know how best to further it. In a market economy actions designed to advance self-interest are limited by market possibilities while, in a highly planned economy they are likely to be limited by laws and regulations.

We owe it to Adam Smith that we have understood how an economy in which agents pursue their own interest need not be chaotic – indeed can be as orderly as it would be if an all-seeing planner had planned it. By 'orderly' we mean the following. In the light of market opportunities for buying and selling and producing, each agent decides on his/her optimum action – i.e. that action which is most to its interest. If all agents find that they can indeed carry out these actions then we say that the economy is orderly or, more usually, that it is in equilibrium. Another way of putting this is that supply is everywhere equal to demand. It is possible to construct a picture of a market economy for which it can be shown that such an equilibrium is indeed possible – i.e. it exists. This picture is a pretty abstract one and I shall return to that. But here we note, provisionally, that market economies and orderliness are not compatible. This is a much more surprising conclusion than many people appreciate. After all, our first instinct is surely to suppose that millions of people pursuing their self-interest must lead to disorder.

I hope that my phrasing of the above proposition has been noted: a market economy and order need not be incompatible. This is not equivalent to the claim that a market economy will achieve order. That claim has never been proved to be correct even for the abstract economy although there are are, alas, economists who proceed as if this were not so.

Adam Smith thought that order would be established by forces which he likened to an 'invisible hand'. Suppose that the best action of agents, given the price of apples and the prices of everything else, leads to the apples demanded exceeding apples supplied. Competition between buyers for the limited supply of apples will lead to a rise in their price. This has two effects: consumers who are less devoted to apples than are others will reduce their demand. Apple growers will see that their profits can be increased by raising the supply of apples. So one can imagine a process by which the price of apples is raised to the point at which the demand and supply of apples match and order is attained. This is the simple story which many call 'the law' of supply and demand. There is, as has been said, 'no bucking the market'.

But this account of the invisible hand is quite incomplete. In the first instance we must note that price and output changes take place in real time and not instantaneously, and that there may be many prices and outputs which are being moved by the forces I have just sketched. In other words, the question of whether the invisible hand will or will not restore order is one of dynamics. To study dynamic processes one needs to capture them in the form of dynamic equations – differential and or difference equations. Mathematicians know a good deal about such equations. Here I can do no more than assert our conclusion: the invisible hand may in certain circumstances guide the economy to its orderly state and in other circumstances it may not. This conclusion holds before taking account of further complications which I shall now discuss.

One of the complications which will feature a good deal in this chapter is that many decisions of agents taken at one date have consequences at some later date. Suppose the apple grower can store apples. Today's decision to store or to sell apples out of store will depend not only on today's price but on the price expected to rule tomorrow. It is therefore perfectly possible that apple growers taking the rise in the price of apples today as a signal that they will rise further tomorrow will reduce the apply supply to consumers in order to hold bigger stocks. If consumers have similar expectations they may actually increase their demand for apples in the face of rising prices in order to store them for the future when they expect prices will be even higher. We can see that the invisible hand may now guide the apple market away from order. Certainly speculative episodes of this sort are frequently observed.

Now economists have argued that this sort of perverse behaviour is due to our not having described a market economy properly. As far as agents are concerned a Granny Smith today is not the same thing as a Granny Smith tomorrow. Accordingly we should regard them as two different goods and so we should think of a present market for present apples and a present market for tomorrow's apples. Suppose such futures markets existed. Then there would be no need to form expectations about future prices at all. We could all carry out all the transactions we would ever wish to make today, and the speculative story which I have sketched could not unfold.

Let us consider this rather important point further. Given today's price for the delivery of apples tomorrow, both consumers and apple growers following their optimal self-interested course will decide how much of future apples to demand and supply today. If supply and demand match there plainly would be no need for the apple market to reopen tomorrow. For it could only be in equilibrium at the quantities and prices already established yesterday. So in such an economy where goods are distinguished not only by physical characteristics but by date of delivery, and where all these goods had current markets, all market transactions would take place at one date only. There could be no speculation. Moreover orderliness now implies that there is order in all markets and so for all future dates.

Adam Smith thought of markets as devices to co-ordinate the self-interested actions of a vast number of agents. Once we recognise the intertemporal aspects of economic choice of agents it is clear that for Smithian co-ordination we require intertemporal markets of the kind I have described. If some of these markets do not exist co-ordination through markets will be incomplete. That is why in the pure theory of market economies we first postulate that markets are complete. In that case the speculative aberrations I have noted will not occur. But even so our first conclusion remains intact: the invisible hand may or may not guide the economy to an orderly, that is equilibrium, resting place.

In actual economies markets are incomplete. One reason for this is that markets are costly to run. We need retailers, wholesalers, brokers and middlemen of all sorts if transactions between agents are to occur smoothly. In the absence of these middlemen, agents would have to search for partners to exchange. Another reason for incompleteness is moral hazard. Futures are promises to deliver or buy and they may not be kept. But also for goods which are not highly standardised there is the moral hazard that the quality of goods actually delivered will differ from what the futures buyers thought to obtain. For these and other reasons we should expect there to be fewer markets than are required for market economies to carry out their co-ordination task.

But that conclusion may be premature. Suppose one group of traders plan to buy oranges tomorrow at the price of oranges which they expect to hold then. Another group plans to sell oranges. If there were a futures market for oranges they would make their contract today. If that market does not exist but there is a forward market for money then the first group could sell money forward for delivery tomorrow (i.e. they could lend today) and the other group could buy money forward (borrow today). When tomorrow comes, provided everyone was correct in their forecast of tomorrow's orange price, the lenders could use the money delivered to them to buy just the amount of oranges they had planned yesterday and the borrowers could repay their loan from the proceeds of the orange sales which too would yield exactly the amount planned.

This illustrates a general conclusion: it is possible to economise in the number of markets required for co-ordination *provided agents can correctly predict* the prices which will equate demand and supply in the future. Call this the *perfect foresight* proviso. You will now notice that we have gone from the frying-pan into the fire. We started with a requirement for more markets than actual economies have. So we found a way in which a forward market in money was really all that co-ordination requires. But this in turn needed perfect foresight of future market clearing prices. It is a triumph of wishful thinking that a number of economists – mostly American – are prepared to take perfect foresight or its slightly more complex brother, rational expectations, as descriptively satisfactory. Indeed it is not too much to say that recent British economic policy sought its intellectual justification in the work of these optimistic economists.

Whatever one may think of the perfect foresight hypothesis it is now clear to all economists that the co-ordinating power of market economies depends crucially on the expectations of the participants. When the invisible hand moves it must not only perform its role of co-ordinating demand and supply but it must also somehow teach agents to have correct expectations. The agent who expected oranges to sell at six pence and found the actual price to be seven pence must learn from this and revise his next forecast. If co-ordination is to be achieved the learning process must lead to perfect foresight. One is not at all surprised by the fact that we have found it singularly difficult to establish such convergence even for very highly simplified models.

But once we have recognised the crucial role of expectations a new, and somewhat unpleasant, possibility arises: that is the possibility of an equilibrium of self-confirming beliefs. Keynes called them 'bootstrap equilibria'. Consider the following example. The economy is in equilibrium, that is, at the ruling prices there is no excess demand anywhere. Prices are correctly expected to remain constant. However, there are unemployed workers who are indifferent between working and unemployment at the going real wage. All goods are produced under constant returns. All agents hold a stock of money which is proportional to the value of their transactions. Now suppose the government increased every agent's money stock by 1 per cent in the form of a gift. It is easy to see that if everyone expects prices to rise by 1 per cent and they do so rise, nothing will have changed in the economy. If on the other hand everyone expected prices to remain constant but producers expected to sell 1 per cent more and so produced 1 per cent more, that too would be a possible new equilibrium in which expectations are fulfilled. The newly employed workers would come to hold the extra money and buy the extra output. In both cases expectations are confirmed. The example is not particularly realistic but it is only one of many. For instance, one can show that there are perfect foresight equilibria based on the self-confirming belief that the occurrence of sunspots determines prices even though sunspots have no effect on the resources of the economy. Keynes, in a somewhat looser model of the economy than the one I have been considering, thought that the belief by firms that demand was low could be self-confirming since that belief would lead to low employment and to low investment. All these examples illustrate the possibility that the outcome of market co-ordination may not reflect the true or 'fundamental' opportunities open to an economy.

I shall return to some of these matters again. But now it is time for a preliminary summing up. It is possible to demonstrate the following proposition for an ideal market economy: there are prices for present and future goods such that if they ruled, each agent can exactly carry out the actions which, in the light of these prices, are optimal for him. There is no proof that the invisible hand will lead to these prices and many non-pathological theoretical examples where it does not do so. In actual economies, because of the paucity of markets for future delivery of goods, one requires the hypothesis of perfect foresight to make Smithian co-ordination possible. But even then one cannot exclude the possibility of 'bootstrap' equilibria when beliefs rather than 'fundamentals', such as availability of resources, determine economic events.

I shall now proceed to some further discussion of the positive theory of market economies before I turn to evaluation. But before I do so I want to conclude this section with a warning. We have seen that there is no guarantee that market economies will co-ordinate as satisfactorily as one might wish. This finding may have policy implications to which I shall turn later. But it is quite insufficient to support an argument in favour of largely abandoning the system. The faults of one economic arrangement do not imply the virtues of another.

IV

I have been concerned with the question of whether a large multitude of self-interested economic decisions could be consistent with order and, if so, whether market economies would bring it about. This is an important question. For instance if it were true that often more work was supplied than is demanded – that is, if the market for labour were disorderly – then that would be of considerable concern. So would be a conclusion that the invisible hand leads to cycles in output and employment. It would also be rather serious if we concluded that certain goods and services which we collectively want would either not be provided at all or in smaller amounts than we all want. Indeed many matters of practical economic importance can be studied as aspects of the co-ordinating power and failure of market economies.

Evidently this is a large topic once we leave the general for the particular, and I shall have to concentrate on essentials. But before I do that I shall have to modify the rather abstract account which I have given so far.

So far I have described an economy in which the market opportunities of agents are known to them once they know market prices. They simply take these as given and independent of their own actions. It will have occurred to you that this leaves the question of how prices change in order to attain the values consistent with equilibrium, hanging in the air. This is indeed so and it is a difficulty which economists have resolved so unsatisfactorily that I shall refrain from describing it. The fact of course is that not all agents take prices as given and indeed that prices are set and changed by agents.

What this means is that some agents have market power. That is, they can influence the price at which they transact. In fact in a market economy agents will seek such power. For instance, producers say of motor-cars will seek to differentiate their product from that of other motor-car producers because in doing so they may, for example, raise price without losing all their customers. Workers will find that by forming unions they may do better than if their wage were fixed by an auction such as used to take place in the docks. But apart from seeking power some agents have power thrust upon them. This occurs when in some lines production is carried out under significantly increasing returns to scale. Suppose that in such a firm price were equal to the average cost of production so that there are zero profits. If such a firm could sell a little more its average costs would be lower. If a small reduction in price is all that is required for increased sales then that will be profitable. But it is clear that if it took its selling price as independent of its sales that it would have an inducement to increase its output as long as average costs are falling. That is, absence of market power is inconsistent with increasing returns.

Increasing returns to scale are also connected with some production units becoming rather large relatively to the size of the market. A monopoly is an extreme example of this. Large firms are in a strategic relation to each other in that they must calculate the reactions of competitors to their own actions. We have some interesting theories of such interactions. But one possible outcome, of which Adam Smith was very much aware, is that they will act together rather than compete by price or anything else. Competition is a strenuous and risky activity and entrepreneurs and managers, if they can, will generally prefer to do without it. In particular there is a strong incentive to discourage the entry of new potential competitors.

All of this will become relevant when we return to evaluation. Here I want to stress the modification required in the earlier discussions. Many agents in taking their decisions at any date will have to make forecasts not only of future prices but of demand at these prices. Intertemporal coordination is now more difficult because the occasions for mistakes are greater. But there is a further modification required. So far I have taken the single agent as the decision maker and forecaster. But when firms are large it is not at all clear how decisions and forecasts are made. Much of economics is still based on a picture of the nineteenth-century entrepreneur and, although work is now proceeding on understanding organisations, we are still largely ignorant.

However, a certain paradox concerning large firms has not escaped our attention. These firms typically are miniature 'command economies'. That is, they are hierarchical and are run by command. Certainly they are not market economies. But why not? If, as I have argued, markets can co-ordinate economy-wide decisions, why cannot they co-ordinate those of a firm? The favoured answer turns on transaction costs. It is argued that if, say, workers in a firm sold a good at different stages of production to each other and rented equipment from owners that this would be a slow and costly process. Moreover the 'market' inside the firm would be small and not only would time be spent on bargaining but bargaining outcomes might be unfavourable – say to the capitalists. Hence there is also an obvious Marxian explanation for the command structure of the factory system.

These explanations have merit. But they surely lead one to consider whether there are not similar arguments regarding the market economy as a whole. Economists have much neglected transaction costs in the past. But we are now taking them increasingly into account. For instance we now take account of search costs – that is, costs incurred, say, by an unemployed worker in searching for a satisfactory job or by the consumer in searching for the lowest priced good. If workers were allocated to jobs and if similar goods were similarly priced these costs would not be incurred. I think the reason why (questions of liberty and so on apart) these transaction costs in the economy as a whole would not be expected to induce a transition to an economy much more governed by command turns on information. Most large firms (but not all) are small enough to allow those in command to be reasonably informed. This is not true of the economy as a whole.

I now return to the main theme and a further aspect of market economies which I have so far neglected. When earlier I discussed the dearth of futures markets I did not consider other cases of missing markets. Here is a famous example: an apple grower and a bee keeper have their businesses close together. Each takes decisions with respect to apple output and honey so as to be most profitable for himself. But the apple grower does not only produce apples – he also produces nectar which the bee keeper can take advantage of. The bee keeper in turn does not only produce honey but also supplies pollination services to the farmer. Neither nectar nor pollination services have a market, largely because it is difficult to establish property rights in them. This is an example of externalities. They are very widespread, and occur when the action of one agent directly affects the well-being of some others. When these others are future generations who cannot participate in current markets it is clear that we cannot expect co-ordination between the generations unless one believes that parents can represent children who in turn are taken to represent their children and so on.

Externalities may be an obstacle to market co-ordination. Suppose for instance that every fisherman in a given fishing area is aware that there is overfishing which endangers his future livelihood and that he would prefer that less were caught. However unless all the fishermen involved have agreed to reduce their catch and their agreement is trustworthy, there is no sense for any one fisherman to reduce his catch. The market here fails to co-ordinate the desired actions of fishermen because the contribution each fisherman makes to reducing future stocks is not priced. There are very many such cases in practice and some of these will be discussed in subsequent chapters.

But it is once again worth noticing that it is the lack of some markets which leads to these problems. Another very striking example concerns the production of information. Such production can be costly, for instance Research and Development. However, unless they have property rights in information, self-interested agents may not go to the expense of producing it. For information can be used by anyone without reducing the amount of it available to anyone else. It is an example of a public good. Once a piece of information is available its market price would by zero. There is co-ordination failure. In actual economies some of these problems are dealt with by patents and copyright but in introducing these one recognises that failure.

V

I have been successively modifying the abstract Adam Smith economy in an attempt at greater realism. I now want to return to the question whether, even when market economies can more or less co-ordinate private decisions, they can be relied upon to do so. For a long time following Keynes it was believed that they could not without the aid of government. Now there has been a counter-revolution, especially in America, and it is claimed that market economies are sufficiently well adjusting to allow governments to do no more than hold the ring. Mrs Thatcher, for instance, has heard of this and believes it.

Once again I shall have to be rather dogmatic since these questions require lengthy attention. They are also complicated. But I believe that one can assert that both the theoretical and empirical evidence is, to put it somewhat mildly, ambiguous. No government would license a new drug given the quality of the evidence and no sensible government would pursue economic policy as if either of the claims were true. But politicians seem to need to claim certainty and then sadly come to believe their claims.

To illustrate my argument I shall concentrate on one particular problem. That problem is the market for labour.

Suppose we start with a situation where, for whatever reason, the amount of work offered exceeds the demand for it. We know the Adam Smith account of what will happen. Money wages will fall due to the competition for work. At lower money wages firms will find it profitable to employ more labour and it will be less profitable to work. Demand is increased, supply is decreased and we are on the road to co-ordination on the labour market.

But as it stands this analysis is incomplete and Keynes was quite unambiguously right in claiming this. For if, when wages fall, firms employ more labour they will wish to sell more goods and to sell more the prices of their products will also fall. Indeed theory would claim that prices will fall in more or less the same proportion as wages do. But when that happens firms have no incentive to employ more labour. It is, as Keynes argued, a fallacy of composition to go from the effect of lower money wages on a single firm to the effect on the economy as a whole.

Even now the story is not complete. When prices are lower money balances held by agents will buy more and that may have two effects. Demand for goods may increase because of higher wealth and the willingness to lend may increase because smaller money balances are required to finance transactions. The increased demand will mean that firms can sell more without prices being lowered in the same proportion as money wages and increased willingness to lend will reduce interest rates and further increase demand by encouraging more investment.

We see that lower money wages increase employment only indirectly via raising the agents' wealth represented by their money stock. Keynes argued that therefore the same outcome could be achieved by monetary policy directly without going through the risky process of money wage and price reductions. This requires some comment.

Recall that wages and prices are *falling* and distinguish that from a situation when wages and money prices are *lower*. As I have already argued, in studying adjustment processes expectations play a crucial role. Here when prices are expected to fall – that is, if the process is foreseen – at any nominal interest rate lending will be discouraged and so will be investment. That is because the expected deflation now yields a positive return to just holding money stocks. Moreover agents who expect prices to fall will tend to postpone their purchases. It can be shown that even if agents have correct expectations the *process* of adjustment may never be completed or, if it is, it will only be so after a rather lengthy and generally cyclical path has been traversed. That is why Keynes thought the invisible hand operating in the labour market to be pretty unreliable and costly and why he preferred his alternative.

You can reverse this story and study the case of an excess demand for labour. Wages and prices are now rising. If the government keeps control of the money stock the real wealth of agents will now be falling. But here too the process may be a long and chequered one. In particular it may 'overshoot' and involve the economy in lengthy episodes of excess supply of labour. Looking at the current economic situation in the United Kingdom these conclusions may not surprise you.

To all of this must be added the fact that money wages rise more rapidly than they fall and that considerations of equity – relativities – are of considerable significance. The market for labour is not like an auction market for fish. Typically workers have long-lived relations with their employers and this in itself will mean that wages will not respond rapidly to market conditions. Lastly we must remember that there is no such thing as 'labour' but a complex distribution of skill and location amongst those available for work. It may thus happen that while relatively unskilled labour is looking for work a scarcity of certain skills which are required to complement the unskilled makes the demand for the latter small. In due course relative wages may move but that may take a long time.

VI

Before turning to normative issues I shall now give a brief summary of what has gone before and discuss one further characteristic of market economies.

It can be shown that market economies and the co-ordination of the choices of a multitude of agents need not be inconsistent. Even so the co-ordination achieved is likely to be only partial. This is particularly true for public goods, for intertemporal choices, and for cases of significant increasing returns and externalities. In a later section of this paper I shall be more precise about the evaluation of co-ordination achieved by markets.

But this is only half an answer. The possibility of achieving co-ordination is not the same as the claim that it has been achieved. In general capitalist economies are in a continual process of adjustment. Partly this is so because agents are correcting mistakes and partly because new situations which had not been properly foreseen, like inventions and political changes, keep arising. Economists have been unable to show that, even on average, such adjustment processes lead to orderly outcomes. The evidence in my view is strong that market economies rarely become chaotic or even very disorderly. But I believe that it also shows, especially when combined with the theoretical evidence, that such order as is achieved may often be unsatisfactory – a point which I shall elaborate later. Taking just the one case which I have discussed, that is the labour market, I consider it quite clear that, for instance, recent arguments which discuss what one may call 'Keynesian' problems are quite insufficient for their task. The *Independent* recently labelled those who hold this view 'Bourbons'. The ignorant leader writer really meant that for a while they were not in the height of fashion. Serious economists all over the world are becoming increasingly aware that the brief intellectual episode of wishful thinking concerning the smooth running of market economies is now at an end. I re-emphasise that this does not imply any certainty of how to make them run more smoothly leave alone that there is some grand alternative.

This leads me to my last point. I have been stressing the power of markets in bringing about an orderly allocation both a-temporally and intertemporally. But anyone who has listened to Mrs Thatcher or recent American Presidents knows that this is not what makes the government marketeers. It is doubtful that they have a glimmer of the allocation problem. What, liberty apart, they find important is the efficiency and dynamism of markets. In market economies the drive for profits will see to it that producers do not produce more dearly than technological know-how and markets allow. This drive also will lead to a restless search for better ways to produce given goods and to finding new goods to produce. The economist who described these features most satisfactorily was Schumpeter. It has been difficult to formalise his analysis but there can be little doubt that he characterised an important feature of market economies. Mrs Thatcher and the Presidents are not wrong in singling out these dynamic processes.

But while market economies may be a necessary precondition for such processes to occur, they are not sufficient. One need only look to, say, Latin America to see this. Innovations for instance create at least temporary monopolies because to call them forth we require patents and in any case it takes a longish time for imitators to get their act together. As Schumpeter noted, if these monopolies grow large they become miniature states and the innovation process will be routinised in Research and Development and indeed will often be hindered. The role of the single dynamic and innovative individual will start to disappear. It is the very search for profits which carries the seeds of encouraging combinations and, importantly, reductions in competition. Paradoxically then it may well be that the virtues of dynamism of a market economy can only be preserved by non-market means such as government competition policy.

Closely connected with these arguments are the needs for incentives. Innovators take risks and so innovations must be paid for by suitable inducements. What these are is by no means clear. It can be argued that there is no absolute standard by which to judge whether one is rich or poor. These concepts seem intrinsically to involve comparisons. If no one has more than twice average earnings then those who do have twice average earnings may regard themselves as rich and be willing to take trouble to become so. The empirical evidence on these matters is poor. But there are strong indications that after a certain level the incentives are not pecuniary but rather things like power and job satisfaction. None the less it may be true that the Schumpeterian rewards only go to economies which tolerate a rather high degree of income inequality.

There is one last matter to take into account. The Schumpeterian process is not costless and indeed has many costs not adequately reflected in markets. This is quite an obvious point and I need not labour it. Not only will rapid growth make demands on exhaustible resources which will only be properly reflected in their prices if people have fairly accurate expectations. It also quite often gives rise to vast externalities. You need only think of Manchester in the nineteenth century or of many congested and polluted towns today to make further argument unnecessary. These externalities do not imply that growth and innovations are bad – indeed they may often provide the means for improved methods of dealing with externalities – but rather that they cannot be left to the market.

VII

I now finally turn to evaluation. As I warned at the beginning, one must not expect conclusive judgement. Nor is my question concerned to compare non-market economies with market ones on some scale of worthiness. Rather it is my intention to show how an argument of evaluation of aspects of market economies might proceed. I stress 'argument'. I am not interested in matters of faith.

There is a beautiful result of economic theory which I begin with. Suppose all agents take market prices as given and suppose the economy possesses all the markets which I have discussed. Then if there are no externalities and no public goods an equilibrium – that is, an orderly state of the economy – has the following property: it is impossible to improve the welfare of any one without reducing the welfare of someone else. The economy is said to be Pareto-efficient.

It is of some importance not to misunderstand this result. It requires only a weak value judgement to argue that if someone's welfare can be increased without any one else's being diminished, that it would be good to go ahead and do so. Hence for most people Pareto-efficiency may be a necessary condition for a good society. But it is not sufficient. The reason is that, as the definition makes clear, there will be a Pareto-efficient allocation for every distribution of welfare we care to have. Thus an economy with people starving in the streets may be Pareto-efficient. This kind of efficiency is a very weak tool for judging.

Now a market economy will of course generate a distribution of income and wealth. Suppose we judge it to be unsatisfactory by some moral criterion. We may then support a government policy of redistribution by means of taxes and subsidies. Here I have to report a sad fact: it can be shown that such redistribution cannot be accomplished without sacrificing some efficiency. That is, the equilibrium of the economy after redistribution will not be Pareto-efficient. In some sense then we must pay for our moral concerns – there is a trade-off between efficiency and changed income and wealth distribution. This affords an opportunity for each of us to give a more precise expression to our moral judgement: how much efficiency are we willing to sacrifice in order to attain a given distribution?

Now, still sticking to the abstract economy, we ought to see how we might argue about distributional policies. One argument which is often heard strikes me as morally illiterate. In the abstract economy it will, under certain conditions, be true that each person gets paid an amount which exactly reflects the value of his or her property's contribution to the value of total output. Everyone receives what he contributes. Hence it is maintained the distribution is just. One need only think of the cripple who can contribute nothing or of the genetically disadvantaged who can only contribute a very little to see how extremely odd this view is. After all in sport it is quite customary to impose a handicap on the ablest.

One suggestion of how an argument on these matters with oneself or others might be conducted is the following, which owes much to the insights of John Rawls. Imagine that you were to decide the question of a fair distribution in a society before you joined it or knew what position in it you would occupy. Even if you are totally self-interested, provided you are not an outright gambler, you would not vote for an extremely unequal distribution because of the risk that you would be at the bottom. One moral principle would then be that when you do join the society you should support the distribution you voted for before you knew the position in the society you would occupy. Like all moral principles this may be disputed but I believe that prolonged argument would lead this one to be accepted.

In a sense this line of argument leads to the exercise of imaginative sympathy: 'if I had been born a cripple would I have wanted to receive what an actual cripple now receives?' The idea is that much of what we are is accidental: our genes, our home life, etc. None of these seem to qualify for 'reward' in the usual sense and all of them could have been different from what they are.

Whatever the outcome of such arguments, unless they lead to what I have called the morally illiterate conclusion, we cannot expect market economies to deliver. It is quite impossible to leave this important matter to the invisible hand. Of course part of our judgement will depend on how we think distribution changes brought about by governments affect the amount which there is to distribute. I have already discussed both the efficiency loss and the possible 'Schumpeterian' loss. But even here great care must be taken to keep the argument honest. A society which for some time has been more egalitarian may also find that incentives can be provided at lower levels of inequality. Incentives, as I have already argued, depend much on comparisons. These in turn affect self-esteem which in turn will be much influenced by social norms. I have to confess that I regard the nurturing of an exclusively self-regarding norm by the government as not only unnecessary for its purpose but also as unhelpful.

Let us now return to the abstract economy. In very many respects which I have discussed it does not correspond to actual economies. These have externalities and many agents cannot take prices as given. In addition there are many public goods which we might want and which the market does not provide. In subsequent chapters a number of these matters will be examined in more detail. In this chapter I simply want to make clear in what sense the market may fail us. As before, I shall restrict myself to examples.

Consider television. One person watching does not restrict any one else's ability to watch. Nor does his watching affect the cost and use of resources in transmitting. Since, however, transmitting programmes is costly, it needs to be financed. One market solution is to do so by selling advertising time. But this means that viewers may now pay in the form of being forced to consume unwanted advertisements. Incidentally it may also adversely affect programmes. Another solution would be metered television. The consumer now pays directly. This may prevent his viewing some programme because it is not worth the price to him although if he were charged only the cost of his viewing – that is, zero – he would view. This is not Pareto-efficient. If some means could be found whereby the consumer pays a fixed charge independently of his viewing that would be consistent with efficiency, although distributional considerations may lead one to object to this. None the less the efficient market solution is closer to the present method of financing the BBC than it is to that of financing independent television. But it is doubtful that the market would have led to this. One sees here how it may be possible for public policy to improve on the market as far as efficiency is concerned.

Or take roads. As long as they are not congested the cost imposed by any car travelling on it is very small. Pareto-efficiency then tells us that any toll levied should not exceed this small cost. The income from the small toll may not suffice to finance the building of the road. It may then not be built even though everyone using the road together would have been willing to finance the initial investment and then travel at the small toll. The market cannot co-ordinate these people and so we either sacrifice the road or efficiency.

There are of course very many examples and most of them are important to the quality of life. One should notice now that while it is true that there should not be a disparity between private and public rates of return, at the time of decision to provide such a good it is very important that these returns be properly calculated. In particular, externalities of all kinds must be taken into account. For instance a low pecuniary return on railways is not a reliable signal telling us to put less into them. The externalities in saving congestion on the roads, reducing pollution and providing social cohesion need to be calculated.

What all of this amounts to is this. There are some things markets either cannot do or do only inadequately. I have tried to give a general characterisation. The conclusion does not mean that we should do without markets but rather that we should devise means of filling gaps and making them work better. The view, for instance, that public investment is always less productive than private is a sign that the mechanism of market economies has not been understood.

Lastly, and briefly, there is the vast question of macro-policies. It is of course mistaken to believe that a government can renounce them. Whatever it does even when, for instance, it stabilises the money supply, amounts to a policy. The question is not: should we have a policy?, but what kind of policy should we have? I have several times stressed our ignorance and it is proper that any policy should take it into account. But it is not true that market economies left to themselves must lead to there being excess or insufficient demand. In either case some use of fiscal and/or monetary policy may aid the adjustment process. Indeed, if such a policy is known in advance it may make maladjustments rarer or lead to their more rapid disappearance. The view which you may have encountered that such policies are bound to be ineffective is based on the hypothesis that the economy is already perfectly orderly. But of course that is precisely the case when such policies are not needed.

The reason why we should not give up our search for good policies of this sort is this: fluctuations in economic activity create uncertainty and often randomly distributed losses in welfare. The uncertainty may inhibit Schumpeterian forces. There is no convincing argument that these are inevitable concomitants of a market economy which could not be improved upon without destroying the latter. The arguments here are somewhat akin to those that in previous centuries regarded disease as beyond control. I do not claim that economists have now watertight policy suggestions. But I do claim that it is important that the search for policies which reduce the unwanted costs of market processes should continue.

VIII

My theme has been large: too large for a single chapter. But I hope to have whetted the appetite for serious thinking of non-economists and reminded economists how important their habit of analysis can be to us. The failure of command economies and the comparative success of many market economies have evident lessons. But they will not be understood unless the bounded possibilities of market economies are understood. Just as, in the thirties, many wrongly took the depression as not only evidence against markets but in favour of command economies and took it so, as we know, mistakenly, so the failure of command economies is not evidence for unblemished market economies. We must learn to think of these issues with a cool head, a sober eye, and no faith.

2 Privatisation

KEN GEORGE and EDWARD LYNK

INTRODUCTION

One of the main interests of economists is in the performance of firms. There are two major themes in the literature, one concentrating on the interrelationships between industrial structure and business conduct and performance; the other looking at the way in which business performance might be influenced by the form of ownership and control. It is with the second of these themes that privatisation is most directly concerned, but the first theme is also important because every major privatisation has been accompanied by debate on whether or not there should be some measure of industry restructuring. It is instructive therefore to sketch very briefly some of the main findings of theoretical and empirical work on the interrelationships between structure, conduct and performance, before turning to an examination of the effect of ownership on efficiency.

STRUCTURE, CONDUCT AND PERFORMANCE

For around a century, up to about 1970, the conventional wisdom was that the causal relationship ran in the main from structure to conduct to performance. In particular, it was argued that in highly concentrated industries, and especially where dominance is combined with high barriers to entry, firms are able to employ a variety of anti-competitive practices which result, amongst other things, in excess profitability. Over the past twenty years, however, the new theorising in industrial organisation has challenged this mono-causal relationship. There has been much emphasis, for instance, on the efficiency-enhancing effects of business conduct leading to the conclusion that high concentration may well be the result of the superior efficiency of large firms. In particular, the new thinking has challenged the view that vertical price and non-price restraints can be adequately explained by appeal to anti-competitive motives, emphasising instead the efficiency-enhancing effects of these restraints. Another development has been to view conduct strategically. Expenditure decisions relating to research and development (R & D), product differentiation, and capacity extensions may all contain a strategic element designed, for instance, to deter entry. Most recently considerable prominence has been accorded to contestable markets. If a market is contestable the desirable goals of cost minimisation and allocative efficiency are achieved whatever market structure happens to exist. However limited contestability theory might be in its practical applications it has served to emphasise the importance of entry in determining industry performance.

Although there are several points of conflict between the old and the new theorising (Shepherd, 1989), there are also important areas of agreement and some useful pointers that arise from the sum total of accumulated theoretical and empirical work.

First, competition is important in achieving internal and allocative efficiency. But competition can also be excessive, i.e. some degree of monopoly power also has a positive role to play. The concept of an optimal balance between competition and market power is an elusive one but none the less important; and given that the detailed circumstances of individual industries differ, so the optimal balance will vary across industries. For instance, in summing up the evidence on the relationship between R & D and industry structure, Scherer (1980) concludes: 'What is needed for rapid technical progress is a subtle blend of competition and monopoly, with more emphasis in general on the former than the latter, and with the role of monopolistic elements diminishing when rich technological opportunities exist'.

Second, entry conditions are important. All industrial organisation theories are agreed on this. However, once again theory suggests that under certain circumstances there can be too much entry lending to destructive competition and lower welfare (von Weizsacker, 1980).

Third, the new theorising has pointed to the possible efficiency enhancing effects of many business practices that were traditionally regarded as anti-competitive. For instance, in a world in which there are information costs and transactions costs it will pay a firm to commit resources to advertising and other activities which enables it to build up a clientele. It will do so by establishing a reputation for reliability, value for money, and a willingness to emphasise long-term relationships with customers rather than to pursue a policy of making the most of every short-run profit opportunity. These efforts at developing the firm's goodwill inevitably create barriers to entry. In his analysis of advertising expenditure as a barrier to entry Demsetz (1982) argues that 'it is the combination of information costs, the creation of a reputable history, and the commitment of industry-specific investment, not advertising, per se, that constitutes the barrier'. He goes on:

a reputable history is an asset to the firm possessing it and to the buyer who relies on it because information is not free. A property right system that affords patent, copyright and trademark protection, and that makes antitrust divestiture difficult is one that encourages investment in permanence and discourages investment in fly-by-night operations.

In a similar vein Okun (1981) argues that

> the customer market view . . . accepts the attachment between buyer and seller as an inherently desirable institutional arrangement that economises on the expenses of shopping, trying out products, and otherwise engaging in transactions. . . . Society pays the cost of monopoly elements and collects the benefits of genuine economies of transactions.

This emphasis on continuity and long-term commitments is important because many of the most important efficiency benefits are achievable only when firms adopt a long enough time horizon in decision making. At the same time however the policy dilemma increases because it becomes more difficult to distinguish anti-competitive from innocent business responses. For instance, carrying excess capacity may be a sound business strategy in a growing market with lumpy investment, especially in one where there is an obligation to supply. But it may also be an example of strategic entry deterrence. Similarly, brand proliferation may be an effective way of deterring entry but it may be no more than a response to consumer demand: at what point does product differentiation become excessive and anti-competitive?

The dilemma is partially, but only partially, resolved by the fourth pointer. Both the old and the new schools of thought suggest that the finger of suspicion should point more confidently at firms in positions of dominance and where dominance has been persistent. Summing up the current state of knowledge on strategic entry deterrence Ordover (1990) concludes that

> policy prescriptions in this area must be imprecise indeed. The rule of reason approach suggests that antitrust policy ought not to interfere with the conduct of firms with small market shares. It should impose more stringent demands on dominant firms, although what constitutes dominance is a matter for policy to resolve.

In general, policy has indeed focused on dominancy, and when abuse of a dominant position has been unearthed the policy solution, more often than not, has been to control some aspect of business conduct. Occasionally a structural solution has been adopted as in the cases of Standard Oil and AT & T in the USA and the brewing industry in the UK. But what if there are technological or other benefits in having one supplier? In the UK the answer in the past was public ownership. This, it was hoped, would preserve the benefits of single firm supply without exposing the consumer to monopoly abuse. Reality, however, did not match up to theory. In particular, through the 1960s and 1970s there was a growing conviction that public ownership and internal efficiency were incompatible.

OWNERSHIP AND EFFICIENCY

What is the relationship between internal efficiency and the form of ownership and control? Are there good reasons to expect internal efficiency to be more easily attainable under private than under public ownership? These questions belong to a more general set of problems known as *principal–agent* or *agency* relationships. A principal–agent relationship exists when one party (the agent) agrees to act in the interests of another party (the principal). Thus managers are appointed by shareholders to run companies on their behalf. Likewise the government appoints managers to run nationalised undertakings in accordance with policies laid down by Parliament. Two conditions are necessary for agency relationships to pose interesting problems. First, the agent's objectives must differ from those of the principal. Second, the principal must have access to less information than is available to the agent, e.g. on cost, market conditions and the agent's behaviour. There is in other words a problem of asymmetric information and thus a need for monitoring the agent's behaviour and performance.

Agency-type relationships exist between managers and other employees as well as between owner and manager. At the latter level, which is the one that interests us here, these relationships pose no problem in firms where there is no divorce between ownership and control, e.g. the single proprietor who also manages the firm. A problem does exist, however, in large firms where, typically, there is a degree of divorce between owner and manager and where organisational complexity together with imperfections in product and capital markets allow managers to pursue objectives other than the maximisation of shareholders wealth. On the face of it the agency problem would appear to be more acute under public ownership and this forms an important aspect of the argument in favour of privatisation. In large part this is due to the fact that there are more layers of responsibility and thus more opportunity for directives to be distorted, messages misunderstood and grievances left unresolved. The management board is given directives by a government minister who is answerable to Parliament, which in turn represents the owners, who are the taxpaying public. In addition there are civil servants who advise the minister and the rest of the Cabinet who may not support him on key issues. There are more principal–agent relationships therefore than one would find in a typical large private company. The objectives of the various parties involved are also liable to display more variety, so the potential for conflict is greater. For instance, in transport, social as well as economic objectives are likely to be important to the 'owners'. Governments have indeed often set nationalised industries social as well as economic objectives but the trade off between the two has never been entirely clear. This reflects the fact that, given the different weights attached to these objectives by members of the public, the trade off *is* not clear. This in turn allows politicians wide discretion and ample opportunity to manipulate the weights accorded to economic and social objectives in decision making for maximum political advantage. The setting of several, possibly conflicting, goals also increases the scope for managers to exercise discretion.

It would seem, therefore, that there is an *a priori* case in favour of privatisation. The argument rests upon the incentives structure and constraints implicit in the operation of markets. More specifically, the following arguments can be advanced.

1. The profit motive provides *incentives* which are largely absent in state-owned corporations; generally, rewards are more closely linked to performance.
2. Privately owned firms have a clearly defined objective – the maximisation of profits – which is easy to monitor. This aids the co-ordination of effort within the firm. State owned firms, however, have to pursue a mixture of economic and social goals which results in inefficiency in day-to-day operations and ambiguities in pricing and investment decisions.
3. Private companies are more responsive to market conditions and will more readily take advantage of new opportunities such as diversification into new growth areas. This is aided by the fact that privately owned firms have greater freedom in raising capital.
4. Private companies are not plagued by government intervention when making decisions on prices, wages, investment, location etc., whereas such intervention is common in the public sector.
5. Private companies are more accountable to their owners who are better

able to monitor performance and organise a revolt against inefficient management.

6. Efficiency is encouraged in privately owned companies not only by the profit motive and clearly defined objectives but also by the threat and occurrence of take-over.

There are a number of comments that can be made about these alleged advantages of privatisation. In the first place many of the weaknesses of public bodies could be remedied without change of ownership, by, for instance, the use of performance targets and the putting in place of more effective monitoring systems. These have been regular themes in the Monopolies and Mergers Commission (MMC) reports on public sector bodies. In addition, remuneration could be linked more closely to results, there could be greater freedom in raising capital, and the government could adopt a more arm's length approach to day-to-day operations. There is no doubt that if there has been a failure on the part of public corporations to respond to new opportunities, this has in part been government imposed. For instance, while under ownership British Gas had successfully diversified into oil exploration but was forced by the government to divest itself of this activity. In the run-up to privatisation one of the advantages which the minister claimed for the change of ownership was the freedom which the new company would have to diversify into new areas, including oil exploration! Having said this, however, there is no disputing the fact that it has proved difficult under public ownership to find an effective arm's length regulatory mechanism with a consistent set of objectives. This difficulty provided one of the more compelling arguments in favour of privatisation.

The second observation is that many of the advantages claimed for private ownership have been much exaggerated, especially in relation to large firms, which is the appropriate comparison to make. Managerial incentives may be severely attenuated in large companies; and the vested interest of different groups within the firm may make it difficult to set clearly defined objectives (Williamson, 1963; Cyert and George, 1969). For a variety of reasons, shareholders may fail to exercise effective control on management. For instance, where shares are widely dispersed the incentive for any group of shareholders, who hold a small proportion of a company's equity, to intervene in managerial decisions is weakened by the free rider problem. Furthermore, the alternative to getting deeply involved with management is to dispose of shares, and in Britain the choice which institutional shareholders in particular have between active supervision and passive portfolio adjustment has generally been exercised in favour of the latter. As far as the discipline of the takeover mechanism is concerned it is true that not even very large companies are immune. Even so it is not a credible threat to the very largest of the public utilities. In any case as a mechanism for enhancing efficiency the market for corporate control works very imperfectly (Singh, 1971; Meeks, 1977; Kumar, 1984). There is also some evidence to suggest that too high a threat of takeover induces firms to take an unduly short view in decision making with adverse effects on long-run efficiency.

The evidence on business performance also falls short of giving unqualified support to private ownership. The UK manufacturing sector is littered with examples of firms that have failed to respond to market forces. Several of the companies that went bankrupt (e.g. British Leyland – later the Rover Group now part of British Aerospace; Ferranti – now part of GEC, and Rolls-Royce –now part of Vickers) were rescued out of public funds. Other companies, now privately owned, such as Britoil, Enterprise Oil and Amersham International, would not have existed but for initiatives taken in the public sector. The post-privatisation performance of companies operating in competitive markets has also been mixed (Yarrow, 1989; George, 1990). Finally, comparisons of productivity performance in the public and private sectors suggest that nationalised industries have performed well – at least relative to the average performance of all manufacturing. The results of two such studies are shown in Table 2.1. Particularly

TABLE 2.1 *Productivity changes (output per head)*

	1960–75 (% change) (a)		1968–78 (% per annum) (b)	1978–85
British Airways	150	British Airways	6.4	6.6
British Gas	242	British Gas	8.5	3.8
Electricity	127	Electricity	5.3	3.9
Coal	25	Coal	−0.7	4.4
Postal services	−6	Post Office	−1.3	2.3
Telecommunications	169	British Telecom	8.2	5.8
		British Steel	−0.2	12.6
		British Rail	0.8	3.9
All manufacturing	51	All manufacturing	2.7	3.0

(a) Source: National Economic Development Office, *A Study of UK Nationalised Industries* (London: HMSO, 1976).
(b) Source: R. Molyneux and D. Thompson, 'Nationalised Industry Performance: Still Third Rate?', *Fiscal Studies*, 8(1) (1987), 48–82.

striking is the remarkable improvement in the performance of British Steel and to a lesser extent of coal and rail after 1978. True, the improvement in steel was from a very low base in the mid 1970s when there was a very high level of overmanning. But the transformation of the company from the bottom end to the top end of the worldwide efficiency league table demonstrates what can be achieved under public ownership. It is tempting to attribute part of the improved performance of publicly owned corporations in the 1980s to the threat (or, to managers, the lure!) of privatisation but this is an unlikely explanation for coal, rail, and postal services, or indeed for steel, which was not privatised until 1988. A more likely explanation is the simpler one of greater government resolve to increase efficiency.

On the yardstick of financial performance, however, the public sector has performed badly. For instance, over the ten-year period 1970–79 the gross trading surpluses, net of subsidies, of all public corporations averaged 4.3 per cent of the net capital stock at replacement value. By comparison, for all industrial and commercial companies, gross trading profit as a percentage of net capital stock at replacement cost averaged 17.1 per cent. This discrepancy was undoubtedly due in part to the low level of internal efficiency already alluded to. However, it is also due in part to monopoly price distortions in the private sector and government price controls in the public sector – the latter being justified in some cases at least as a policy response to externalities. More generally, the use of profit as an indicator of efficiency is valid only if the price of a good or service reflects society's valuation of it relative to other commodities, and if the cost of inputs reflects the social value of those inputs. When these conditions do not hold as a result of monopolistic price distortions or externalities, financial measures may be a poor indicator of relative performance.

Whatever the relative importance of internal inefficiency and market failure in explaining the poor financial performance of the public corporations up to 1979 it is clear that after 1979 the policy emphasis was to improve that performance and to progressively reduce subsidies. Internal efficiency was the goal and allocative efficiency was pushed into the background. This was evident during the dispute over pit closures in the early 1980s when financial performance clearly dominated wider economic and social concerns (George *et al.*, 1988). It is also evident in the government's policy towards the railways. Here, as elsewhere, the drive for greater efficiency is commendable, but the goal of eliminating all public subsidy will be achieved at a high cost in terms of allocative efficiency. During the last decade subsidy has become a dirty word and wider economic efficiency arguments have stood little chance when confronted with the virtues of financial rectitude. Another aspect of this problem is that emphasis on profitability and measurable productivity improvements may be at the expense of the quality of service. This is an important issue in both the privatised utilities and in many activities in the public sector. We will be returning to the problem later in the chapter.

THE PRIVATISATION OF MONOPOLIES

The public asset sales that have attracted most attention have been those, and in particular the major utilities, where the firm has considerable market power. The first such privatisation was that of British Telecom (BT) in 1984. This was followed by British Gas (1986), the British Airports Authority (1987), the regional water authorities (1989) and Electricity (1991). In these cases the degree of market power enjoyed by the monopoly incumbents is such that there would be general agreement that some exposure to competition would have a beneficial impact on both allocative and internal efficiency. There is a problem, however, in that the opportunity for introducing competition without losing some of the benefits of scale may be limited by natural monopoly elements in industry structure.

The monopoly problem was recognised in the deregulation legislation of the early 1980s. The Telecommunications Act 1981 and the Oil and Gas (Enterprise) Act 1982 heralded the introduction of more competitive markets. In some areas of telecommunications, such as the retailing of customer apparatus and certain value-added network services, a substantial increase in competition has occurred with noticeable benefits to consumers. In BT's core network operations, however, the government has deliberately restricted competition. Mercury was licensed as a new network operator in 1982, its aim being to take a small percentage of the lucrative business market. The privatisation of BT in 1984 was seen by some commentators as an ideal opportunity for creating a more competitive industry structure along the lines of AT & T divestiture in the US. However, the government announced that no new licences for network operation would be issued before 1990. Thus the market structure was left with a dominant supplier facing limited competition from the much smaller Mercury Communications Co. (now part of Cable and Wireless), and a local network company operated by Hull City Council.

In the case of gas, the Gas Act 1986, which privatised the British Gas Corporation, gave the privatised company a monopoly in the supply of tariff (mainly domestic) customers but, in line with the 1982 legislation, allowed new entrants into the contract business (generally large industrial and commercial users). Any new entrant would of course have to use

British Gas (BG) pipeline systems and would have to negotiate terms including matters relating to safety of supply. In the event deregulation failed to induce any new entry.

BG also has very substantial vertical market power. It has been a monopoly purchaser of gas from UK gas fields, a monopoly which, a recent MMC report recommended, should be ended (see below). Another MMC report in 1980, on the supply of domestic gas appliances, was highly critical of the Corporation's conduct as a dominant buyer, and concluded that its retailing monopoly was against the public interest. The MMC offered two possible solutions. Either the Corporation should withdraw from the retailing of gas appliances, or a number of restrictive practices should be abandoned which would have the effect of reducing its power as a retailer. In July 1981 the Minister of State for Consumer Affairs announced that the Corporation would be required to cease selling domestic appliances and dispose of its showrooms over a five-year period. However in October 1981 the Secretary of State for Energy announced that the sale of gas showrooms would be delayed until complex safety legislation had been debated in Parliament, but that the Government remained fully committed to breaking up the monopoly as soon as possible. The management of the British Gas Corporation argued vigorously against enforced division and four years later the government announced its intention to privatise the corporation intact!

The government also set its face against restructuring in the case of the British Airports Authority (BAA). BAA owns and operates seven airports in Britain – Heathrow, Gatwick and Stansted near London, and Prestwick, Glasgow, Edinburgh and Aberdeen in Scotland. Competition between airports is bound to be blunted by the inevitable government involvement in this sector. In view of the sensitive environmental issues, and other externalities, it would be naive to imagine that airports could be allowed to engage in unfettered competition. Even so a beneficial increase in competitive pressure by, for instance, privatising the three London airports as separate companies, could have been achieved without jeopardising the government's legitimate concern with wider issues. The possible benefits, which are examined in detail by Starkie and Thompson (1985), include more competition for off-peak business thus making better use of capacity, and more information to the regulatory authority which would be beneficial in the setting of regulatory standards. However, the government argued that any benefit from a more competitively structured industry would be very limited and would be more than offset by efficiency losses. Doubtless, the government was also concerned with the proceeds of the asset sale. In addition, and as in the case of British Gas, the management of BAA campaigned vigorously against enforced division of the company.

For telecommunications, gas, and airports it would appear that a more competitive industry structure could have been achieved without loss of efficiency. In view of the MMC's highly critical 1980 report on the sale of gas appliances more effective measures would have been justified at that end of the market. The area gas boards could also have been privatised as separate companies – a policy which has been adopted in the case of the electricity supply industry. The same can be said of BT and the privatisation of local networks as separate companies, and also of the division of BAA into two or more separate entities. In all three cases reducing the size of the company would have reduced the scope for anti-competitive behaviour. Decision making would have been spread more widely and the existence of a number of separate companies would have allowed performance comparisons to be made which would have facilitated the setting of standards for regulatory purposes.

Empirical Evidence on Costs

To what extent, however, would restructuring be achieved at the expense of economies of scale or of scope. The privatisation programme was initiated with virtually no information concerning the nature of cost conditions within the industries concerned. The purpose of this section is to examine the empirical evidence that has been collected on the nature of the cost functions in those industries that have been privatised or are canvassed as potential candidates for privatisation. In particular we are concerned with the extent to which the chosen (or hypothesised) industry structure post-privatisation is consistent with the pre-privatisation cost configuration, and hence the extent to which privatisation can be expected to yield efficiency savings.

In order to assess the appropriate structure of an industry information is needed on the nature of cost and production conditions within the industry. Of particular importance is an assessment of the extent to which the industry cost function exhibits subadditivity. Until fairly recently conventional wisdom suggested that the existence of substantial economies of scale for a given level of demand was sufficient to confer natural monopoly status upon an industry. However, advances in the theory of the multi-product firm together with a more precise definition of cost complementarities have revealed the inadequacies of such a definition for modern multi-product industries. A multi-product firm is a (static) natural monopolist if, and only if, the cost function defined over all outputs is globally subadditive. That is, for any given level of production of (two) outputs Y_1, Y_2, the following holds:

$$C_a(Y_1, Y_2) + C_b(Y_1, Y_2) > C(Y_1, Y_2)$$

where $C_a(\,.\,)$, $C_b(\,.\,)$ refer to the costs associated with hypothetical two-firm production. Hence an industry is a natural monopoly for a given vector of outputs if single firm production is more efficient than multi-firm production. Baumol, Panzar and Willig (1982) have shown that the simultaneous existence of economies of scale and of scope between a set of outputs is sufficient to ensure local subadditivity of the cost function. Significant scale economies are believed to characterise the production technologies of several major utilities. It is also believed that many enjoy the benefits of joint production, with economies of scope characterising the production of a range of outputs. Joint production generally arises because factors of production which are required in the production of one output are available costlessly for the production of another, i.e. these factors exhibit the characteristics of a 'public' input. Hence an economy of scope is essentially an unavoidable externality in multi-product production. Major sources of scope economies and cost complementarities are believed to be found in the high levels of fixed and sunk costs implied by the network operations of the public utilities.

In the UK, analysis of joint production has been carried out for telecommunications (BT was privatised in 1984), water (privatised in 1989) and the Post Office which is a possible future candidate for privatisation.

In the case of telecommunications restructuring proposals have taken three forms. One of these, advocated by Beesley and Laidlaw (1989), involves the liberalisation of entry and the introduction of competition into several service areas. Underlying these proposals is the belief that technical advances in making network facilities compatible with more than one carrier has removed the significant sunk cost elements likely to deter entry. More radical proposals (Beesley and Littlechild, 1986; Vickers and Yarrow, 1988) involve the restructuring of BT. Beesley and Littlechild advocate the separation of internal (local and trunk) from external (international) voice telephony services. 'The starting structure for the successor private company or companies is extremely important . . . . If, for example, British Telecom's international division were separated from the inland division, each would encourage alternative sources of supply . . .' Vickers and Yarrow recommend the separation of local and long distance (inland trunk and international) services, and point to the efficiency gains that have resulted from the divestiture of AT & T in the United States. Important efficiency gains from this form of restructuring also appear to have occurred in Japan.

Foreman-Peck and Manning (1987) and Hunt and Lynk (1990a, 1990b) have analysed these proposals using similar time-series data sets from the

Reports and Accounts of the Post Office for the period 1951/52 to 1980/81 before telecommunications was hived off as a separate business. Foreman-Peck and Manning estimate a straightforward translog cost function that permits the identification of cost complementarities between local and long-distance voice services. They find no evidence of joint production. Hunt and Lynk address both the Beesley–Littlechild and Vickers–Yarrow proposals using recent advances in non-stationary time series analysis. In particular they use the correspondence between 'error-correction' and cointegration mechanisms as elucidated in the Granger Representation Theorem (Engle and Granger, 1987) to estimate dynamic disequilibrium multi-product cost functions with steady state solutions that permit the identification of cost complementarities between outputs (see appendix for details). Hunt and Lynk (1990a) find no evidence of joint production between local and long-distance services thus confirming the results of Foreman-Peck and Manning. However, they *do* (1990b) find evidence of cost complementarities between internal and external services. Therefore, whereas joint production appears to occur between trunk and international services there is no evidence of such a relationship between all three types of services, suggesting that the divestiture of local from long-distance services would not involve efficiency losses.

In water privatisation a major issue has been the removal of the environmental activities from the regional water authorities to the National Rivers Authority. This has meant the abandonment of the principle of 'integrated river basin management' (IRBM) the virtues of which were extolled in the 1986 Water Bill.

> The catchment-based structure of the water industry has worked well in practice. It has been recognised throughout the world as being a good and cost effective model for other countries to follow. It is the main reason why the Government intends to retain the structure of the water authorities essentially as they stand in the transfer to private ownership (Department of the Environment, 1986).

The rationale for the change in the government's thinking was that self-regulation of environmental issues was unacceptable under private ownership because of the danger that financial targets might be met by relaxing environmental standards. However, although IRBM *does* imply the integration of water supply, sewerage, and environmental activities it *does not* imply self-regulation of any of them. Though privatisation necessitated the setting up of an external regulatory body it did not require the separation of services. Hunt and Lynk (1989) estimate a multi-product cost function which permits the identification of cost complementarities between the three activities, using pooled cross-section time series data for the period 1979/80 to 1980/87. They find substantial cost complementarities between water supply and environmental activities and also between water supply and sewage treatment. These findings suggest that divestiture of environmental activities has resulted in efficiency losses.

Finally, several proposals have been made concerning the restructuring of the Post Office (cf. Senior, 1989; Albon, 1987, 1988). These include the separation of mail from counter services and the separation of letters from parcels. Indeed within the Royal Mail, letter, parcel, and counter services are already operated as separate divisions. Hunt and Lynk (1991) estimate a dynamic disequilibrium multi-product cost function for the period 1951/2 to 1987/8. They find no evidence of joint production between mail and counter services. In fact, the evidence suggests that joint production of these services results in diseconomies. Within mail service activities, however, they do find evidence of significant cost complementarities between letters and parcels suggesting that separation of these activities leads to higher costs.

Empirical work suggests considerable differences in the nature and form of the pre-privatisation cost functions of public utilities. Joint production seems to characterise certain areas of water, telecommunications and postal services, but not others. A major concern is that policies of divestiture may have been applied in areas where they should not have been, and have not been applied where substantial benefits might have been available. Thus BT was privatised intact, with all its massive market power, yet the evidence strongly suggests that divestiture along the lines of AT & T in America would have resulted in substantial benefits. Conversely, the acknowledged advantages of IRBM were lost when environmental activities were taken away from the regional water companies.

Proponents of the particular path which privatisation has followed will argue that the empirical evidence is relevant to pre-privatisation cost functions, whereas the aim of privatisation is to shift those functions. In other words, the empirical evidence is by no means conclusive, especially in a dynamic context where competitive conditions change and where technical progress is continually influencing cost configurations. However, it is clear that in several cases the post-privatisation cost configurations would need to be radically different to upset the conclusions that have been presented.

REGULATORY PROBLEMS

Even where there is some scope for restructuring utilities along more competitive lines it may well be very limited and still leave the industry far short of being effectively competitive. In major industries, such as the utilities, where firms have substantial market power and/or where there are important externality problems, some form of regulation would still be needed. This section examines some of the problems encountered in regulating monopolists, particularly multi-product monopolists, and looks at the rather limited amount of evidence available in the UK on the effectiveness of the regulatory mechanisms that have been adopted.

Price Controls and Efficiency

A central feature of regulation is some form of price control, and a central objective is the maximisation of allocative and internal efficiency. In setting allowable prices the regulator will want to ensure that the firm will not only be able to recover its costs over the regulatory period, but that it will also earn a 'fair rate of return'.

Since allocative efficiency depends upon relative prices and costs there is a good case for indexing allowable prices to the prices of a suitable basket of other goods and services. In addition, it may be possible to foresee that real costs in the regulated firm should fall as a result of unusually rich opportunities for technological advance or above average growth in demand, in which case these forecasts can be incorporated into the pricing formula. Thus in the case of British Telecom (BT) an RPI-X formula was adopted so that in any one year BT could not increase the average price of its regulated services by more than the increase in the retail price index *minus* a figure initially set at 3 percentage points. The formula can be further elaborated by linking it to changes in the cost of one or more inputs. If these costs are largely under the firm's control the pricing formula would then incorporate the disadvantages of cost plus pricing, i.e. a weakening of incentives to minimise costs. However, if the cost components of the pricing formula are largely outside the firm's control and are competitively determined there is little cause for concern. In the case of British Gas the pricing formula is RPI − X + Y, the Y element allowing the company to pass on changes in gas purchasing costs.

With either of the above formulae there is a danger that over time prices and costs will diverge and so result in allocative inefficiency. From the point of view of allocative efficiency, therefore, the shorter the interval between price reviews the better. Likewise, the shorter the interval the less important becomes the precise formula used for determining allowable prices. On the other hand a short 'regulatory lag' means that the firm gets little benefit from efficiency improvements, and incentives to reduce costs may be seriously weakened. The choice of time interval between price reviews is thus a compromise in which the desirable goals of allocative and internal efficiency have to be weighed in the balance.

As already intimated, the allowable increase in prices in a multi-product firm generally relates to a basket of goods/services rather than to individual goods/services. This can be defended on grounds of administrative simplicity and also as a way of minimising the problem of allocating sunk and joint costs. However this approach also raises several problems, including that of determining which goods and services should be included in the regulatory basket, and the extent to which the relative prices of regulated goods/services are to be permitted to vary. Ideally, the prices that are regulated should be those where the danger of monopoly abuse is high. However, abuse is a matter of degree and the regulatory authority may not choose an appropriate dividing line. If there is no control over relative prices within the regulated basket the firm has an incentive to loosen the regulatory constraint by increasing the output of low-priced goods/services and reducing the output of high-priced goods/services, thus changing the weights of the price index.

What evidence is there that any of these problems have surfaced in the UK? Looking first at internal efficiency, the evidence for BT is not that reassuring. Molyneux and Thompson (1998?) and Bishop and Kay (1988) conclude that BT's productivity performance has not changed materially post-privatisation. The latter estimates that total factor productivity increased at an average annual rate of 2 per cent between 1979 and 1983 and at 2.5 per cent between 1983 and 1988. Allowing for the faster growth in demand for BT services over the latter period, implying scale economy benefits rather than shifts in cost functions, the authors conclude that there is no evidence of a significant improvement in productivity performance. This conclusion has to be seen against the productivity gains that BT could have been expected to achieve. It is not possible to put precise figures on this but there is sufficient evidence to suggest that BT's performance has been disappointing. For instance, immediately before privatisation a major network modernisation programme was planned. Foreman-Peck (1989) suggests that, using North American experience as a benchmark, a 50 per cent productivity gain was feasible. Similarly, Beesley and Laidlaw (1989) argue that in local network operations BT has, on the basis of international comparisons, some 75 000 more employees than would be needed with best practice techniques. That the Office of Telecommunications underestimated attainable productivity gains is indicated by the fact that in 1989 the X component in the pricing formula was increased from 3 per cent to 4.5 per cent.

Although there is little sign of a positive impact on the total volume of telephone services or on overall efficiency, the composition of output has changed. Foreman-Peck, using an econometric model designed to simulate the dynamic impact of liberalisation and the change of ownership, estimated that business connections were 26 per cent higher and residential connections 12.5 per cent lower than would otherwise have been expected. This reflects not only a re-orientation of the business towards more profitable segments, but also a response to the presence of Mercury which has concentrated mainly on the business section of the market.

Evidence on tariffs suggests that BT is making substantial relative price changes within the basket of regulated services. In July 1990 the company announced a new price structure, effective from September 1990. Though there were a number of changes to the structure of call charges (e.g. cheap rate calls became more costly relative to peak rate calls), the major change was a substantial increase in line rental and connection charges relative to call charges. BT argued that the re-adjustments were necessary to bring charges more closely into line with costs, but in the absence of detailed cost information this is impossible to verify. What is clear is that an increased loading of costs on to line rental will increase competitive pressure on Mercury, since trunk calls, where the two companies are in competition, are included in the regulatory basket.

The evidence does not, however, suggest that BT and Mercury are aggressive price competitors. It is more consistent with a model of non-collusive oligopoly in which the smaller firm is content to live under the monopoly price umbrella of the dominant firm, setting prices somewhat lower but not so low as to trigger a price war. This has been particularly noticeable in the unregulated international calls market. Since Mercury's entry into the market international call charges have increased substantially at the same time as costs have fallen dramatically. In March 1990 it was disclosed that BT was a member of an international cartel and that gross profit margins on international calls averaged 60 per cent.

Evidence of allocative inefficiency also exists in the supply of gas. Contract business (i.e. supplies to users with annual gas consumption in excess of 25 000 therms) is not regulated. In 1988, just two years after privatisation British Gas's (BG) contract business was referred to the MMC following complaints about abuse of monopoly power. The MMC criticised BG for, amongst other things, extensive discrimination in the pricing and supply of gas, and for failing to provide adequate information on the costs of common carriage. The MMC was of the view that BG's behaviour served to deter new entrants and to inhibit the development of competition.

In June 1990 the regulatory body Ofgas announced a review of the formula governing the prices set for tariff customers (i.e. those consuming up to 25 000 therms annually). Ofgas has also completed a study of cost structures and is believed to have concluded that BG loads too many costs on to its unregulated customers.

As with the case of telecommunications so with gas, experience suggests that the monopoly supplier will make use of whatever discretion is available in the price control formula, and will often do so anti-competitively. Experience also shows that in attempting to tackle this problem the regulator is drawn into ever more detailed scrutiny and control of pricing behaviour.

Price Control and Quality of Service

Even if price regulation is successful in reducing costs there is a danger that this may be at the expense of service quality. The incentive to improve quality is weakened because, though such improvement will benefit the firm in so far as it increases sales, the firm is unable to appropriate any of the benefit to the main body of consumers who purchased the good/service before the quality improvement was made. In the absence of competition failure to maintain or improve quality will not threaten the firm's position.

In principle, the problem of service quality can be met head on by linking allowable prices to indicators of service quality. In practice there may be great difficulty in the choice of suitable indicators and in determining their weights in the pricing formula. Furthermore it involves yet more detailed intervention by the regulator. An alternative approach is to introduce some form of contractual liability whereby customers receive compensation if service levels fall below predetermined levels. A scheme of this sort was introduced by BT in 1988 following an upsurge in customer complaints. Even so complaints to Oftel in 1989 were up a third on the previous year. The director-general of Oftel commented that BT's procedures for handling complaints remains one of his biggest continuing concerns.

A general concern in the area of service quality lies in the use of inadequate efficiency and productivity indices. It is a matter for concern not only in the newly privatised utilities but also in many areas that remain in the public sector, especially the caring and nurturing services such as health and education. In these sectors productivity gains tend to lag behind those in the rest of the economy. One possible reason for this is the inefficient use of labour. But even if labour were efficiently used productivity gains would lag behind because of fewer opportunities for factor substitution and technological advance. For instance, in Wales over the period 1974–85 the average growth in output per employee for all economic activity averaged between 2.0 and 2.5 per cent. In both health, and education, however, crude measures of labour productivity showed a decline (George and Rhys, 1988). Although productivity tends to lag behind the same is not so true of wage and salary movements. This has important cost and financial implications. Unit costs will tend to increase faster in these services than elsewhere in the economy. A widespread response to this is a reduction in contact between supplier and customer – a tendency that is observable in retailing, restaurants, postal services, bus services, health, and university education. As a result of these adjustments measured productivity will increase but 'real' output per employee will not increase so quickly and may even decline. In the health service, for instance, an increase in the number of in-patients discharged per consultant might be used as an indicator of increased efficiency, but this would be a totally misleading indicator of the standard of health care if patients were being discharged too quickly because of a shortage of hospital beds.

The low level of productivity growth and escalating costs in the provision of many public sector services has placed a growing financial burden on central and local government funds. One response to this has been an attempt to increase efficiency by putting services out to tender. One advantage of putting services out to competitive tender is that the same level of service, supplied in exactly the same way, may be obtained at lower cost. But possibly more important is the effect which this policy has had in making public sector administrators think more carefully about work practices and the level of service required. This seems to be borne out by the experience of the West Glamorgan Health Authority. Over the four-year period from August 1986 the Authority put 25 services (domestic, laundry, gardening, catering and portering) out to tender. The gross annual outset value of the contracts was £7.5 million, and the Authority calculate that the tendering system has yielded gross annual savings of just under £1.2 million (16 per cent) on pre-tendering service costs. Twenty out of the 25 contracts were won by an in-house team, and the Authority's view is that the savings generated are the result of two main factors: changed work practices and changed service specifications, with the latter probably accounting for most of the savings made.

The experience of the West Glamorgan Health Authority shows that substantial cost savings are possible from a more competitive environment. Even so, the problem remains that costs can always be reduced at the expense of service quality, especially if most of the available savings are secured from a change in service specifications. Of course there may well be genuine waste in the form, for instance, of overmanning; i.e. service is overprovided. But once obvious waste is eliminated difficult judgemental decisions have to be made, and what may be perceived as an adequate provision of service by a hospital manager may be viewed quite differently by a ward sister. However the clearest indication of all of a decline in the quality of service in these areas is the failure to keep expenditure at a high enough level to maintain standards, as is evident for instance in hospital waiting lists and the deteriorating condition of school buildings.

Price Control and Investment

A major concern in the analysis of regulatory problems has been the adverse incentives which regulatory control might imply for investment decisions. In analysing the effects of rate of return regulation Averch and Johnson (1962) showed that the result might be an adverse choice of technique, with too much capital being employed relative to other factors. The incentive to employ too much capital exists because this enlarges the rate base, so that for a given allowable *rate* of return the firm achieves a higher *level* of profit.

The circumstances under which this tendency exists is where the allowable rate of return (r) exceeds the current cost of capital (c). This is because setting $r > c$ is equivalent to a subsidy on capital. The firm therefore perceives the cost of capital to be less than the market cost. In Figure 2.1, I is the relevant isoquant which shows the combination of labour and

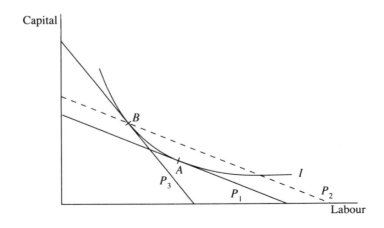

FIGURE 2.1

capital capable of producing a given output. P_1 is an isocost line whose slope gives the ratio of the market price of labour to that of capital. The optimal combination of inputs is thus A. However, if the firm perceives the cost of capital to be lower than the market rate it will decide its factor input combination on the basis of an isocost line such as P_3 which shows capital to be cheaper relative to labour. The firm will then select the input combination at point B. In terms of market prices point B is inefficient, and this is shown by drawing isocost line P_2 parallel to P_1 so that it too reflects market prices. Clearly the output given by isoquant I is being produced at higher cost at B than at A. The degree of distortion in factor proportions depends on the elasticity of factor substitution. It will also depend on the elasticity of demand for the final product, a high elasticity making it difficult for the higher costs associated with non-optimal production techniques to be passed on to customers in the form of higher prices.

Research in the US, however, has produced little evidence of the 'rate-base' padding, effect. There are several possible reasons for this. The incentive to extend the rate-base uneconomically depends on the allowable return on capital being in excess of the market rate for new funds. There is no difficulty in showing this in theory but in practice, given capital market imperfections, the relationship between the two rates may be less than clear cut. In addition the technical possibilities of substituting capital for labour may be very limited – and in the extreme case of zero elasticity of substitution there will be no factor proportion distortion. Another important consideration is that although an allowable rate of return may be an objective, what the regulator actually sets is prices. The rate of return enters as an input into the determination of maximum prices but it may not be the only input into the price formula. As suggested earlier, the regulator may also take into account performance indicators designed to measure operating efficiency, and this may have the effect of depressing prices. The firm also has to allow for the effects of *regulatory lag* – the time interval between price reviews. The longer the lag the longer the time period over which the firm has to absorb cost increases before it has a chance to pass them on in the form of higher prices and the less inclined it will be to engage in wasteful capital expenditure. Caution will be reinforced if it is thought that the regulator, aware of the possibility of rate-base padding, will scrutinise investment decisions and perhaps disallow some items of capital expenditure. Where sunk costs are important the perceived dangers of over-investment by the firm are particularly acute since once the investment has been made the firm's bargaining power at rate-setting time will be considerably weakened. This consideration is particularly important given the specificity and durability of public utility assets and the very long pay-off periods that are involved. In sum, investment decisions have to be made on the basis of the firm's expectations of future allowable prices and of what the regulator will accept as a reasonable rate base. These and other uncertainties are likely to act as a powerful offset to any forces tending in the opposite direction.

Too short a period has elapsed for any reliable analysis to be made of the effects of the UK privatisation programme on investment. An examination of BT's post-privatisation investment does not, at first glance, suggest any reason to suspect underinvestment, since real capital expenditure has grown steadily since 1984. However, this may indicate that price control generally has been too slack and that BT has been allowed to earn an excessive rate of return. One area where BT is closely regulated is that of value added services such as the provision of cable TV, where it has been barred from entry. It is interesting to note that BT has recently announced that it is shelving a £200 million investment programme to provide local optical cables because the profitability of the investment depends upon the telephone network being allowed to carry TV services. Doubts about permission to enter profitable markets have the same effect on investment as doubts about the extent to which future allowable price increases will cover full cost – the tendency will be to underinvestment. The BT example parallels the 'investment strike' of the Bell operating companies in the USA who are delaying the modernisation of their networks whilst they are barred from several service areas, including cable TV.

Regulating Entry

We have already mentioned that where competition exists the regulatory burden is lightened. In the utilities, however, access to consumers is via a network which is largely controlled by a dominant supplier. This raises problems of devising terms of access to the network which will be sufficiently attractive to induce entry and at the same time gives the network owner fair compensation. If the incumbent monopolist operates a range of services with a substantial measure of cross-subsidisation new entrants may well target the profitable services leaving a large part of the remaining network unprofitable to supply. A further problem is that unregulated 'hit and run' entry may have disruptive effects which reduce welfare.

These problems arise not only in the provision of services such as gas and electricity but also in road and rail transport. This section examines the issues in relation to local bus services and examines some of the changes that have taken place in South Wales since services were deregulated by the 1985 Transport Act. The operation of local bus services up to 26 October

1986 (deregulation day) may, in broad terms, be described as follows. Bus undertakings with a monopoly or near monopoly of local services, operated a network which could be divided into three parts: (a) profitable services; (b) unprofitable services subsidised by the profits made in (a); (c) other unprofitable services. Parts (a) and (b) made up the break-even network; (c) were other 'loss-making' services regarded by the county council as essential for satisfying social needs and thus subsidised from local authority funds. The larger the break-even network the smaller the support that had to come out of public funds. Cross-subsidisation was therefore regarded by many local authorities as an important part of policy.

The means of achieving cross-subsidisation was the application of a common fare policy. That is, in spite of substantial cost variation between individual services, the fare for travelling a given distance was the same regardless of the route travelled. With such a pricing policy low-cost services made a profit while high-cost ones made losses.

The common fare policy had the advantage of being easy to administer; it was also widely regarded as a fair method of charging for bus services. The general arrangements for the supply of bus services enabled local authorities to secure the supply of unprofitable but socially desirable services and, especially in the large metropolitan areas, facilitated the co-ordination of public transport.

However, the old system was open to a number of criticisms.

1. The resources used in providing local bus services were misallocated because of the common fare policy and thus the failure of fares to reflect the relative cost of providing individual services.
2. The fairness of the system was open to challenge especially in the cities where some of the most profitable services were to and from areas with a high proportion of low-income households. In these cases the common fare policy meant that low-income households were subsidising those on higher incomes.
3. The combination of cross-subsidisation and revenue support in the form of a general subsidy for a whole network weakened incentives to minimise costs on individual routes especially in those areas where revenue support was sufficient to meet the full network deficit.
4. The protection given to the monopoly supplier meant that there was a weakening of incentives to relate services more closely to passenger needs, to introduce more economical mini and midibuses, and generally to exercise the managerial authority needed to increase efficiency.
5. The problems facing management were exacerbated by the political element in decision making. Management could be hamstrung by the

need to consult not only county officers but also county councillors on any change in service however small.

In principle there is no reason why desirable changes such as increased use of passenger surveys, more flexible use of manpower, and more rapid introduction of smaller buses could not have come about under the old regime. Recommendations to this effect were made by the MMC's report on stage carriage services (1982). In reality, however, change was often inhibited by a combination of management weakness and the political element in decision making. Management at both Swansea and Cardiff agree that deregulation at the very least gave an impetus to much needed reforms.

The purpose of deregulation was of course to expose incumbent monopolists to competitive pressures. But how was this competition likely to manifest itself? Would it be widespread and permanent or localised and sporadic? Entry into commercial services was expected to occur on the most profitable routes, i.e. there would be a substantial amount of 'cream skimming'. It was also expected that the incumbent would respond aggressively to any attempt at entry. Overall profitability in providing bus services is, at best, modest and loss of the more profitable services would have serious consequences. The incumbent could therefore be expected to react to entry by matching lower fares and increasing service frequency, very often with the use of smaller, more economical, vehicles. A sharp response could be expected even to very small-scale entry on profitable routes because by establishing a reputation for toughness other potential entrants might be deterred.

If the incumbent is efficient and reasonably strong financially, entry by small operators with very limited financial backing can not be expected to succeed in this market. Certainly this has been the experiences to date in both Cardiff and Swansea. In Cardiff, new entry occurred following the 1980 Transport Act. Cardiff City Transport reacted sharply and the new competition was short-lived. Deregulation has not encouraged any other attempt at entry even though the fare structure has remained largely unaltered. In Swansea, there have been several attempts at entry since 1985 but most have been short-lived. Here too, South Wales Transport (SWT), the incumbent monopolist, responded to entry by lowering fares and increasing service frequency with the use of smaller buses. Two small competitors remain but on routes which are 'acceptable' to SWT. The fare structure has changed substantially since deregulation with fares reflecting more closely than hitherto the relative costs of operating individual services, thus reducing the scope for cream skimming.

On commercial services the only real threat to a reasonably efficient incumbent is one that comes from another large operator. However, there is evidence that suggests that this form of potential competition is blunted by mutual self-interest in avoiding destructive confrontations. It is not surprising to find, therefore, that a great deal of the new competition that has occurred has focused on the subsidised contract market such as the supply of school services, for if a new entrant is successful in winning a tender in this segment of the market it is then sheltered from competition for the duration of the contract.

Post-deregulation performance in many other areas, however, has by no means been as problem free as it has been in Swansea and Cardiff. One important reason for this has been that the incumbent dominant supplier has been ill-prepared to meet competition. In Merthyr Tydfil, for instance, the absence of a strong incumbent led to substantial new entry, fierce competition between rival operators, and substantial disruption of services.

In bus services it is important that the customer is able to enjoy, at minimum cost, the benefits of a network of services operating to a regular and dependable timetable. In the larger metropolitan areas the ability to integrate public transport to form a coherent long-run strategy is also important. While there has to be flexibility to meet changing market requirements there also has to be a long-term commitment from bus operators who are prepared, in Demsetz's words, to invest in permanence rather than in fly-by-night operations. One of the less fortunate aspects of the 1985 Act is that by encouraging cream skimming and hit-and-run entry it failed to recognise sufficiently clearly the importance of the network. While competition is important in minimising costs the most appropriate form of competition will vary according to the circumstances of individual markets. Under the 1985 Act there is virtually unregulated entry. Operators have to meet minimum safety and other criteria but many well established firms would argue that these are not rigorously enough enforced. A more regulated and less disruptive form of entry would exist if, for those bus operators under municipal control, greater use was made of the tendering system. For privately owned bus operators it would be more appropriate if management inefficiency was punished by takeover rather than by piecemeal sniping at parts of the business.

CONCLUDING COMMENTS

The privatisation programme in the UK was launched as part of a strategy for strengthening the supply side of the economy. Agency theory suggests that there should be some reason to expect internal efficiency to be higher in privately owned firms than in public corporations. Although privatisation has given management the opportunity to break away from entrenched and inefficient procedures there is no clear evidence that privatisation has led to a noticeable and widespread improvement in performance. Even if some of the evidence is favourable to privatisation there is also evidence which shows that efficiency can be increased substantially under public ownership.

There would be general agreement that some exposure to competition has an efficiency-enhancing effect. There is also a considerable body of theoretical and empirical work that warns of the anti-competitive dangers inherent in markets which are characterised by dominancy. It is, therefore, to be regretted that in privatising certain corporations the government did not also take the opportunity of restructuring the industries along more competitive lines, especially where the evidence suggests that this could have been achieved without loss of economies of scale or of scope.

However, although some exposure to competitive pressure is invariably beneficial the optimum balance between monopoly and competition is difficult to establish. Competition can be destructive in the sense that short-run price competition and the threat of new entry can be so intense that firms are unwilling to commit themselves sufficiently to activities such as R & D expenditure and labour training, which are necessary for long-run efficiency. One of the major regulatory problems is that of erecting a market environment which is at once both sufficiently competitive to foster managerial efficiency in the use of existing assets and also conducive to investment in permanence. In striving to attain this goal it will sometimes be necessary to reduce entry barriers, but in some circumstances it may be necessary to limit entry.

We are also concerned about the emphasis which, since 1980, has come to be placed on various measures of internal, or operating, efficiency, and on the attainment of financial targets. Efficiency indicators are often based on seriously incomplete measures of output and can give a misleading impression of movements in consumer welfare. More generally, financial targets and efficiency standards may be attained at the expense of service quality and allocative efficiency. Commenting on the problems facing the nationalised industries Sir Dennis Robertson (1957) commented: 'a right distribution of productive resources between employments is a "good thing" economically but not the only good thing, even economically'. Today it would appear that the pendulum has swung too far and that the warning needs to be amended. Internal efficiency is a 'good thing' economically but not the only good thing, even economically.

APPENDIX

Several of the empirical studies reviewed in the text used the recent advances in non-stationary time-series analysis as a methodology. The purpose of this appendix is to provide a brief and simple explanation of this methodology for non-specialists. A more detailed and rigorous account can be found in a series of papers in the *Oxford Bulletin of Economics and Statistics, Special Issue,* August, 1986.

It is a fundamental assumption of the classical linear regression model that the linear properties (mean, variance, etc.) of any time-series are constant through time. If this is not the case then this causes problems for conventional econometric analysis and may lead to the estimation of a spurious regression. Most time-series data on economic variables is time-trended over the post-war period. This implies that the data is non-stationary and that its linear properties evolve over the sample. A stationary time-series is defined to be integrated of order zero, $I(0)$, and so a series of x_t of order k implies that $\Delta^k x_t$ will be $I(0)$. So kth order differencing will produce a stationary series. Granger (1986) and Engle and Granger (1987) have shown that if two series y_t and x_t are $I(1)$ then although, *in general*, a linear combination of them say $z_t = x_t - \alpha y_t$ will also be $I(1)$, there may exist a value for α which ensures that z_t is $I(0)$. If this is so then the two series are said to be cointegrated and α is the cointegrating vector.

The intuition behind the above is very straightforward. If two or more economic variables have a long-run relationship of the form $x_t = \alpha y_t$ then this implies that through time they will not drift too far apart from each other. Granger (1986) gives, as examples, wages and prices and spot and official commodity prices. If the variables do not drift too far apart then this implies they must have similar time-series properties (i.e. be of the same order of integration) and the error between them over the time period must itself be stationary. If this were not the case then the gap between x_t and y_t would itself be time-trended. So for cointegration to occur we require z_t, the error term in

$$x_t = \alpha y_t + z_t \tag{2.1}$$

to be integrated of order zero, i.e. stationary. If z_t is $I(0)$ then a long-run relationship exists between the set of variables. The Granger Representation Theorem then states that if cointegration occurs then this implies the existence of a valid dynamic error correction representation of the form

$$\Delta^k x_t = -p z_{t-1} + \text{lagged } (\Delta^k x_t, \Delta^k y_t) + \varepsilon_t \tag{2.2}$$

In (2.2) z_{t-1} is the 'error correcting' variable. In other words the departure from equilibrium experienced in the previous period acts as a stabilising influence on future variation of the series. Hence (2.2) indicates that the amount and direction of change in x_t and y_t take into account the size and sign of the previous equilibrium error, z_{t-1}.

Estimation of (2.1) will provide long-run equilibrium values of the parameters of interest. Since some of the tests for cointegration are still in their infancy it is advisable to check for consistency before estimating (2.2). Consistency demands that p be negative, significant and less than one in absolute value. Finally, it is possible to derive long-run parameter values which are directly comparable to those in (2.1) by 'releasing' the error correction variable. That is, from (2.1) we have

$$z_t = x_t - \alpha y_t \tag{2.3}$$

Substitution in (2.2) yields

$$\Delta^k x_t = -p(x_t - \alpha y_t)_{t-1} + \text{lagged } (\Delta^k x_t, \Delta^k y_t) + \varepsilon_t \tag{2.4}$$

In steady-state equilibrium where all adjustment has ceased then (2.4) reduces to:

$$\begin{aligned} 0 &= -px + p\alpha y \\ \text{or} \quad x &= \alpha y \end{aligned} \tag{2.5}$$

Note that in the absence of a constant term in (2.1), then (2.5) is identical to (2.1). This implies that the long-run steady state parameter values derived from (2.5) should closely approximate those recorded in (2.1). (See Jenkinson (1986) for an example of this procedure.) Hence consistency demands that if cointegration is found via estimation of (2.1), then in estimating (2.2), p should be negative, significant and less than unity, *and* the implicit parameter values in (2.4) should closely approximate those derived in (2.1).

The above methodology is utilised in several of the studies reviewed in the text. Equation (2.1) corresponds to a multiproduct cost function where y_t is a vector of output variables, input prices and a technology term. Broadly speaking these studies pass the consistency criteria discussed above with minimal sign reversal, appropriate error correcting variable values, and acceptable statistical performance.

REFERENCES

Albon, R. (1987) 'Privatise the Post: Steps towards a Competitive Service', *Centre for Policy Studies,* Policy Study 82.

Albon, R. (1988) 'Liberalisation of the Post Office', in C. Johnson (ed.), *Privatisation and Ownership,* Lloyds Bank Annual Review (London: Pinter Publishers).

Averch, H. and Johnson, L. (1962) 'Behaviour of the Firm under Regulatory Constraint', *American Economic Review,* vol. 52, pp. 1052–1069.

Baumol, W. J., Panzar, J. C. and Willig, R. D. (1982) *Contestable Markets and the Theory of Industry Structure* (New York: Harcourt Brace Jovanovich).

Beesley, M. E. and Littlechild, S. (1986) 'Privatisation: Principles, Problems and Priorities', in J. Kay, C. Mayer and D. Thompson (eds), *Privatisation and Regulation: The UK Experience* (Oxford: Clarendon Press).

Beesley, M. E. and Laidlaw, B (1989) *The Future of Telecommunications: An Assessment of the Role of Competition in UK Policy* (London: Institute of Economic Affairs, Research Monograph 42).

Bishop, M. and Kay, J. (1988) 'Does Privatisation Work? Lessons from the UK', London Business School, mimeo.

Cyert, R. M. and George, K. D. (1969) 'Competition, Growth and Efficiency', *Economic Journal,* March.

Demsetz, H. (1982) 'Barriers to Entry', *American Economic Review,* vol. 72(1).

Department of the Environment (1986) *Privatisation of the Water Authorities in England and Wales,* Cmnd 9734 (London: HMSO).

Engle, R. F. and Granger, C. W. J. (1987) 'Cointegration and Error Correction: Representation, Estimation and Testing', *Econometrica,* vol. 55, pp. 251–76.

Foreman-Peck, J. and Manning, D. (1987) 'Natural Monopoly and Telecommunications Liberalisation in the UK', Communications Policy Research Conference, European Telecommunications Policy.

Foreman-Peck, J. (1989) 'Ownership, Competition and Productivity Growth: the Impact of Liberalisation and Privatisation upon British Telecom', Department of Economic History, University of Hull, mimeo.

George, K. D. *et al.* (1988) 'Coal', in K. D. George and L. Mainwaring (eds), *The Welsh Economy* (Cardiff: University of Wales Press).

George, K. D. (1990) 'Public Ownership vs. Privatisation', in Peter de Wolf (ed.), *Competition in Europe: Essays in Honour of Professor Henk W. de Jong* (Amsterdam: Kluwer Academic Publishers).

George, K. D. and Rhys, D. G. (1988) 'The Service Sector', in K. D. George and L. Mainwaring (eds), *The Welsh Economy* (Cardiff: University of Wales Press).

Granger, C. W. J. (1986) 'Development in the Study of Cointegrated Economic Variables', *Oxford Bulletin of Economics and Statistics,* vol. 48, pp. 213–228.

Hunt, L. C. and Lynk, E. L. (1989) 'Privatisation and Efficiency in the UK Water Industry: an Empirical Analysis', Department of Economics, University College of Swansea, mimeo.

Hunt, L. C. and Lynk, E. L. (1990a) 'Telecommunications Industry Structure in the UK: an Empirical Examination of the Case for Restructuring BT', Department of Economics, University College of Swansea, mimeo.

Hunt, L. C. and Lynk, E. L. (1990b) 'Divestiture of Telecommunications in the UK: a Time Series Analysis', *Oxford Bulletin of Economics and Statistics,* August.

Hunt, L. C. and Lynk, E. L. (1991) 'An Empirical Investigation of the Case for Post Office Divestiture in the UK', *Scottish Journal of Political Economy*, May/August.

Jenkinson, T. J. (1986) 'Testing Neo-Classical Theories of Labour Demand: an Application of Cointegration Techniques', *Oxford Bulletin of Economics and Statistics*, vol. 48, pp. 241–252.

Kumar, M. S. (1984) *Growth, Acquisitions and Investment* (Cambridge, Cambridge University Press).

Meeks, G. (1977) *Disappointing Marriage: A Study of the Gains from Merger* (Cambridge, Cambridge University Press).

Molyneux, R. and Thompson, D. (1987) 'Nationalised Industry Performance: Still Third Rate?', *Fiscal Studies*, vol. 8(1) pp. 48–82.

Monopolies and Mergers Commission (1980) *Domestic Gas Appliances: a Report on the Supply of Certain Domestic Gas Appliances in the United Kingdom*, HC 703 (London: HMSO).

Monopolies and Mergers Commission (1982) *Bristol Omnibus Co., Cheltenham District Traction Co., City of Cardiff District Council, Trent Motor Traction Co., West Midlands Passenger Transport Executive*, HC 442 (London: HMSO).

Monopolies and Mergers Commission (1988) *Gas: a Report on the Matter of the Existence or the Possible Existence of a Monopoly Situation in Relation to the Supply in Great Britain of Gas through Pipes to Persons other than Tariff Customers*, Cmnd 500 (London: HMSO).

National Economic Development Office (1976) *A Study of UK Nationalised Industries* (London: HMSO).

Okun, A. M. (1981) *Prices and Quantities: a Macroeconomic Analysis* (Oxford: Basil Blackwell).

Ordover, J. A. (1990) 'Economic Foundations of Competition Policy', New York University, mimeo.

Robertson, D. H. (1957) *Lectures on Economic Principles*, Volume 1 (London: Staples Press) p. 168.

Scherer, F. M. (1980) *Industrial Market Structure and Economic Performance*, 2nd edn (Boston: Houghton Mifflin) p. 438.

Senior, I. (1989) 'Liberating the Letter', in C. Veljanowski (ed.), *Privatisation and Competition: a Market Prospectus* (London: Institute of Economic Affairs).

Shepherd, W. G. (1989) 'The Process of Effective Competition', Department of Economics, University of Massachusetts, Working Paper (1989–1).

Singh, A. (1971) *Takeovers: Their Relevance to the Stock Market and the Theory of the Firm* (Cambridge: Cambridge University Press).

Starkie, D. and Thompson, D. (1985) 'Stansted: a Viable Investment?', *Fiscal Studies*.

Vickers, J. and Yarrow, G. (1988) *Privatisation: an Economic Analysis* (London, MIT Press).

von Weizsacker, C. C. (1980) 'A Welfare Analysis of Barriers to Entry', *Bell Journal of Economics, 11*.

Williamson, O. E. (1963) 'Managerial Discretion and Business Behaviour', *American Economic Review*, December.

Yarrow, G. K. (1989) 'Privatisation and Economic Performance in Britain', Carnegie-Rochester Conference Series on Public Policy, 31 (Amsterdam: North-Holland).

3 Financial Markets

CHARLES A. E. GOODHART

INTRODUCTION AND SUMMARY

The most dramatic event of recent years has been the revolution in Eastern Europe. This revolution, and the attempts at political and economic reform in Russia, and China, owed much to the perceived failure of the centralised, command system of economic organisation. The progress that an economic system, such as Marxist socialism or capitalism, can generate depends largely on the investment in physical and, probably more important, human investment that is undertaken. Within command economies the choice of all major investment projects is part of the centralised plan, and its financing is achieved through savings largely enforced on economic agents. Whereas the proportion of GDP allocated to investment in command economies appears generally to have been high, the quality and subsequent management of the capital stock has been depressingly poor.

Apart from the monitoring and accounting functions of the monopoly State Bank, financial markets and intermediaries played virtually no role in the economic systems of the command economies. One of the reasons for the comparative failure of such economies has been that the incentives (both positive incentives to maximise returns and negative incentives to avoid failure, bankruptcy and unemployment) for the achievement of economic success are less pronounced in Socialist economies (Kornai's soft budgets, see his *Economics of Shortage*, 1980). The emotions that drive markets may, indeed, be greed and fear; but it is the incentives to maximise returns and to avoid failure that makes the economy function relatively satisfactorily. It is, therefore, against the dramatic background of recent events in Eastern Europe, that the first section of this chapter addresses the question of the role and functions of financial markets within a capitalist economy. Indeed, the revolution in Eastern Europe, and the reforms in USSR and PRC, have led swiftly to the perceived need there to establish some forms of Western-type financial markets and intermediaries, of which more later.

A second dramatic event in recent years was the Stock Market crash of October 1987. There are several facets of this event that we do not properly understand. The sell-off did not appear to be triggered by the arrival of any clearly identifiable adverse major item of 'news' (see Friedman, 1990; Shiller, 1987). If the crash in the New York Stock Exchange was instead caused by some market failures specific to the USA, e.g. a dysjunction between the futures market and the NYSE and the potential role of 'portfolio insurance', why then did virtually all other stock markets around the world collapse in tandem like a house of cards (see Roll, 1988, 1989; King and Wadhwani, 1988)? King, Sentana and Wadhwani (1990) have shown that only a tiny proportion of the fluctuations over time in the degree of covariance between the movements in national stock markets can be accounted for by (their selected set of) observable economic variables. Instead, such common fluctuations 'are driven primarily by movements in unobservable variables', but quite what these unobservable phenomena are, or what determines them, remains to be discovered.

This episode demonstrated all too clearly that our understanding of the basic characteristics of financial markets is still rather limited. In Section 2 I shall survey a small proportion of recent research which has been undertaken on the nature and characteristics of these markets, e.g. hypotheses about how financial markets determine asset prices, how risk is perceived and priced, and the extent and nature of volatility in asset markets.

There are many further facets, and issues, that could be explored in a study of financial markets; indeed a fully satisfactory study would, perforce, be voluminous. I have chosen to end the chapter by concentrating on three issues that have become subjects of public concern. First, many observers regard financial markets, especially but not only stock markets, as being subject to myopia, short-termism; but what exactly is meant by short-termism, and what is the justification for this claim? Second (and obviously related to the preceding issue), financial markets and financial intermediaries are sometimes in a position to control the ownership and management of companies, the market in company governance. What is the best mechanism for exercising such controls? Does the possibility of hostile takeover invigorate or disrupt the process of management?

Markets do not exist in a pure vacuum. There is always some market structure (market microstructure) and a system, whether self-determined by the market members or imposed by outside (State) intervention, of rules and regulations. The third issue that I shall consider is the nature of the structure and the associated regulations, against the background of the ongoing discussions about the effect, identification and treatment of insider trading.

Even having restricted attention to a limited number of issues within a much wider field, the above subjects cover a far broader range than I can cover with any personal expertise. I have been greatly helped and assisted in the preparation of this chapter by my membership of the Financial

Markets Group, and, if a proportionally large number of the references relate to the Papers of the FMG, this is because I am naturally familiar with, and close to, this impressive body of work.

THE FUNCTIONS OF FINANCIAL MARKETS

If borrowers cannot persuade potential net savers to transfer funds voluntarily through the medium of financial instruments via financial markets and/or financial intermediaries, they are limited to the use of resources that they can raise privately, from their own means, family and friends, or the resources that can be extorted from those over whom the borrower is in a position of power, via feudal charges, taxes, tithes, etc. The first source of funds is too small to finance the investment requirements of any developing economy. The second source of funds can be comparatively large. The resources devoted, for example, to the construction of the great medieval cathedrals may have represented a sizeable proportion of GDP at the time. More immediately, the power of governments in command, centralised economies has generally been sufficient to divert comparatively large (relative to Western countries) percentages of GDP to investment projects. A good discussion of this may be found in Ellman (1989, p. 183).

The problems in the command economies have not been so much of obtaining control over resources for investment purposes, but in their capacity for choosing between alternative investment projects, successful monitoring of the efficiency of the projects actually financed, and the maintenance of appropriate incentives for economic success (see, e.g., Johnson, 1990).

It is, indeed, just these latter functions which financial markets, and ancillary professional services, such as accountancy, credit rating agencies, etc., attempt to serve. It is not an easy exercise. Exactly how does one persuade someone voluntarily to hand over command of resources and money to someone else of whom he/she has very little personal knowledge, or direct contact? If I was to ask you to lend me £1000 against my word that I would repay you £1500 in two years time, would you do so? The incentive for, and possibility of, fraud in financial markets has always been obvious; the borrower issues a false prospectus, raises money for a bogus purpose, and decamps without repaying, or alternatively invests your money in a much riskier project than advertised, creaming off the residual profits if successful, and leaving the investor with the loss if not.

Because of the inherent information, monitoring and enforcement problems associated with financial markets, primary financial markets in which private sector agents would borrow *directly* from private/personal lenders, e.g. equity and corporate debt markets, were historically quite slow to develop. The first large primary financial markets were those for Government bonds, where the information problems were less acute and whose value rested, sometimes uneasily, on governments' expected future power to raise taxes.

The crucial innovation was the development of banks as financial intermediaries specialising in the assessment of information about alternative investment projects, monitoring the outcome of such projects, and enforcing penalties for failure to repay on the terms due. The banks would therefore act as the specialist agent of the principals, the savers (depositors), to carry out such functions, which would be impossibly difficult/expensive for each agent to undertake individually (e.g. Diamond, 1984).

Fama (1985) has noted that, since bank deposit interest rates are usually closely in line with the rates offered on (equivalent maturity) company sector paper, e.g. commercial bills, the spread between the deposit and lending rate (enhanced by any required reserve ratios or (tax) burden on banks), is paid by the bank borrower. Hence there must be a credit assessment/monitoring function undertaken by banks, which bank borrowers cannot avoid by going directly to primary markets. (Garber and Weisbrod (1990) have recently, however, made the counter-claim that the cost to companies of issuing paper is above the direct interest cost offered to lenders because of their need to arrange, with banks, for contingent future access to cash should the future roll-over of their borrowing prove difficult.) Some recent evidence (James, 1987; Lummer and McConnell, 1989) has been reported that company share prices rise when it is publicly announced that they have raised sizeable lines of bank credit, perhaps because the specialist credit assessment functions of banks are so highly regarded that a bank loan is regarded as a good signal.

Because of the asymmetric information whereby the borrower knows much more about the project than the banker, the banks may not be in a position to distinguish better, safer loans from riskier projects, and may be forced to ration credit; see the large literature on equilibrium credit rationing (e.g. Stiglitz and Weiss, 1981; Gale and Hellwig, 1985): in practice, however, most credit rationing, especially in less developed countries has been due to the imposition of (interest rate) controls by the authorities (Fry, 1988), and other market imperfections (e.g. cartelised constraints on price adjustments, as in the case of UK Building Societies until recently).

Not only is information-gathering often difficult, time consuming and expensive, but the exercise of continuous monitoring of borrowers would be even more so. If banks were required to take an equity participation in borrowers' projects, as actually occurs in Islamic banking with Mushariqi loans, since the Koran bans the practice of interest (Ali, 1988; Ahmed,1989), how would they be able to ensure that the outcome of the project was being accurately reported, and, if the banks had put up much/most of the equity finance, how would they be able to maintain incentives for the borrower to apply sufficient effort to the conduct of the project? (This latter remains a concern in the case of start-up venture capital, when the entrepreneur may have no source of personal equity. Hansen (1990) suggests that the solution may reside in a combination of debt/equity instruments which can be adjusted, e.g. convertible, as the project develops.) The more that banks, as in Germany and Japan, are prepared to maintain long-term, quasi equity, relationships with (corporate) clients, the more they will require access to privileged (inside) information on the clients' operations, e.g. a seat on the Board of Directors.

Accordingly, the standard form of financial contract issued by banks is in fixed interest debt form, often supported by collateral, liens on objects of value, and buttressed by the threat of enforced bankruptcy, which imposes certain additional penalties for failure. (The role, functions and optimal institutional and legal form of bankruptcy in a capitalist economy is a fascinating subject, see for example the papers by Webb (1987, 1990a, b), but that would take us too far afield to pursue here.) This contract form enables banks to reduce monitoring costs, so long as the terms of repayment are being met, taking comfort from the fact that the contract form maintains the incentive on borrowers to make the project succeed. Only if difficulties, even so, arise, do the banks then need to monitor intensively in order to seek to avoid the extra costs involved in repossession and bankruptcy proceedings. By similar analogy, the problems of asymmetric information and monitoring costs lead the saver to prefer a fixed-interest deposit with the banks, which suits the bank, which can thereby relate its fixed interest assets to liabilities of a similar form, even though of a generally shorter maturity.

Models of financial structure, such as Modigliani and Miller (e.g. 1958, 1961, 1963), that abstract from bankruptcy costs throw out an important baby with the bathwater. With virtually all bank lending being in fixed interest form, (small) borrowers could find that tapping available outside finance (initially predominantly through banks) would have the effect of raising their debt/equity ratio to levels that would increase the risk of (costly) bankruptcy unduly. If bankruptcy is, indeed, such a costly procedure both for creditor and debtor, why cannot alternative (financing) strategies be found to avoid it? The answer lies in large part in the impossibility of distinguishing bad luck (bad states of nature) from bad management, and the difficulty of monitoring managerial effort and efficiency.

There has remained a perennial problem of how (smaller) entrepreneurs, without a presentable track record, could obtain sufficient extra equity beyond their own personal sources and retained funds (e.g. Macmillan Committee, Wilson Committee etc.). With both banks and borrowers being unwilling to allow debt/equity ratios to rise beyond a certain level, fluctuations in profits, and hence in equity values, can have a considerable knock-on effect in influencing financial constraints, e.g. on the expenditures undertaken on investment, of middle/small companies without access to primary capital markets (see for example Greenwald, Stiglitz and Weiss, 1984; Greenwald and Stiglitz, 1988; Gertler, 1988; Gertler and Hubbard, 1989; Calomiris and Hubbard, 1989).

There is, therefore, an incentive for larger companies to pay the sizeable costs involved in making additional information available about their past profits and future prospects, that could reduce the information and monitoring costs of lenders, in order to give such borrowers access to the equity market. But once again, how can one avoid, or at least reduce, the incentive for companies to exaggerate, if not falsify entirely, what has been happening to them, and their future prospects. There are, of course, legal remedies against fraud, but recourse to the law tends to be slow and expensive. Consequently, a standard response has been for companies to pay some independent body, an accountant, credit rating agency (or to lunch investment analysts!), to provide an 'independent' guarantee that the recorded accounts give a 'fair and true view' of the business. The accountant, a key figure in financial markets, is then placed at times in the delicate position that the accounting firm's future depends on its reputation for independent and unblemished veracity, while its present fees depend on its relationship with clients who may at times be in some difficulties. Examples of creative accounting, and failures of firms whose prior accounts gave no hint of trouble, suggest that this solution to information problems, while the best available, can be less than perfect!

Other partial solutions to such information problems are for the firm to signal confidence in its position in a manner which would be too expensive for bad firms to copy, e.g. by paying dividends (despite the tax cost of so doing, see John and Williams, 1985; Miller and Rock, 1985; Ross, 1977; Roell, 1987c) or by the directors buying their own equity (see Leland and Pyle, 1977) though there can be a danger both of market manipulation and insider trading (see later section) from such latter actions.

Access to the primary equity market not only allows entrepreneurs to adjust their debt/equity ratio, but also allows them to diversify their wealth, and even to exit from a (prosperous) on-going business without having to close down the firm. Over time, this process has, of course, resulted in most major public firms being run by managers who have only a relatively small equity stake in the firm themselves, and whose remuneration is often more largely met by salary than by profit share. This can lead to company managers seeking to maximise a different objective function, than the outside equity holders. Managers may well value the continuity of their own jobs, status and size, as much as profit maximisation.

For such reasons, and also because certain managers may be assessed by equity holders as being comparatively poor, the equity market has come to serve not only a role as a primary market for the allocation of investable funds, but also as a market for corporate control and governance. If an outsider can successfully bid for a majority of the shares of a company, he is then able to (and frequently does) replace the existing management by a completely new set. Whether this facet of the equity market is functioning satisfactorily will be further considered in the final section of the chapter.

A successful economic system needs to solve, *inter alia*, an information problem, how to ensure a sufficiently wide distribution of accurate information on the prospects of potential users of external finance, and an incentive problem, how to structure the pattern of incentives to persuade agents to report information honestly and to perform efficiently. I have tried to show how financial markets in capitalist economies help to resolve, more or less, such problems.

Against that background we can point to certain failings in a command economy, though this is not the occasion to attempt any comprehensive analysis. The attempt at over-centralisation resulted in an arbitrary and inefficient price system. With such 'wrong' prices, it would not in any case have been sensible to aim for cost minimisation, and managers were generally told to aim for quantitative growth rather than profitability. Given this absence of incentive for profit maximisation, in part also because managers might have little share in any resultant 'profits', there will be a tendency in command economies for managers to exaggerate the inputs required to achieve a planned output target, whose quality the manager may be further induced to lessen in the pursuit of that quantitative target. Again the absence of both greed (for profit maximisation) and fear (of bankruptcy, takeovers, and sacking) is likely to lessen pressures on managers to perform.

It is, therefore, not surprising that some of the first reforms to be introduced in East European countries, and considered even in USSR and China, have been to seek to renovate financial intermediaries and markets more along Western lines. Certain of these reforms have been widely accepted in principle, such as the need to replace the mono-state-bank with competitive commercial banks, who should make independent credit assessment; though the desire by the politicians/bureaucrats in power to maintain control over both the direction and price of credit has in practice stultified the extent of reform in several of those countries, and often led to inflationary excesses in addition to their other problems.

Another step widely accepted in principle has been the introduction of markets in the debt of governments and para-statal bodies.

While there has also been general appreciation that incentives for efficiency require profit-related pay for managers of large companies, and private ownership of (small) service enterprises and farms, greater political objections and concerns have been raised about further moves to the establishment of private ownership, e.g. over large scale concerns in manufacturing, property, etc. But if fixed interest debt markets are to be established, and bankruptcy laws/provisions seriously introduced, how can debt/equity ratios be adjusted, and a market in corporate governance established (i.e. takeovers of bad managers by good managers), without an equity market? One suggestion that has been quite widely canvassed is that new equity shares in all the previous socialist companies be created, and vested in a number of competing investment-holding financial companies. This has an added advantage, since the change from a command to a market economy will be so extreme that virtually no one, *ex ante*, could price the shares of the individual basic companies accurately (Blanchard and Layard, 1990). The investment-holding managers, whose pay should be related to their success in achieving asset value appreciation, would then trade these shares on some form of equity market, and could choose to accept, or even originate, take-over bids for control of company management. There remains, however, some dispute about how far the investment-holding management companies should be enabled, or encouraged, to reach positions of corporate control. If they are to operate the market in corporate governance, they must be able to achieve such positions, but might they not also then attain too much monopoly power? See the article by Bobinski and Wolf (1990) on 'Radical options for privatisation'.

Such a fund-management holding company solution need not breach the objections against private ownership of large concerns, if that were deemed still politically objectionable. The holding companies *could* offer private savers fixed interest deposits, rather than shares in themselves, presumably with more successful (riskier) holding companies offering higher interest rates. Then the State could still absorb any surplus accruing to holding companies from the excess of dividends and realised capital appreciation, over interest and running costs. Nuti (1987, 1988, 1989), has suggested such an approach as a means of reconciling continuing ultimate State ownership of the main means of production with an efficient system of financial markets. Others (e.g. Winiecki, 1989, 1990) have rejected such a half-way house as untenable, and/or unacceptable. Thus there remains dispute whether such financial holding companies are only the first step along the road to Western style private ownership in all respects, or could help to provide a satisfactory accommodation between the need for a financial market (able to achieve the key functions outlined above), on the one hand, and a political desire to maintain State ownership on the other. Whatever the outcome of that debate, it seems likely, at the present juncture, that the establishment of financial holding companies in formerly command economies will be a prospective future development.

THE CHARACTERISTICS OF FINANCIAL MARKETS

A. Rational Efficient Markets and the Pricing of Assets

The present fundamental value of an asset depends on the future flow of services available from holding it, discounted back to the present. The services identified in the case of financial assets are usually restricted to the flow of future cash payments of dividends, in the case of equities, and interest and principal in the case of bonds, discounted back to the present at a discount rate, the choice of which is discussed further below.

The market value of assets may, however, also be affected by the (differing) incidence of tax, on different groups of investors, falling on both the interest/dividends and on the capital gains/losses, (see for example Auerbach and King, 1983). The valuation of the latter is particularly complex since the owners of the asset can make the choice of when to realise capital gains/losses, which provides an option value to the asset (see for example, Constantinides and Scholes, 1980, and Constantinides and Ingersoll, 1984).

Again the asset may provide the owner with certain other services. Some assets, e.g. pictures, land, may provide non-pecuniary services. Financial assets which can be realised quickly, at little cost, and close to some known value, also allow the owner the opportunity to rearrange overall portfolios of assets quickly and flexibly, and hence may provide liquidity services.

The main hypothesis in this area is currently the rational efficient market (REM) hypothesis which posits that market members will use information efficiently to estimate the future flow of services, the appropriate discount rate, and hence the present fundamental value of assets, see for example Marsh and Merton, 1986. Information will only be fully utilised, however, if it is costless – in time, effort and money – to acquire, store and manipulate. Accordingly if information-gathering is, indeed, costly, such activity will only be pursued to the point that the costs are balanced by expected benefits, e.g. in excess returns. Hence prices will not generally reflect *all* potentially available information (Grossman and Stiglitz, 1980).

If the REM hypothesis holds, asset prices should only change in response to 'news', affecting the future flow of services, or the appropriate discount rates. It is often difficult to identify the 'news', the surprise element, in events and announcements, e.g. how much was expected or 'leaked' beforehand, but the growth of surveys of expectations of future economic and political events – and econometric estimates of what rational expectations should be – allows the research worker to make some estimate of the division of announcements into anticipated and unanticipated parts. The hypothesis then tested is that the anticipated element in announcements should not cause changes in asset prices, while the unanticipated would do so. It is, however, usually difficult to give much greater precision than this to the issue of what kind of quantitative effect a macroeconomic announcement, such as monetary growth or trade figures, will have on asset prices since this will depend, *inter alia*, on market perceptions about the policy regime in operation, and hence the authorities' own response to the 'news'.

Since the future stream of dividends, the future path of riskless interest rates, and the market's future evaluation of risk are all stochastic uncertain variables, it is not possible in general to examine directly whether the market's assessment of fundamental valuation is correct, or not. One area of research, which would seem to allow such a test, relates to the pricing of an asset, whose value depends on its backing by other assets whose own market value is observable, i.e. an investment trust, a closed-end trust in US parlance.

This research has, however, shown that the market value of the shares of such trusts regularly (though not always) stands at a substantial discount to the market valuation of the supporting/backing assets. While there are some explanations for this that are consistent with a rational, efficient market, e.g., agency costs, illiquidity, capital gains tax liabilities on unrealised appreciation, Lee, Shleifer and Thaler (1990) argue that none of these can plausibly account for the size and pattern of these discounts. Instead, following the line of argument advanced by De Long *et al.* (1990), they argue that the discounts reflect shifts in the 'sentiment of individual investors'. Even when a proportion of investors are capable of making a rational, efficient assessment of fundamental values, they still have to be concerned about the changing moods of other investors in the market, whose decisions to buy/sell may be driven by other considerations, fashions or fads.

I shall revert to this possibility, of the market being partly driven by fads/fashions at several points later. For the moment, however, if asset values did only adjust in response to 'news', then they should not vary in response to information that has already been made available. This hypothesis is often presented, in the literature, in three forms, weak, semi-strong and strong. The weak form tests the proposition that excess returns cannot be achieved from investing on the basis of information about past movements in own asset prices. In high data frequencies this approximates to the proposition that asset prices follow a martingale; and at lower frequencies that returns will be appropriate for the risk category of asset. This hypothesis is generally supported by econometric research (e.g. unit roots), see Fama (1976), for example, but the continued use of Chartism, at least in forex markets, provides some presumptive contrary evidence. Moreover, there have been some faint signs of excess returns being available by investing on certain days in the week, the 'Monday' effect, or in certain months, the 'January' effect (see French, 1980; Gibbons and Hess, 1981; Keim and Stambaugh, 1986; Condoyanni, O'Hanlon and Ward, 1988; Dimson, 1988; Jaffe and Westerfield, 1985; Campbell and Hamao, 1990).

Semi-strong efficiency holds when it is not possible to make excess returns on the basis of prior publicly available information. There is increasing evidence that it *is* possible to predict some small part of future asset returns on the basis of currently available data, e.g. on the dividend/price ratio on equities, by the level of interest rates and by the long-term yield spread, see for example, Beltratti (1990), Campbell (1990), Campbell and Hamao (1990), Campbell and Shiller (1988), Campbell (1987), Fama and French (1988), Attanasio and Wadhwani (1989), Sentana and Wadhwani (1989), King, Sentana and Wadhwani (1990). Although it does now seem possible to predict a small proportion of future variations in return, how far it is possible to make money from such predictive capabilities, and hence refute REM, after taking account of time-varying risks, transaction costs, etc., is still uncertain.

Strong efficiency holds when the current value of assets rationally reflects all available information, private information as well as publicly available data. This is harder to test since it is not possible to observe private information. However, event studies on takeover announcements frequently show a sustained upward movement in the stock price of the target company in advance of the announcement, which may be due to a widening circle of informed insider dealing.

The apparent conclusion of the econometric studies, i.e. that it is not, or only barely, possible to make systematic excess returns in financial markets from an analysis of publicly available prior information, notably including the past history of the assets themselves, should not, perhaps, surprise anyone. If information enabling excess returns to be made is costless, it should be used, and in the process the excess returns would be arbitraged away.

Yet there are several professional activities whose livelihood would seem to depend in part on the denial of that proposition. I have already mentioned Chartists. In addition some investment advisers/managers purport to go beyond the valuable functions of advising on diversification and the choice of position on the efficient risk/return frontier to be able to achieve excess returns for clients. Studies, however, of the returns achieved by managers of client funds, e.g. investment and unit trust managers, have often indicated that on balance their results underperform the market indices, which is one reason for the growth of passive funds in the USA, which are simply invested so as to achieve the market index outcome. Early studies on the performance of mutual funds in the USA (e.g. Jensen, 1968; Frend *et al.*, 1970) tended to show that, net of expenses, they underperformed the market; but at least one recent study (Ippolito, 1989) has led to a reconsideration of that assessment. Another line of study, pursued by Dimson and Marsh (1984), and Dimson and Fraletti (1986), is to examine whether brokers' and security analysts' recommended purchases/sales would systematically garner excess returns (marginally 'yes' in the 1984 paper; 'no' in the 1986 paper).

Efficiency of this form, i.e. the inability to use prior public information to generate excess returns, does *not,* however, imply that asset prices do provide a 'correct' representation of fundamental values. Summers (1986a, b) has pointed out that the above tests have very low power to discriminate between a market which prices assets efficiently, and one which incorporates some long-lasting and slowly-adjusting fad, or fashion, in the determination of asset prices.

As already remarked in the case of studies of closed-end (investment) trusts, the possible existence of fads, or fashions, in financial markets is a feature that has to be taken into account even by those who may remain rational and capable of more clear-sighted assessment of the fundamentals (Shiller, 1984; Wadhwani, 1988). Furthermore, it is *not* necessarily the case that 'rational' investors will both make more money and also drive 'noise traders out of the market', see De Long *et al.* (1989).

It would be extraordinarily difficult, if not impossible, to detect a mispricing 'fad' that remained constant over time, though we will note below the surprising persistence of a larger differential than can easily be explained by risk factors between equity and bill/bond returns (and how can one explain the differences between equity price levels in NYSE and Tokyo SE?). But most of the proponents of the fads/fashions school believe that such fashions do have a finite life span.

If so, one would expect to see some statistical consequentials. First in the very long run, at low frequencies, there would be a tendency towards mean reversion in asset returns; what is driven up by a fad must eventually subside. Some evidence that such low frequency, mean reversion exists is provided by Poterba and Summers (1987), though the extent of such mean reversion, post-1945 at any rate, has been challenged by Kim, Nelson and Startz (1988). Other possible explanations of such mean reversion are also theoretically possible, e.g. variations over time in required returns, say if individuals became more risk averse when they became poorer when the market had fallen. Poterba and Summers doubt whether the evidence is consistent with the necessary persistence of shocks to required returns for this alternative explanation to be valid, but see Section C. below on measuring the persistence of shocks to volatility, also see Campbell (1990).

Second, in a market influenced by transient fashions, one might expect more volatility than in one characterised solely by rational expectations. There has been a vast, and increasingly technical, literature on this issue of whether equity markets exhibit 'excess' volatility (on which Marsh and Merton, 1986; Kleidon, 1986; Campbell and Shiller, 1987 and West 1988 are good recent references). It is doubtful whether any consensus conclusion can yet be distilled from these myriad studies, but my impression is that there is evidence that equity market volatility is greater than can be easily explained by the REM hypothesis, but that the excess, after taking account of the unit root behaviour of market prices, etc., is considerably less marked than the initial studies (e.g. by Shiller, 1981) had suggested. Nevertheless Bulkley and Tonks claim that, had investors been applying a constant discount rate over time, they could have derived long-term trading rules, to take advantage of such low-frequency stationarity, on the basis of known data that would have made excess returns both in the UK (1987, also see 1990) and in the USA (1988), thereby rejecting market efficiency criteria.

Such results, from equity markets, cannot necessarily be generalised to other asset markets. For example, the response in the price of long-dated fixed-interest Government bonds in the UK and USA to unanticipated movements in short-term interest rates has commonly indicated that the market has expected more mean-reversion in nominal short-term rates to some 'norm' than has actually been the historical case, since 1945 at least. In that sense long-term bond prices have been insufficiently volatile, see for example, Sargent (1972), Mankiw and Summers (1984), Shiller, Campbell and Schoenholtz (1983) and Campbell and Shiller (1989). Goodhart (1988) also claims that the foreign exchange market shows fewer signs of 'overshooting' than the Dornbusch model (e.g. 1976) would have suggested.

Two further academic diversions may also be briefly mentioned. The first is the possibility that asset prices may follow a bubble path, either in a fashion consistent with rational expectations, or not. This was intellectual fun, and was proffered in part as a possible explanation of the earlier findings of 'excess volatility' in stock prices. Nevertheless subsequent analysis indicated that the conditions for rational bubbles to exist were impossibly demanding, e.g. that such a bubble 'can start only on the first date of trading of a stock', Diba and Grossman (1988, p. 753), and West (1988), and such bubbles also appear to be inconsistent with learning rules for agents that were expectationally stable (Evans, 1989). History, however, shows that irrational bubbles can exist in financial markets, e.g. South Sea Bubble, Dutch Tulip Mania. While some wondered whether the Crash of October 1987, or the earlier gyrations in the gold market (1978/9), could be described in terms of the breaking of a bubble, most careful empirical research (for an account of some pitfalls in such research, see Evans (1989)) has not found any clear evidence of bubble-type behaviour in such recent market fluctuations, e.g. in the form of runs of excess positive returns (e.g. Evans, 1986; Mullins, 1989). One recent exception, Froot and Obstfeld (1989), argues that the path of US stock prices can be explained in terms of an 'intrinsic bubble' in which the market overreacts in a systematic way to changes in current dividends. This line of explanation is similar to that of Campbell (1990) who finds evidence of covariance between changes in expected dividends and in expected returns.

The second diversion is whether financial asset markets may exhibit any tendency to non-linear deterministic dynamics, which may superficially appear as stochastic fluctuations. Part of the attraction of this research lies in the exciting terminology involved, chaos theory. There are many who are intuitively attracted to the idea that financial markets exhibit chaotic behaviour. Unfortunately it takes a huge data set, of several thousand data points, and some highly advanced maths to test adequately for chaos. Moreover such early tests, as have been done, have not found much evidence of chaotic behaviour in financial markets (Vassilicos, 1990).

B. The Pricing of Risk

Given a declining marginal utility of income (wealth), investors can normally be expected to be risk averse. If investors are then risk averse, they will require a higher expected return in order to persuade them to assume more risk. This trade-off between risk and return has played a central role in the analysis of financial markets. For an excellent survey, see Ross (1989).

One of the first economists to formulate this trade-off Tobin (1958) compared the choice between holding a riskless short-term monetary asset and a risky longer-term bond. Initially, the riskiness of an asset was frequently measured by the variance of its own return (or price) over time, but it was soon realised that the idiosyncratic risk of individual assets could be eliminated by appropriate diversification, leaving behind certain common risks inherent in the holding of assets, which could not be avoided by such diversification.

This approach was formalised in the Capital Asset Pricing Model (CAPM) as developed by Sharpe (1964), Lintner (1965), and Markowitz (1959). In this model the return on the risky market *portfolio* of assets has to exceed the riskless rate of return by a premium depending on the expected conditional variance of such returns (expectations formed at $t-1$), interacting with the risk premium needed to induce investors to hold the market portfolio, which in turn depends on investors' rates of risk aversion, hence,

$$E_{t-1}R_{mt} - r_t = \gamma(E_{t-1}\sigma_m^2)$$

where E is the expectation operator, R_m is the return on the risky market portfolio, r the safe rate of interest, γ coefficient (depending on relative risk aversion) relating the excess return required in order to assume additional risk, and σ^2 the conditional variance of the market portfolio.

In turn the expected return on (price of), any individual asset depended not on its own (conditional) variance, but on its conditional covariance with the market portfolio. This latter was expressed, and measured, in terms of the beta of each asset, as set out in the standard formula:

$$E(R_i) - r = \alpha_i + \beta_i[E(R_m) - r]$$

and

$$\beta_i = \text{Cov}(R_i, R_m/\text{Var } R_m)$$

where R_i and R_m are the one-period returns on the individual ith asset and the market portfolios respectively.

Assets whose returns varied exactly in line with the market had a beta of one, assets whose returns varied more than the index a beta greater than unity, and assets whose returns were more stable were regarded as defensive, with betas less than unity.

With the removal of exchange controls over capital movements, the assets available to any one investor became effectively worldwide. Investors could, therefore, choose to hold an international portfolio, which would allow them to reduce (perhaps to eliminate) individual risk by appropriate international diversification. So, by extension, it became possible to analyse relative expected returns between assets denominated in different countries through international, or I, CAPM. This introduced certain additional complexities into the analysis, however, since the risks of foreign investment depended on the covariances of both exchange rates, and foreign assets' own-currency returns, with the market portfolio; and also the selection of the safe rate of return would depend on the domicile of the investor, e.g. US three-month Treasury Bill rate would not represent a riskless asset to a Japanese investor, since it would be subject to exchange risk in returning to Yen, with (consumption) expenditures denominated in Yen presumably representing that investor's main source of utility.

The CAPM model was essentially static, in that it involved a single period maximisation process on the basis of current estimates of portfolios variances/covariances, etc., though such variances and covariances, and hence relative risk, could be expected to vary over time, see for example, Hall, Miles and Taylor (1988). The next step was to introduce intertemporal analysis through the Consumption CAPM developed by Breeden (1979) and Lucas (1978). With consumption liable to fluctuate over time, there would be a relationship between the marginal rate of substitution of consumption between periods and the excess return required on risky assets. The lower the rate of substitution of consumption between periods, i.e. the less that consumers were willing to allow their consumption to fluctuate, the greater would have to be the excess return on holdings of risky assets, the variance of whose returns would aggravate such fluctuations in consumption. In so far as the covariance between the pay-off (dividend, interest yield) on the asset (or portfolio) in question and the level of consumption in each period was expected to be low (high), so the required return on that asset would be less (greater). In practice, of course, profits, dividends and interest rates all tend to show a strong positive covariance, over the cycle, with incomes and consumption.

More formally, following Grossman and Shiller (1981), where the present discounted value of utilities of a potential investor can be written as,

$$U_t = \sum_{k=0}^{\infty} \beta^k u(C_{t+k}), \qquad \text{where } \beta = \frac{1}{1+r}$$

and r is the subjective rate of time preference, then the investor will achieve an optimal division between present consumption and holding an asset i, whose price in terms of consumption goods is P and pays a real dividend of D, when

$$U'(C_t) P_{it} = \beta E [U'(C_{t+1}) (P_{it+1} + D_{it+1})| I_t],$$

and I_t is the information set available at time t. Then with the marginal rate of substitution $S_t = \beta U'(C_{t+1})/U'(C_t)$, and the expected return on ith asset, $R_{it} = (P_{it+1} + D_{it+1}/P_{it})$, it follows that $E(R_{it}S_t) = 1$ and that

$$ER_{it} = E(S_t)^{-1}. [1 - \text{Cov}(R_{it}, S_t)],$$

so that the expected return on any asset (or portfolios of assets) must be greater, when the marginal rate of substitution is lower, and when the expected covariance between the return and MRS (which will be low when consumption is low in a slump) is high (i.e. low returns in a slump), also see Hansen and Singleton (1982 and 1983).

Indeed, one could combine CAPM and the consumption CAPM by seeking to analyse the excess return on any asset in terms both of its covariance with the market portfolio and with investors' expected time path, and marginal rate of substitution, of consumption. Together with other possible sources of common risk, some to be discussed below, this led on to the arbitrage pricing theory of capital asset pricing (Ross, 1976), or APT, in which the risk of any asset might be related to several common factors, some observable, some not (see also Dybvig (1983) and Dybvig and Ross (1985)).

Such theories had have great analytical attraction, but have had much less empirical success in explaining observed patterns of asset returns (see the surveys of Jensen, 1972 or Schwert, 1983). Thus one recent survey paper 'Arch Modelling in Finance' by Bollerslev *et al.* (1990, p. 20), noted that 'a simple version of the standard CAPM model seems to be inadequate in explaining the movements in expected stock returns'. This is despite their earlier comment that 'the evidence in Mankiw and Shapiro (1986) and many others, [is] that the static CAPM performs better, from an empirical point of view, than the consumption CAPM'.

There are a variety of reasons put forward to explain the comparatively poor (relative to earlier hopes and expectations) empirical performance of CAPM, ICAPM and CCAPM, in explaining relative asset returns. For most (personal) investors their holdings of housing and land are the largest and most important component of their assets. Data on such holdings, the (conditional) returns and variances on such holdings, are rarely available. Furthermore there are certain indivisibilities relating to home ownership that differentiate it from financial assets. Moreover there may well be barriers, perhaps in the shape of learning costs, that prevent investors diversifying as much as theory would have indicated between different classes of assets. King and Leape (1987) have shown that most personal US investors only hold a small number out of a quite wide range of alternative financial asset types.

Thus CAPM models do not fully account for the heterogeneity of assets, or investors. The same criticism can, perhaps, also be made for Consumption CAPM models, which generally use, as the basis for empirical modelling, a representative agent approach together with aggregate consumption data. Grossman and Shiller (1981, p. 2), however, note that

> The theory of asset returns embodied in [the above] expressions . . . is very powerful because it can be applied so generally. It holds for *any* asset, or portfolio of assets. It holds for *any* individual consumer who has the option of investing in stocks (even if he chooses not to hold stocks) and thus it must hold for aggregate consumption so long as some peoples' consumption is well represented by the aggregate consumption.

One problem with this is that the community is infinitely lived, whereas no individual is; as Attanasio and Weber (1988) note, 'aggregate data may be sensitive to the contemporary presence in the economy of cohorts of different age of birth'. Until recently at least, most people had few net financial assets, so that their consumption was liquidity constrained, with the consumption pattern of stockholders behaving differently from that of non-stockholders (Mankiw and Zeldes, 1989). Moreover, the assumption that utility is additively separable, depending only on current consumption in each period, rather than also on the past history of consumption is dubious (see Constantinides, 1989). As Bollerslev *et al.* (1990) note 'aggregate consumption [might be] providing a poor measure of the fundamental consumption risk'.

One of the main current puzzles in the analysis of financial markets has been identified by Mehra and Prescott (1985) in their paper on 'The Equity Premium: A Puzzle'. They use a simple, formal model to examine whether the differential, of slightly over 6 per cent, between the return on riskier equity than on safer short-term bills (using US data, but much the same premium also holds for the UK), can be explained, given the historical time path and variability of aggregate consumption, in terms of plausible values for the coefficient of relative risk aversion. Their conclusion is that the combination of an apparently low riskless rate of interest, as represented by the (conditionally expected) *real* rate of return on short-term bills, which has on average been close to zero over recent decades, indeed over the last century, is hard to square with a much higher average real rate of return on equities (some 6 per cent higher). Nor can this result be explained by a very high preference for liquidity, since the premium between the *ex-post* achieved return on equity and on long-term government bonds is not much less than the equity/bill premium. Thus the decomposition of the equity premium into a 'pay-off' uncertainty premium and a 'term' premium reveals that empirically the former has been the dominant element (Esposito, 1990).

Considering also the risks involved in holding nominal fixed-interest assets in periods of highly variable inflation, the main puzzle may be to explain why investors were prepared to hold government bills/bonds at such low real yields for so long (Weil, 1989). 'Why is it', Weil asks (p. 12), 'if consumers are so averse to consumption fluctuations that the risk free rate is so low?' Again one part of the explanation may relate to the heterogeneity of investors, with a large proportion of such fixed interest debt being absorbed by investors with particular incentives to hold fixed-interest assets, e.g. those required by regulation to do so, those with fixed interest liabilities, etc. But if one tries to explain relative returns in terms of market segmentation, separate customer clienteles, then one would have expected to see more effects on asset prices/returns from variations in asset supply (e.g. the size of the Public Sector Borrowing Requirement) than has been identified so far (Bibolini, 1990; Goodhart and Gowland, 1977).

There are, of course, other kinds of risk as well, in addition to market and consumption risk. One such risk is political, i.e. that the political basis of the system may be so changed that the framework of the economic system, that determines the structure of ownership, distribution of returns between classes of agents, penalties for default, etc., may be redesigned. Such risks will have influenced investors in wartime, times of civil strife and times when the existing capitalist system appeared to be working badly, or under pressure from other sources, e.g. in the USA, 1931–3, or in the UK 1973–5. (Note: it is not plausible to adduce any increase in political risks as the explanation for October 1987.)

Besides those traders who try to assess fundamental values there will be those operating in response to prior changes in price. These may be of several kinds. First there are those who are forced to sell as prices fall (e.g. traders on margin, who cannot, or choose not to, put up additional margin requirements), or choose to sell to protect their wealth, e.g. portfolio insurance. Second, there will be those who try to buy after price declines, perhaps on the grounds that, though actual fundamental values are hard to observe clearly, the actual price change has exceeded the plausible shift in fundamentals occasioned by recent news. The demand of such feedback traders for assets is then a function of the prior excess return on the asset (price change at high frequencies), i.e. that:

$$D_2 = \gamma R_{t-1}$$

$\gamma > 0$ (for type 1), $\quad \gamma < 0$ (for type 2)

The demand for assets of those seeking to assess fundamental values is

$$D_1 = r_t + \rho(\sigma^2)$$

With market equilibrium requiring that

$$D_1 + D_2 = 1$$

then

$$E_{t-1}(R_t) - r_t = \rho(\sigma^2) - \gamma\rho(\sigma^2)R_{t-1}$$

(see Sentana and Wadhwani, 1990). Accordingly expected returns will be raised or lowered (and returns subject to negative/positive autocorrelation) depending on the comparative weight in the market of the feedback traders of the two types. Intuitively one might expect fear to be the strongest emotion at times of crashes and general depression, so that the presence of type 1 feedback investors would be most obvious in such circumstances, and both survey evidence (Shiller, 1987) and data on time variation in the auto-correlation properties of stock returns (Sentana and Wadhwani, 1990) is consistent with that hypothesis.

Nevertheless our present ability to explain relative asset returns in terms of premia related to certain identified sources of risk remains undeniably weak. A recent study by King, Sentana and Wadhwani (1990) sought to identify the relative returns from holding stock market indices in sixteen different countries on the basis of some ten monthly macroeconomic variables (the observables) and a (small) set of unobservable common factors affecting these markets. The results showed that the contribution of the observables was tiny (with the partial exception of Japan). Thus the main contribution to conditional volatility in these markets comes from the unobservable elements, in particular the first unobservable common factor which exhibits sharp, but temporary, spikes (little persistence) at certain turbulent occasions (notably October 1987). This is, perhaps, a sophisticated way of quantifying our current ignorance of what causes asset returns to exhibit relative variation over time. Indeed, the concept of time-varying risk premia involves one of the most conspicuously 'empty boxes' of modern economics.

Given that economists find it so hard to relate asset returns to identified forms of risk, there must remain some question whether the pricing of risks, of various kinds, e.g. 'political', market-variation, counter-party, settlement, etc., is satisfactorily done in financial markets. Thus the Cross Report (Cross *et al.*, 1986) was concerned whether the risk inherent in new instruments, e.g. various fancy kinds of derivatives, was always properly priced, e.g. by competitive banks. Indeed, the experience of losses on LDC lending by multinational banks in the period 1979–82, at least, suggests that prices then were not properly adjusted for risk. Miles (1989) notes that 'There is no difficulty in showing that spectacular misperceptions of risk, even by specialist credit raters, are often made', and he cites the Texas real estate market in the mid 1980s. This is not to suggest, however, that the authorities are necessarily better than financial intermediaries, or markets, at this exercise; the authorities often regard themselves as largely unable to price relative risk at all, e.g. with common premiums for deposit insurance, or apply very broad-brush and often simplistic measures, as in the case of the BIS bank capital adequacy requirements.

C.   The Volatility and Higher Moments of Asset Markets

In the analysis of the risks inherent in financial markets, theory appears to have out-run empirical support. In the case of studies of the time-varying volatility, and higher moments, of asset markets, empirical econometric work has been out-distancing theory. It has long been appreciated that asset markets are characterised by periods of extreme volatility and turbulence, interspersed with periods of calm, i.e. that the conditional variance of asset markets is autocorrelated, and time-varying, heteroscedastic, rather than constant, homoscedastic.

Thus the error term, ε_t, in a discrete time stochastic process, such as an asset market, may be a function of an iid error term ζ_t, $E(\zeta_t) = 0$ Var $(\zeta_t) = 1$, and σ_t which is a time varying, positive and measurable function of the time $t - 1$ information set, such that

$$\varepsilon_t = \zeta_t \, \sigma_t,$$

see the original papers by Engle (1982) and Bollerslev *et al.* (1990).

In his original work Engle suggested estimating σ_t^2 as a linear function of past squared errors, hence

$$\sigma_i^2 = \omega + \sum_{i=1}^{q} \alpha_i \varepsilon_{t-i}^2$$

where $\omega > 0$ and $\alpha_i \geq 0$, since σ^2 must be positive. With financial data, this captures the tendency for large (small) price changes to be followed by other large (small) changes, but of unpredictable sign. This model is known as the linear autoregressive conditional heteroscedasticity (q) model. In practice the imposition of the non-negativity constraint, with a long lag length q, caused certain estimation problems, and a simpler more flexible lag structure was achieved through a generalised ARCH, or GARCH model, whereby

$$\sigma_t^2 = \omega + \sum_{i=1}^{q} d_i \varepsilon_{t-i}^2 + \sum_{i=1}^{p} \beta_i \sigma_{i-i}^2$$

Again all the parameters have to be non-negative. In practice, most attempts to fit GARCH models to financial markets have indicated that it is possible to do so with low orders of both p and q, often with $p = q = 1$.

The generalisation from a univariate to a multivariate ARCH or GARCH model is conceptually straightforward, but the rapid multiplication of parameters, and the observation that many assets, and asset markets, tend to be disturbed at the same time, have led to the use of multivariate latent factor ARCH models, in which the variances and covariances are modelled as a function of a smaller number of common factors.

It is apparent, both from simple observation, and from the success of fitting GARCH models to many (most) asset markets, that the conditional variance is time varying. In so far as the time-varying conditional variance is a satisfactory representation of the riskiness of an asset, then the expected conditional return itself should be functionally related to the conditional variance so that:

$$E_{t-1} R_t = \alpha + r_t + b E_{t-1} \sigma_t^2 + c X_t$$

where X is a vector of other supposedly relevant variables. The joint modelling of expected returns as a function of the conditional variance, together with the estimation of that variance, is described as an ARCH in Mean model, or ARCH M model. Again many tests of such models have been made, and the value of *b* has frequently been found to be significant, e.g. French, Schwert and Stambaugh (1987), Chou (1988) and Attanasio and Wadhwani (1989).

Even with an ARCHM model, the simultaneity between the two equations necessitates that the full model be correctly specified in order to obtain consistent estimates (Pagan and Sabau, 1988; Pagan and Hong, 1988). So attempts to apply a multivariate ARCHM model become technically complex.

One of the questions raised by the October Crash was how far any shock to the market, possibly even arising from a chance event, would feed on itself, because the shock would cause (expected) higher volatility to persist in future for a long time. Clearly if there was such persistence, then the applicable risk premium would rise, requiring a rise in future expected returns from asset holding; this would then be achieved by a fall in current asset prices relative to expected future cash flows. The greater the expected persistence, the more (downwards) shocks feed on themselves. In practice the additional volatility observed in stock markets after 19 October 1987 had largely reverted to normal by the opening months of 1988 (Schwert, 1989).

More generally, ARCH type models are an excellent way of estimating the extent of such persistence. The results of such exercises have not, however, produced any clear consensus. There may be some evidence that there are differing kinds of shocks to the market, with really large shocks (outliers) having little persistence (Friedman and Laibson, 1990) with a rapid reversion to the norm, but certain kinds of other shocks, perhaps due to shifts in market structure, having much more persistence with an approximately unit root (non-stationary) effect on market volatility, i.e. in a GARCH (p, q) model,

$$\alpha_1 + \ldots + \alpha_q + \beta_1 + \ldots + \beta_p = 1$$

in the simpler, and common GARCH (1,1) model, the unit root occurs when $\alpha_1 + \beta_1 = 1$. Engle and Bollerslev term this an integrated in variance, or IGARCH, model, and some empirical tests of asset markets have not been able to reject such IGARCH effects. As with all cases of lagged dependent variables, the model is covariance stationary if and only if $\alpha(1) + \beta(1) < 1$.

There is no question but that ARCH type models have been found to be highly successful in modelling certain patent features of asset markets, i.e. time varying volatility (through Pagan and Schwert (1989) have compared several different models of stock return volatility, and found that patterns of change over time exhibit important non-linearities not easily captured by ARCH models). Consequently, there has been an explosion in the number of such empirical exercises, and a profusion of new varieties and versions of ARCH models, with various modifications, on offer. The present state of play in this respect is well described in Bollerslev *et al.* (1990). What is less clear is the nature of the (market) behaviour that drives such clustering effects in volatility. It is, of course, known that volatility is highly correlated with other measures of market activity, such as trading volume, frequency of price revisions (e.g. by market makers), but it seems most probable that some common factor drives both volatility and activity, rather than having one way causation from volume to volatility, or vice versa.

The standard explanation of the initial shock to markets is the arrival of 'news' (though Goodhart (1990) has shown how few public announcements of economic 'news' actually seem to move markets, and it is difficult to relate the October crash to any such news; also see Roll (1988).) Be that as it may, it is certainly possible to view some part of the subsequent high levels of volatility (following shocks) as inherent in the process of information dissemination and absorption (together with the working-out of the consequential operations of feed-back traders), and this seems a reasonable line of approach for a persistence in volatility lasting minutes, hours or even, at a pinch, days. But information processing is now extremely rapid, and is it really feasible to envisage an absorption/adjustment process lasting for weeks/months?

Another micro-market approach, developed by Admati and Pfleiderer (1988) and by Barclay, Litzenberger and Warner (1989), shows how there may be a tendency for market traders (both those with some 'inside' information on appropriate market prices and liquidity traders) to cluster together at certain occasions, e.g. at the close and open of markets with discrete opening/closing times. There is some evidence of this in stock markets, but much less so in continuously operating (during weekdays) forex markets (Goodhart, 1990). Anyhow, while such micro-market factors might explain intra-day clustering of volume/volatility, it would not seem such a strong basis for the explanation of inter-day clustering. French and Roll (1986) noted that volatility dropped away when markets were shut; initially they tended to the view that there was some internal market dynamic whereby trading activity itself generated further trading, but subsequently they retreated to the view that the patterns of volatility/trading volume that they perceived was a function of the more frequent arrival of 'private' news during trading hours. Obviously, it would be hard to test this latter hypothesis.

Thus, while the observed time path of the variance of asset markets can be reasonably well modelled by ARCH-type models, the behavioural rationale for this phenomenon – at least at the lower frequencies, beyond intra-day periodicities, e.g. over weeks and months – is not yet so clear.

That said, the ARCH models cannot account for *all* the observed statistical characteristics of asset markets. One of the features of asset markets is that they exhibit more extreme movements (in both directions) than normal, i.e. the distributions of returns (price changes) have fat tails; they are leptokurtotic. Some considerable part of such leptokurtosis is due to time-varying volatility, and hence is eliminated by the application of ARCH models. Even so, the residuals from ARCH models themselves are frequently, perhaps generally, leptokurtotic and non-normal. One response to this in econometric exercises is to adopt conditional distributions with fatter tails than the normal tail, e.g. Baillie and De Gennaro (1990) following a suggestion by Bollerslev.

Nevertheless the question still arises about what causes the fat tails. One curious feature of ultra-high frequency data, e.g. tick by tick continuous data in the forex market, is that the observed leptokurtosis declines as the frequency of observation becomes even higher than about ten minutes (Goodhart and Figliuoli, 1988). This may suggest that the pace of arrival of information is more nearly captured by ultra-high frequency data, allowing the price change per unit of new information to revert to a normal distribution. With time aggregation, however, the distributions, i.e. of news arrival and of price change per unit of news, become inextricably mixed. So, the leptokurtosis may result from a mixture of distributions (see for example, Clark, 1973; Epps and Epps, 1973; Tauchen and Pitts, 1983; Harris, 1986, 1987) with which ARCH models cannot fully cope.

We have already noted that the persistence of shocks to volatility, as evidenced in ARCH models, is likely to reflect back on the conditional expected return, since it will raise the required risk premium. In that sense any large shock (positive or negative) to expected future cash flows should raise the applicable discount factor. This implies that stock markets should exhibit skewness, with 'jump' drops being greater than 'jump' rises. Evidence that this is indeed so, and an explanation on the above lines, is available in Campbell and Hentschell (1990) and Friedman and Laibson (1990). Since an upwards shock for one side of the forex market is a downwards shock for the counterparty, there is no such reason for expecting skewness in those markets, and indeed none has been reported in the empirical studies.

In this section of the chapter we have noted how asset markets are characterised by time-varying volatility, more extreme movements (than normal), i.e. leptokurtosis, and negative skewness in stock markets. While such features have been modelled with some considerable success by one, or other, of the growing family of ARCH models, there remains a challenge how to account for the behaviour that leads to such features.

CRITICISMS OF FINANCIAL MARKETS

A. Short-termism

I have not seen an exact and precise statement, set out in a rigorous fashion, of the main elements of this criticism. In the earlier section on asset pricing, I noted that the present price of an asset should reflect its future stream of services (e.g. dividends, interest, non-pecuniary services) discounted back to the present at a discount rate applicable to its risk class. Under the rational efficient markets theorem all (publicly available) information is already incorporated into this price, so that expectations of future asset returns (note: not asset prices, nor the returns themselves which both will tend to be time-varying, even in the absence of 'news' shocks) will only change in response to 'news'.

The general implication of this, though subject to some quite stringent conditions about transactions costs, etc., is that an investor seeking to achieve the best long-term outcome, risk/return combination, should be seeking also to achieve the best short-term results, since (changes in) long-term expected future developments should be immediately and efficiently reflected in current asset prices.

One strand of the criticism of short-termism resides in the complaint that City investors are *too* concerned with maximising short-term returns, at the expense – it is implied – of having a worse long-term outcome. But, current theories of asset pricing would suggest that the way to achieve long-term success is by trying to achieve the best available outcome in each short-term period. It is, of course, true that higher returns may be made, for a time, by the assumption of more risk or just by luck, so it must take several periods before it is possible, or sensible, to seek to discriminate between 'good' and 'bad' investment managers on the basis of their records. Nevertheless, the idea that the pursuit of short-term success in investment management will be at the expense of long-term values only holds up if somehow the correct valuation of future flows of services, or the appropriate discount rate, are *not* being applied in the pricing of present assets.

Another, and perhaps, more plausible strand of argument is that the evaluations by investment managers on the basis of fairly short-term horizons, e.g. two years, may lead to mispricing in those cases where there is a small probability of a *very* good (bad) outcome, balanced by a much larger probability of a repetition of a rather poor (good) outcome. In such cases investment managers may not be prepared to take a fair bet to hold the asset with a small probability of an outstanding outcome, and too prepared to hold assets with a small probability of a crash. If they did the former for example, they would on average underperform their competitors, with just an occasional offsetting chance of a killing. But the average underperformance might well lead to being sacked, while the incentive for portfolio managers (often paid on a salary) to go for a killing may not offset the fear of sacking. For such reasons bank portfolio managers may have gone on lending to LDCs in the late 1970s and 1980s. It had been profitable, and everyone else was doing so. Even if the risk of a crash was recognised, it would affect every other investment manager also.

Keynes noted the incentive towards such a herd instinct among portfolio managers in his usual memorable manner in his paper on 'The Consequences to the Banks of the Collapse of Money Values' (1931, Part 2, p. 17b), 'A "sound" banker, alas!, is not one who foresees danger and avoids it, but one who, when he is ruined, is ruined in a conventional and orthodox way along with his fellows, so that no one can really blame him.' Also see Froot, Scharfstein and Stein (1990), 'Herd on the Street', wherein they show that, when investors/speculators have short horizons, informationally inefficient equilibria may result.

There is, I believe, considerable public support for the claim that portfolio managers are subject to such herding type behaviour, with the probable corollary that assets with low probabilities of extreme outcomes (good or bad) may be mispriced. On the other hand there are theories, e.g. Shackle (1949, 1955), that suggest that people, including investment managers, may focus excessively on memorable, extreme events, and thus allocate an exaggerated importance to low-probability, extreme outcomes. Moreover there have been few empirical studies (for one example, see Jain and Gupta, 1987), of, and no consensus about, the extent of herd behaviour.

Although concern about the prevalence of herd-type behaviour may play a part in the claims about short-termism, the core of the accusation would appear to lie instead in a direct denial of the rational efficient market hypothesis. The suggestions are, I think, three. First, that current news about prospective future long-term cashflows, brought about, say, by current R & D expenditures or other investments with a long-term horizon are *not* given the weighting that they really should, on the basis of what should be the best possible estimation, in the calculations of present asset prices. Second, that announcements of current changes in earnings/dividends are given a greater weight in the revision of present asset prices than should be the case in an efficient estimation, i.e. that took the historical auto-correlation properties of earnings/dividends correctly into account. Third, that the discount rates applied to the prospective stream of earnings are too high. In many cases it is not suggested that the rates used are incorrect, just that they are higher than comparable rates, e.g. in West Germany and Japan, and hence may place our (UK, US) corporate competitors at a relative disadvantage. It is not, however, clear what forces maintain international differences between costs of capital to firms in separate countries in a world without constraints on international capital flows.

People must be expected to believe in the value of what they are doing; otherwise they would move elsewhere. Hence there must be a presupposition that existing firm managers will see a rosier future for their own firm, than independent assessors. There is almost bound to be a bias among corporate managers to believe that the 'true' value of their firm is above the market value. Consequently, much of the reported dissatisfaction among corporate management about the failure of the market to respond adequately, e.g. to the glorious prospects glowingly outlined in company reports, announcements about future activities, etc., should be taken with a considerable pinch of salt. Some (large) part of the concern about short-termism rests on such shaky foundations. There have been relatively few empirical studies of the effects on current asset valuations of announcements of expenditures that could be expected to produce longer-term future cash-flows (e.g. R & D), but the few known to me, e.g. one undertaken by the SEC a couple of years ago, do not provide any strong, consensus support for the accusation of short-termism.

There has been much more empirical study of the effects of current earnings/dividends announcements on asset prices. There does appear to be some fragile evidence (Nickell and Wadhwani, 1987) that share prices may react excessively (relatively to what would occur in a fully efficient market), to such current announcement (also see De Bondt and Thaler (1985), and the earlier mentioned papers of Froot and Obstfeld (1989) and Campbell (1990)). But the empirical results are mixed, and sensitive to minor variations, e.g. in econometric methodology. On the other hand, as already noted, in government debt markets the change in price of long-term bonds has generally under-reacted to (unanticipated) changes in short-term interest rates (i.e. investors appear to have expected more mean-reversion in short rates than has actually been the case). So, it remains far from clear whether financial markets do, or do not, generally tend to revise present prices excessively on the basis of immediate, short-term 'news' announcements (and see Merton, 1986).

Nevertheless, accusations about short-termism have been, and remain, common. For example, Chancellor Lawson claimed that, 'The big institutional investors nowadays increasingly react to short-term pressure on investment performance. [They] are unwilling to countenance long-term investment or a sufficient expenditure on research and development . . .'. Similar sentiments have often been expressed by industrialists, e.g. one survey found that 85 per cent of managers felt that the market took too short-term a view of their investment decisions; also see Wadhwani and Mullins (1988). But such accusations are only supported by hard, rigorous empirical evidence to a limited extent. They may quite largely rest on the unhappiness among corporate managers that markets do not assess their companies' future in the same rosy light that they themselves do.

B. Takeovers

The next major criticism is that (hostile) take-overs have become too common (for a factual account of recent European developments, see Smith and Walter, 1990) and been too easy, partly as a consequence of the inappropriately low level of the share price of the target companies, since their future prospects are not properly priced, owing to short-termism. For a survey of the subject and literature, see Hughes and Singh (1989). The suggestion is then made that various changes be made to regulations, e.g. on voting rights, to make take-overs more difficult, namely, the articles by Plender in the *Financial Times*, 20 and 24 July 1990.

There are several reasons for seeking to initiate a take-over. There can be configurations of relative equity prices, tax loss arrangements, etc., which makes take-overs a more (tax) efficient form of expansion than direct physical investment (e.g. see King, 1987; Roell, 1987(a); Morck, Shleifer and Vishny, 1988) Companies may seek to merge with others in the same industry in order to reduce competition and to achieve a dominant, monopolistic position. This latter is against the public interest, and in those cases where such motives are suspected, the merger proposal will be referred to the Monopolies and Mergers Commission. Some economists, e.g. Eckbo (1985, 1990) have questioned whether the effects of intra-industry mergers (in the USA) have been as anti-competitive as the regulators have tended to assume.

The most dramatic take-over battles (BAT, Guinness, etc.) have, however, occurred when the bidding company has based its case primarily on its ability to achieve a higher return to shareholders from its prospective management of the target company, than existing management can. Moreover, it has to support its claim with an announced willingness to pay a higher market price than currently available for the target company, otherwise it cannot get control. Indeed, evidence on the comparative movements in share prices of the bidding and target companies (Franks and Harris, 1986; Jensen and Ruback, 1983) indicate that virtually all the increase in market valuations resulting from the take-over go to the shareholders of the target company, and very little or none to the bidding company (also see Bradley, Desai and Kim, 1988). Indeed, the asymmetry is so pronounced that many who regard takeovers as a healthy incentive towards efficient management are concerned that present regulations, e.g. on the percentage of shares that can be bought before announcing a public bid, unduly inhibit take-over activity (King and Roell, 1987), and such asymmetries may have been significantly enhanced by the adoption of various forms of anti-takeover state laws, and of 'poison pill' defences, in the US recently, see Herzel (1990).

The objections to such takeover activity are several. First, the activity is expensive in the use of scarce and costly professional advisers, which is undoubtedly true (Roell, 1987c) though the professionals involved (in M & A) hardly see it as a real social cost. Second, there is a concern that market asset mispricing forces existing management to skimp on activities (e.g. R & D) that would raise true asset values and spend excess effort in padding current earnings (dividend) figures to deter raiders; and that when a 'raider' does appear that once again scarce and expensive managerial time is given over to the battle for corporate control (on both sides). Third, that there are better and cheaper ways to ensure efficient management, i.e. by giving large financial institutions the power and (inside) information to replace 'bad' management, as in Japan and Germany (see Franks and Mayer, 1990).

The main thrust of these latter arguments depends on one's view of the efficiency of asset pricing in markets. Thus the second objection above is largely based on the presumption of short-termism, discussed earlier; and the third point essentially involves allowing, indeed encouraging, an 'imperfection' in asset markets whereby certain participants obtain, and act on, private information not widely available. If markets anyhow work imperfectly, allowing the banks such a privileged position is not such a serious worry.

Where there are strong legal constraints against allowing institutional investors a privileged position in financial markets, this alternative approach to corporate governance is, however, hardly possible. Thus Herzel in a paper entitled, 'Institutional Investors Unlikely to Replace the Take-over Market', July 1990, reports that 'In the US institutional investors are discouraged (sometimes specifically prohibited) by the legal system from exercising control over portfolio companies . . . . Exercise of control by an institution would subject it to insider trading restriction and class action and derivative suits . . . .' Another proposal, sometimes aired, is to look to non-executive directors, or a stronger Board, or an independent Chairman, to remove inefficient management (see Herzel, ibid., and King, 1986); as noted in these references, the idea that such an approach would be efficacious in this respect is wishful.

The counter-claim of those who believe that hostile takeovers are a healthy symptom is that some managers are 'poor', and most managers would, without external pressure, seek to achieve objectives, e.g. a quiet life, status, continuing employment, company size, etc., that may be at odds with the wishes of shareholders. In particular, cash-rich companies in mature sectors, e.g. oil, tobacco, may use their cash to acquire physical assets in other industries (without any real qualifications to manage them).

Most supporters of takeover activities, e.g. Jensen (1986), see markets as being relatively efficient, e.g. in pricing assets. Consequently, the rise in asset prices (of the shares of the bidder and target companies taken together) following takeover announcements is treated, *ipso facto*, as evidence that there must be a rational basis for assuming that the future cash flows (and productivity) can now be expected to be higher (Jensen, 1984). Thus take-overs are seen, on this basis, as a central and valuable element of a desirable (and efficient) market in governance. On the other hand, accounting studies and 'Comparisons of pre- and post-takeover performance . . . suggest that at best the impact of takeover on "efficiency" or profitability is neutral' (Hughes and Singh, 1989, p. 259).

Even if it is true that the rise in equity prices, following a takeover bid, does reflect a correct appreciation of a future rise in cash flows and dividends, it does not necessarily also imply that overall economic efficiency has risen commensurately. As pointed out by Shleifer and Summers (1987), the higher dividends may result from a redistribution of revenues towards profits away from wages, pensions, interest payments, etc. If a takeover bidder, such as Carl Icahn, can, for example, break existing (explicit or implicit) company contracts, e.g. to maintain employment, then he may be able to raise profits without any increase in value-added. Because raiders are not bound by Okun's 'invisible handshake' (Okun, 1981), they may well be in a much stronger negotiating posture. It is for such reasons that many 'target' companies (e.g. Pilkington) can rely on the vocal support of their work-force to help them repel raiders. For a recent empirical study of the gains from takeovers, see Bhagat, Shleifer and Vishny (1990); they show that many of the takeovers involved a redistribution of assets from conglomerates to related industrial companies, with 'raiders' and MBOs acting more as 'brokers' than long-term holders, and they suggest that many of the gains from takeovers represented a better return to specialised management than to conglomerates (also see Lichtenberg, 1990). Hall (1990) has studied 'The Impact of Corporate Restructuring on Industrial Research and Development', and has concluded that, whereas the assumption of more debt in a highly-leveraged condition does tend to reduce R & D expenditures, mergers and acquisitions and LBOs of themselves do *not* significantly do so.

Another argument is that the discount rate applied by the market to future dividends, though not necessarily incorrect, may be higher than that used by corporate managers, who thus give growth a higher priority (than current profits). In so far as commentators have a preference for the application of such lower discount rates, e.g. by Japanese company executives, they will welcome the limitation of market-driven takeovers.

Exactly where the right balance lies in assessing whether hostile takeovers are beneficial, or not, is a difficult and complex issue. Perhaps because I am sceptical about the claims that markets do exhibit severe short-termism, my own inclination is to side with those who see them as generally beneficial to the working of the economic system as a whole.

C. Insider Trading

A market, such as a financial market, cannot operate efficiently without certain conventions, rules that establish its micro-market structure, e.g. conventions relating to the dissemination of information, trading technology (e.g. auction or market maker, order or quote driven), settlement process, etc. (see for example, Stoll, 1990; Amihud, Ho and Schwartz, 1985; Kyle, 1988; the various papers by Roell in the Financial Markets Group series, e.g. 1987b, 1988). One important purpose of these conventions is to ensure that the trading process is (reasonably) honest and provides fair treatment for all participants. That concern is particularly acute when the participants are not operating on a commensurate level of information/expertise. In such cases the participant with (much) less information/expertise is particularly exposed to malpractice.

The ordinary investor (liquidity trader) is inherently at an informational disadvantage in dealing with financial market professionals. Indeed, that informational asymmetry is one of the main reasons why the (retail) investor has to use professionals to act on her behalf. The advance of information technology may increasingly allow professional (institutional) investors to operate screen-based trading without the intermediation of trading brokers, etc.; but the retail investor, as principal, will have to continue to rely on professionals.

There are many ways in which the poorly informed investor may be ripped-off, e.g. unnecessary churning of investor portfolios (purely to generate extra commissions/fees for professional agents), and investors will be hesitant to use markets in which they feel at risk. Accordingly there are various rules, and regulations, such as time-stamping the execution of deals to allow accurate audit trails, the use of independent custodians for clients' money, etc., whose purpose is to protect the retail investor.

The question for discussion here is whether the prevention of insider trading comes in to the same category, and, if so, what kind of regulation, if any, on such trading would be appropriate. On one level the need for any regulation looks somewhat odd. After all, 'inside' information is presumably accurate information about the appropriate fundamental value of the asset; if not, the investor with, in practice, incorrect 'inside' information will lose money and leave the market. The objective of financial markets is to move asset prices rapidly and efficiently to a new equilibrium; the use of inside information will do so. Surely that is beneficial. Clearly there will be a trade-off between such benefits and the costs from insider trading, considered below. Such trade-offs have been modelled by Ausubel (1990) and Dennert (1990).

There are four main reasons for being concerned with insider information, despite the above. First, information is clearly valuable in many circumstances, and can be made private property. (There are associated normative questions about the extent to which information *should* be covered by private property rights, but these take us beyond the range of this discussion.) Consequently private information covered by property rights, which the owners have chosen not to announce, may be misappropriated and used for personal gain, e.g. the official who trades in advance of known trade figures, the company executive who trades in advance of planned takeovers. Such misappropriation is clearly theft.

Greater complications arise with the question of handling stolen private property. If the information arrived on my doorstep, e.g. a paper fell off a lorry, or someone told me without being pressed, so I 'obtained' it without seeking it, am I guilty of the use of stolen goods if I use and profit from such information, in any case? Or only if I know that such information is stolen? And exactly how does one define information? If an investment analyst lunches with a company director who is in an ebullient mood, is the inference that the company is doing well properly the private property (of the company?), or not. There are obviously some clear examples of misappropriation of property, but there is a large fuzzy penumbra of dubious cases, which if interpreted strictly would require all information producers to live in monastic cells and could bring information about the economic system and market efficiency to a shuddering halt. As Kay (1988) in his comment on King and Roell noted, 'If there is to be a common level of disclosure to all actual or potential shareholders, that common level is necessarily very low. The price of this ruling would be that shareholders would have very little basis for assessing the quality of a company's management.'

The next concern about the use of inside information (even when such is quite legal, e.g. company directors dealing in their own company's shares within the confines of the rules laid down to control such transactions), is that the transactor is likely to be better informed about fundamental values than the market maker. King and Roell (1988, Sections 3.1/3.2) survey the empirical evidence on excess returns from legal reported insider trading, which indicate that 'shares purchased by company insiders perform abnormally well over a considerable period following the disclosure of the transaction'. Presumably the returns from unreported, illegal insider deals are even higher. Consequently the market maker will find that he has dealt at a 'wrong' price, and after a sale (purchase) to an insider will have to rebuild (reduce) his inventory at a higher (lower) price, thereby losing money (Glosten and Milgrom, 1985). In order to recoup such losses, the market maker will widen his bid/ask spread, thereby increasing the costs of transactions/lowering liquidity of investment in this market to ordinary traders. In turn such traders may refrain from investment until they obtain on average a higher return (see Wyplosz (1988), comment on King and Roell).

So, there may be a trade-off between allowing some restricted forms of insider trading, which may represent a relatively *efficient* way of compensating entrepreneurs, because 'salaries are inappropriate for stimulating entrepreneurial flair, bonuses are too conspicuous, and stock options too inflexible' (King and Roell, 1987, p. 17) and Manne (1966), on the one hand, and a higher cost of capital on the other. Schmidt (1989, p. 34), however, noted that

> Any German company at any time may decide to discontinue the insider restrictions without affecting its status as a limited company. If the net

benefit [to insider trading] proposition is correct, then shareholders could gain by passing at the general meeting a motion to discontinue the insider restrictions relating to the company executives. . . . However, no such motion was ever presented at a general meeting.

This, perhaps, suggests both that companies find the trade-off such that they prefer a lower cost of capital to managerial compensation through this route and that the definition of rules on insider trading could be left more to the discretion of the individual companies.

The third main criticism of insider trading is that large resources are put into attempts to obtain an informational advantage, to achieve an inside information status, in cases where there may be a high private return, but lower social value, from such a use of resources. Thus any investor, who by expending time and money can discover (legally or otherwise) the precise economic news figure to be announced at, say,11.30 a.m. might be expected to obtain a large return, but as King and Roell (1987, p. 166) note the social benefits from advancing the asset price effects of the publication by a short time are probably trivial.

On the other hand exactly how does one quantify the social costs/ benefits of trying to anticipate future outcomes? As Kay (1988) put it, 'it seems plausible to conclude that expenditure on research into anticipating the impact of economic information not yet publicly released exceeds expenditure on all other kinds of economic research in the UK'. If research worker X reckons that inflation, say, will rise more than currently forecast, and hence sells, or suggests the sale of, gilts is she guilty of insider trading, unless she publishes her findings to all and sundry? As Kay again notes, if all information has to be disclosed to the public at large, it would enforce the closure of the business of security analysis.

The fourth argument is ethical. As Easterbrook (1985) put it, 'insider trading is unfair and immoral, the economics do not matter, and anyone who says they do is immoral himself'. Against that, there is the common market dictum that virtually *all* trading is driven by some perceived informational advantage, except for those now investing in 'passive' trusts designed to mimic the market as a whole, and that those who invest blindly without having, or seeking, appropriate information, are fools.

My own view is that the key issue is to define property rights in information, and the appropriate treatment of those who handle stolen information. Insider information should be redefined as theft of private information. The definition of what information is to be treated as private could be delegated within quite wide bands to the bodies involved in information production, e.g. governments, Stock Exchanges, companies. It is both impossible and counter-productive to try to eliminate asymmetries of information, which do not arise from such thefts, any more than one can eliminate asymmetries of talent.

CONCLUSIONS

Financial markets play an essential role in a modern economy. Constructing a system of markets and intermediaries that will encourage lenders voluntarily to transfer resources to borrowers, whom they do not personally know, is a complex and essential exercise. Where such transfers of resources are not forcibly made, as in command economies, such markets have to be developed as a matter of urgency, as in Eastern Europe now.

The crash of October 1987 reconfirmed that our knowledge of what determines asset price movements over time remains quite limited. In the second main section, I reviewed a small selection of current research attempts to analyse the characteristics of asset markets. While there are many caveats, and infringements, of the central retained paradigm that markets use all available information rationally to reach an efficient valuation of such assets, after due allowance for relative risk, it certainly remains the best starting-point for analysis.

Finally, I have reviewed some current criticisms of financial markets, short-termism, too many (hostile) takeovers, driven by 'inside' information. While there is a case to answer in each of these, my view is that the accusations are themselves often unbalanced, and not based on sufficient research. Public perceptions of financial markets are often somewhat hostile, viewing them as haunts of yuppies ripping-off small investors in casinos. Such perceptions – on this view – are themselves generally misplaced.

Acknowledgements

Such understanding as I have of financial markets has been fostered by my membership of the Financial Markets Group at LSE. I am grateful to all members of the Group, and for some particular points to Saul Estrin, Elroy Dimson, Mervyn King, Ailsa Roell and Sushil Wadhwani, but neither they nor the FMG have any responsibility for such errors as remain.

REFERENCES

Admati, A. R. and Pfleiderer, P. (1988) 'A Theory of Intraday Patterns: Volume and Price Variability', *Review of Financial Studies*, vol. 1, pp. 3–40.

Ahmed, S. (1989) 'Islamic Banking and Finance', *Journal of Monetary Economics*, vol. 24, pp. 157–67.

Ali, M. (1988) 'A Framework of Islamic Banking', in J. R. Presley (ed.), *Directory of Islamic Financial Institutions* (Beckenham: Croom Helm).

Amihud, Y., Ho, T. and Schwartz, R. (eds) (1985) *Market Making and the Changing Structure of the Securities Industry* (Lexington, Mass: Lexington Books).

Attanasio, O. and Weber, G. (1988) 'Intertemporal Substitution, Risk Aversion and the Euler Equation for Consumption: Evidence from Aggregate and Average Cohort Data', Financial Markets Group, LSE, Discussion Paper No. 23.

Attanasio, O. and Wadhwani, S. (1989) 'Risk, Gordon's Growth Model and the Predictability of Stock Market Returns', Financial Markets Group, LSE, Discussion Paper No. 49 (March).

Auerbach, A. J. and King, M. A. (1983) 'Taxation, Portfolio Choice and Debt-Equity Ratios: a General Equilibrium Model', *Quarterly Journal of Economics*, vol. 98, pp. 587–609.

Ausubel, L. M. (1990) 'Insider Trading in a Rational Expectations Economy', *American Economic Review*, vol. 18, No. 5, December, pp. 1022–1041.

Baillie, R. T. and De Gennaro, R. P. (1990) 'The Impact of Delivery Terms on Stock Return Volatility', *Journal of Financial Services Research*, vol. 3, pp. 55–76.

Barclay, M. J., Litzenberger, R. W. and Warner, J. B. (1989) 'Private Information, Trading Volume and Stock Return Variances', Paper presented at NBER conference on 'Stock Market Volatility and the Crash', March.

Beltratti, A. (1990) 'The After-Tax Dividend-Ratio Model: Predictable Returns and Excess Returns in the Stock Market', Financial Markets Group, LSE, Discussion Paper No. 82, (April).

Bhagat, S., Shleifer, A. and Vishny, R. W. (1990) 'The Aftermath of Hostile Takeovers', Financial Markets Group, LSE, Discussion Paper No. 87 (June).

Bibolini, D. (1990) 'The Application of Discount Function Techniques to Government Debt Markets', unpublished M. Phil., thesis, University of London.

Blanchard, O. and Layard, R. (1990) 'Economic Change in Poland', Centre for Economic Performance', Discussion Paper No. 3 (May).

Bobinski, C. and Wolf, M. (1990) 'Radical Options for Privatisation', *Financial Times* (2 Aug.) p. 16.

Bollerslev, T., Chou, R. Y., Jayaraman, N. and Kroner, K. F. (1990) 'ARCH Modelling in Finance: a Selective Review of the Theory and Empirical Evidence, with Suggestions for Future Research', University of Arizona, unpublished paper.

Bradley, M., Desai, A. and Kim, E. H. (1988) 'Synergistic Gains from Corporate Acquisitions and their Division between the Stockholders of Target and Acquiring Firms', *Journal of Financial Economics*, vol. 21, pp. 3–40.

Breeden, D. T. (1979) 'An Intertemporal Asset Pricing Model with Stochastic Consumption and Investment Opportunities', *Journal of Financial Economics*, vol. 7, pp. 265–96.

Bulkley, G. and Tonks, I. (1988) 'Volatility of US Stock Prices', Financial Markets Group, LSE, Discussion Paper No. 36 (August).

Bulkley, G. and Tonks, I. (1989) 'Are UK Stock Prices Excessively Volatile? Trading Rules and Variance Bounds Tests', Financial Markets Group, LSE, Discussion Paper No. 22 (1987), subsequently published in the *Economic Journal* Vol. 99, pp. 1083–99.

Bulkley, G. and Tonks, I. (1990) 'Cross-sectional Volatility of Dividend Yields on the UK Stock Market', Financial Markets Group, LSE, Discussion Paper No. 91 (June).

Calomiris, C. W. and Hubbard, R. G. (1989) 'Price Flexibility, Credit Availability and Economic Fluctuation: Evidence from the United States, 1894–1909', Financial Markets Group, LSE, Discussion Paper No. 58.

Campbell, J. Y. (1987) 'Stock Returns and the Term Structure', *Journal of Financial Economics,* vol. 18, pp. 373–99.

Campbell, J. Y. (1990) 'A Variance Decomposition for Stock Returns', Financial Markets Group, LSE, Discussion Paper No. 78 (March).

Campbell, J. Y. and Shiller, R. J. (1988) 'Stock Prices, Earnings and Expected Dividends', *Journal of Finance,* vol. 43, pp. 661–76.

Campbell, J. Y. and Hamao, Y. (1989) 'Predictable Stock Returns in the United States and Japan: a Study of Long-term Capital Market Integration', Financial Markets Group, LSE, Discussion Paper No. 69 (December).

Campbell, J. Y. and Hentschell, L. (1990) 'No News is Good News: an Asymmetric Model of Changing Volatility in Stock Returns', Financial Markets Group, LSE, Discussion Paper No. 85 (June).

Campbell, J. Y. and Shiller, R. J. (1987) 'Cointegration and Tests of Present Value Models', *Journal of Political Economy*, vol. 95, pp. 1062–88.

Campbell, J. Y. and Shiller, R. J. (1988) 'Stock Prices, Earnings and Expected Dividends', *Journal of Finance,* vol. 43, pp. 661–76.

Campbell, J. Y. and Shiller, R. J. (1989) 'Yield Spreads and Interest Rate Movements: a Bird's Eye View', Financial Markets Group, LSE, Discussion Paper No. 66 (November).

Chou, R. Y. (1988) 'Volatility Persistence and Stock Valuations: Some Empirical Evidence Using GARCH', *Journal of Applied Econometrics,* vol. 3, pp. 279–94.

Clark, P. K. (1973) 'A Subordinated Stochastic Process Model with Finite Variance for Speculative Prices', *Econometrica,* vol. 41, pp. 135–55.

Condoyanni, L., O'Hanlon, J. and Ward, C. W. R. (1988) 'Weekend Effects in Stock Market Returns: International Evidence', in E. Dimson (ed.), *Stock Market Anomalies* (Cambridge: Cambridge University Press).

Constantinides, G. (1989) 'Habit Formation: a Resolution of the Equity Premium Puzzle', Paper presented at the NBER Conference on 'Stock Market Volatility and the Crash', March.

Constantinides, G. M. and Scholes, M. S. (1980) 'Optimal Liquidation of Assets in the Presence of Personal Taxes: Implications for Asset Pricing', *Journal of Finance*, vol. 35 (May), pp. 439–50.

Constantinides, G. M. and Ingersoll, J. E., jr (1984) 'Optimal Bond Trading with Personal Taxes', *Journal of Financial Economics*, vol. 13, pp. 299–335.

Cross, S. *et al.* (1986), *Report on Recent Innovations in International Banking* (Basle: BIS).

De Bondt, W. P. M. and Thaler, R. (1985) 'Does the Stock Market Over-react?', *The Journal of Finance*, vol. XL, no. 3 (July), pp. 793–808.

De Long, J. B., Shleifer, A., Summers, L. H. and Waldmann, R. J. (1989) 'The

Survival of Noise Traders in Financial Markets', NBER Working Paper No. 2715 (September 1988) and 'Positive Feedback Investment Strategies and Destabilising Rationale Speculation', NBER Reprint No. 1330 (December).

De Long, J. B., Shleifer, A., Summers, L. H. and Waldmann, R. J. (1990) 'Noise Trader Risk in Financial Markets', *Journal of Political Economy*, vol. 98, no. 4, pp. 703–738.

Dennert, J. (1990) 'Insider Trading and the Allocation of Risks,' Financial Markets Group, LSE, Discussion Paper No. 77 (March).

Diamond, D. W. (1984) 'Financial Intermediation and Delegated Monitoring', *Review of Economic Studies*, vol. 51.

Diba, B. T. and Grossman, H. I. (1988) 'The Theory of Rational Bubbles in Stock Prices', *Economic Journal*, vol. 98, pp. 746–54.

Dimson, E. (ed.) (1988) *Stock Market Anomalies* (Cambridge: Cambridge University Press).

Dimson, E. and Marsh, P. R. (1984) 'An Analysis of Brokers' and Analysts' Unpublished Forecasts of UK Stock Returns', *Journal of Finance,* vol. 39, pp. 1257–92.

Dimson, E. and Fraletti, P. (1986) 'Brokers' Recommendations: the Value of a Telephone Tip', *Economic Journal,* vol. 96, pp. 139–59.

Dornbusch, R. (1976) 'Expectations and Exchange Rate Dynamics', *Journal of Political Economy*, vol. 84, pp. 1161–76.

Dybvig, P. H. (1983) 'An Explicit Bound on Deviations from APT Pricing in a Finite Economy', *Journal of Financial Economics*, vol. 12, pp. 483–96.

Dybvig, P. H. and Ross, S. A. (1985) 'Yes, The APT is Testable', *Journal of Finance,* vol. 40, pp. 1173–88.

Easterbrook, F. (1985) 'Insider Trading as an Agency Problem', in J. W. Pratt and R. J. Zeckhauser (eds), *Principals and Agents: The Structure of Business* (Boston: Harvard University Business School).

Eckbo, B. E. (1985) 'Mergers and the Market Concentration Doctrine: Evidence from the Capital Market', *Journal of Business*, vol. 58, pp. 325–49.

Eckbo, B. E. (1990) 'Mergers, Concentration and Antitrust', Paper presented at the Conference organised by the Centre for Financial Economics of the Gothenburg School of Economics, Marstrand (May).

Ellman, M. (1989) *Socialist Planning,* 2nd edn (Cambridge: Cambridge University Press).

Engle, R. F. (1982) 'Autoregressive Conditional Heteroscedasticity with Estimates of the Variance of UK Inflation', *Econometrica*, vol. 50, pp. 987–1008.

Epps, T. W. and Epps, M. L. (1976) 'The Stochastic Dependence of Security Price Changes and Transactions Volumes: Implications for the Mixture-of-Distributions Hypothesis', *Econometrica*, vol. 44, pp. 305–21.

Esposito, M. (1990) 'The Term Structure and the Equity Premium Puzzle: A Note', Financial Markets Group, LSE, Discussion Paper No. 89 (July).

Evans, G. W. (1986) 'A Test for Speculative Bubbles in the Sterling Dollar Exchange Rate: 1981–1984', *American Economic Review*, vol. 76, no. 4 (September).

Evans, G. W. (1989) 'The Fragility of Sunspots and Bubbles', *Journal of Monetary Economics*, vol. 23, pp. 297–317.

Fama, E. F. (1976) *Foundations of Finance* (New York: Basic Books).

Fama, E. (1985) 'What's Different about Banks', *Journal of Monetary Economics*, vol. 15, (January) pp. 29–40.

Fama, E. F. and French, K. R. (1980) 'Permanent and Temporary Components of Stock Prices', *Journal of Political Economy*, vol. 96, pp. 246–73.

Fama, E. F. and French, K. R. (1988) 'Dividend Yields and Expected Stock Returns', *Journal of Financial Economics*, vol. 22, pp. 3–25.

Franks, J. R. and Harris, R. S. (1986) 'Shareholder Wealth Effects of Corporate Takeovers: the UK Experience, 1955–85', London Business School, mimeo.

Franks, J. R. and Mayer, C. (1990) 'Capital Markets and Corporate Control: a Study of France, Germany and the UK', *Economic Policy*, vol. 10 (April), pp. 189–231.

French, K. R. (1980) 'Stock returns and the Weekend Effect', *Journal of Financial Economics*, vol. 8, pp. 55–70.

French, K. R. and Roll, R. (1986) 'Stock Return Variances: the Arrival of Information and the Reaction of Traders', *Journal of Financial Economics*, vol. 17, pp. 5–26.

French, K. R., Schwert, G. W. and Stambaugh, R. F. (1987) 'Expected Stock Returns and Volatility', *Journal of Financial Economics*, vol. 19, pp. 3–30.

Frend, I., Blume, M. and Crockett, J. (1970) *Mutual Funds and Other Institutional Investors, a New Perspective* (New York: McGraw-Hill).

Friedman, B. (1990) 'Financial Markets and Monetary Economics', *NBER Reporter*, Spring, pp. 1–7.

Friedman, B. and Laibson, D. (1990) 'Economic Implications of Extraordinary Movements in Stock Prices', *Brookings Papers on Economic Activity*, No. 2, 1989; also available as Financial Markets Group, LSE, Discussion Paper No. 70 (Jan.).

Friend, I., Brown, F. E. Herman, E. S. and Vickers, D. *A Study of Mutual Funds* (US Government Printing Office: Washington, DC, 1962).

Froot, K. A. and Obstfeld, M. (1989) 'Intrinsic Bubbles: The Case of Stock Prices', NBER Working Paper No. 3091, Sept.

Froot, K. A., Scharfstein, D. S. and Stein, J. C. (1990) 'Herd on the Street: Informational Inefficiencies in a Market with Short-Term Speculation', NBER Working Paper No. 3250 (Feb.).

Fry, M. J. (1988) *Money, Interest and Banking in Economic Development* (Baltimore: Johns Hopkins University Press).

Gale, D. and Hellwig, M. (1985) 'Incentive-compatible Debt Contracts. The One-period Problem', *Review of Economic Studies*, vol. 52.

Garber, P. M. and Weisbrod, S. R. (1990) 'Banks in the Market for Liquidity', Brown University, mimeo.

Gertler, M. (1988) 'Financial Structure and Aggregate Economic Activity: an Overview', *Journal of Money, Credit and Banking*, vol. 20, no. 3, part 2 (August), pp. 559–89.

Gertler, M. and Hubbard, R. G. (1989) 'Financial Factors in Business Fluctuations', NBER Reprint No. 1251 (August).

Gibbons, M. R. and Hess, P. (1981) 'Day of the Week Effects and Asset Returns', *Journal of Business*, vol. 54, pp. 579–96.

Glosten, L. R. and Milgrom, P. R. (1985) 'Bid, Ask and Transaction Prices in a Specialised Market with Heterogeneously Informed Traders', *Journal of Financial Economics*, 14 (1), March.

Goodhart, C. A. E. (1988) 'The Foreign Exchange Market: a Random Walk with a Dragging Anchor', *Economica*, vol. 55, pp. 437–60.

Goodhart, C. A. E. (1990) '"News" and the Foreign Exchange Market', Financial Markets Group, LSE, Discussion Paper No. 71 (January).

Goodhart, C. A. E. (1990) 'Reuters Screen Images of the Foreign Exchange Market: the Deutschemark/Dollar Spot Rate', Financial Markets Group, LSE, Discussion Paper No. 96 (August).

Goodhart, C. A. E. and Gowland, D. (1977) 'The Relationship between Yields on Short and Long-Dated Gilt-edged Stocks', *Bulletin of Economic Research*, vol. 29.

Goodhart, C. A. E. and Figliuoli, L. (1988) 'Every Minute Counts in Financial Markets', Financial Markets Group, LSE, Discussion Paper No. 37. (1988), subsequently *Journal of International Money and Finance*, vol. 10, no. 1, March 1991, pp. 23–52.

Greenwald, B. C., Stiglitz, J. E. and Weiss, A. (1984) 'Informational Imperfections in the Capital Market and Macroeconomic Fluctuations', *American Economic Review*, vol. 74, pp. 194–9.

Greenwald, B. C. and Stiglitz, J. E. (1988) 'Imperfect Information, Finance Constraints, and Business Fluctuations', and 'Money, Imperfect Information, and Economic Fluctuations', Chs 7 and 8 in M. Kohn and S. C. Tsiang (eds), *Finance Constraints, Expectations, and Macroeconomics* (Oxford: Clarendon Press).

Grossman, S. J. and Stiglitz, J. E. (1980) 'On the Impossibility of Informationally Efficient Markets', *American Economic Review*, vol. 70 (3) (June), pp. 393–408.

Grossman, S. J. and Shiller, R. J. (1981) 'The Determinants of the Variability of Stock Market Prices', *American Economic Review*, vol. 71, pp. 222–7.

Hall, B. (1990) 'The Impact of Corporate Restructuring on Industrial Research and Development', NBER Working Paper, No. 3216.

Hall, S., Miles, D. K. and Taylor, M. (1988) 'A Multivariate GARCH in Mean Estimation of the Capital Asset Pricing Model', Financial Markets Group, LSE, Discussion Paper No. 39 (September).

Hansen, E. (1990) 'Venture Capital Finance with Temporary Asymmetric Learning: a Mechanism Design Approach', Financial Markets Group, LSE, mimeo (July).

Hansen, L. P. and Singleton, K. J. (1982) 'Generalised Instrumental Variables Estimation of Nonlinear Rational Expectations Models', *Econometrica*, vol. 50, pp. 1269–86.

Hansen, L. P. and Singleton, K. J. (1983) 'Stochastic Consumption, Risk Aversion and the Temporal Behaviour of Asset Returns', *Journal of Political Economy*, vol. 91, pp. 249–65.

Harris, L. (1986) 'Cross-Security Tests of the Mixture of Distributions Hypothesis', *Journal of Financial and Quantitative Analysis*, vol. 21, pp. 39–46.

Harris, L. (1987) 'Transaction Data Tests of the Mixture of Distributions Hypothesis', *Journal of Financial and Quantitative Analysis*, vol. 22, pp. 127–41.

Herzel, L. (1990) 'Institutional Investors Unlikely to Replace the Takeover Market', Mayer, Brown and Platt, Chicago, mimeo, July.

Hughes, A. and Singh, A. (1989) 'Takeovers and the Stock Market', *The New Palgrave: Finance* (London: Macmillan) pp. 252–64.

Ippolito, R. A. (1989) 'Efficiency with Costly Information: a Study of Mutual Fund Performance, 1965–1984', *Quarterly Journal of Economic*, vol. 104, pp. 1–24.

Jaffe, J. and Westerfield, R. (1985) 'Patterns in Japanese Common Stock Returns: Day of the Week and Turn of the Year Effects', *Journal of Financial and Quantitative Analysis*, vol. 20, pp. 261–71.

Jain, A. K. and Gupta, S. (1987) 'Some Evidence on "Herding" Behaviour by US Banks', *Journal of Money, Credit and Banking,* vol. 19, pp. 78–89.

James, C. (1987) 'Some Evidence on the Uniqueness of Bank Loans', *Journal of Financial Economics*, vol. 19, pp. 217–36.

Jensen, M. C. (1968) 'The Performance of Mutual Funds in the Period 1945–1964', *Journal of Finance,* vol. 23, pp. 389–416.

Jensen, M. C. (1972) 'Capital Markets: Theory and Evidence', *Bell Journal of Economics and Management Science*, vol. 3.

Jensen, M. C. (1984) 'Takeovers; Folklore and Science', *Harvard Business Review,* Nov.–Dec., pp. 109–21.

Jensen, M. C. (1986) 'The Takeover Controversy: Analysis and Evidence', Harvard Business School, mimeo.

Jensen, M. C. and Ruback, R. (1983) 'The Market for Corporate Control; the Scientific Evidence', *Journal of Financial Economics*, vol. 11, pp. 5–50.

John, K. and Williams, J. (1985) 'Dividends, Dilution and Taxes; a Signalling Equilibrium', *The Journal of Finance,* vol. 40 (Sept.) pp. 1053–70.

Johnson, C. (1990) 'From Communism to Community', *Lloyds Bank Economic Bulletin*, No. 140 (August).

Kay, J. (1988) Comment on King and Roell, 'Insider Trading'. *Economic Policy*, 6, pp. 187–9.

Keim, D. B. and Stambaugh, R. F. (1986) 'Predicting Returns in the Stock and Bond Markets', *Journal of Financial Economics*, vol. 17, pp. 357–90.

Keynes, J. M. (1931) 'The Consequences to the Banks of the Collapse of Money Values', in *Essays in Persuasion*, Vol. IX of the *Collected Writing of John Maynard Keynes* (Macmillan for the Royal Economic Society).

Kim, M. J., Nelson, C. R. and Startz, R. (1988) 'Mean Reversion in Stock Prices? A Reappraisal of the Empirical Evidence', NBER Working Paper, No. 2795 (December).

King, M. A. (1986) 'Takeovers, Taxes and the Stock Market', mimeo, London School of Economics.

King, M. A. (1987) 'Takeover Activity in the United Kingdom,' Financial Markets Group, LSE, Discussion Paper No. 2, subsequently republished in J. A. Fairburn and J. A. Kay (eds), *Mergers and Merger Policy* (Oxford University Press, 1988).

King, M. A. and Leape, J. (1987) 'Asset Accumulation, Information and the Life-cycle', Financial Markets Group, LSE, Discussion Paper No. 14.

King, M. A. and Roell, A. A. (1987) 'The Regulation of Takeovers and the Stock Market', Financial Markets Group, LSE, Discussion Paper No. 4.

King, M. A. and Roell, A. (1988) 'Insider Trading', *Economic Policy*, 6, 163–94.

King, M. A. and Wadhwani, S. (1988) 'Transmission of Volatility between Stock Markets', Financial Markets Group, LSE, Discussion Paper No. 48 (December).

King, M. A., Sentana, E. and Wadhwani, S. (1990) 'A Heteroscedastic Factor Model of Asset Returns and Risk Premia with Time-Varying Volatility: an Application to Sixteen World Stock Markets', Financial Markets Group, LSE, Discussion Paper No. 80 (May).

Kleidon, A. W. (1986) 'Variance Bounds Tests and Stock Price Valuation Models', *Journal of Political Economy*, vol. 94, pp. 953–1001.

Kornai, J. (1980) *Economics of Shortage* (Amsterdam: North-Holland).

Kyle, A. S. (1988) 'Improving the Performance of the Stock Market', *California Management Review*.

LeBaron, B. (1989) 'Some Relations Between Volatility and Serial Correlation in Stock Market Returns', unpublished manuscript, Department of Economics, University of Wisconsin, Madison.

Lee, C., Shleifer, A. and Thaler, R. (1990) 'Investor Sentiment and the Closed-end Puzzle', Financial Markets Group, LSE, Discussion Paper No. 88 (June).

Leland, H. and Pyle, P. (1977) 'Informational Asymmetries, Financial Structure and Financial Intermediation', *Journal of Finance,* vol. 32, pp. 371–87.

Lichtenberg, F. (1990) 'Industrial Dediversification and its Consequences for Productivity', NBER Working Paper No. 3231.

Lintner, J. (1965) 'The Valuation of Risk Assets and the Selection of Risky Investments in Stock Portfolios and Capital Budgets', *Review of Economics and Statistics,* vol. 4.

Lucas, R. E. jr. (1978) 'Asset Prices in an Exchange Economy', *Econometrica,* vol. 46, pp. 1429–46.

Lummer, S. and McConnell, J. (1989) 'Further Evidence on the Bank Lending Process and the Capital Market Response to Bank Loan Agreements', Working Paper (June).

Mankiw, N. G. and Summers, L. H. (1984) 'Do Long-Term Interest Rates Overreact to Short-Term Interest Rates?', *Brookings Papers on Economic Activity,* pp. 223–42.

Mankiw, N. G. and Shapiro, M. D. (1986) 'Risk and Return: Consumption versus Market Beta', *Review of Economics and Statistics,* vol. 68.

Mankiw, N. G. and Zeldes, S. P. (1989) 'The Consumption of Stockholders and Non-Stockholders', unpublished paper, Harvard University and the University of Pennsylvania.

Manne, H. G. (1966) *Insider Trading and the Stock Market* (New York: The Free Press).

Markowitz, H. (1959) *Portfolio Selection* (New York: Wiley).

Marsh, T. A. and Merton, R. C. (1986) 'Dividend Variability and Variance Bounds Test for the Rationality of Stock Market Prices', *American Economic Review,* vol. 76 (June), pp. 483–96

Mehra, R. and Prescott, E. C. (1985) 'The Equity Premium: A Puzzle', *Journal of Monetary Economics,* vol. 15, no. 2, March, pp. 145–61.

Merton, R. C. (1986) 'On the Current State of the Stock Market Rationality Hypothesis', in Stanley Fischer *et al.* (eds), *Macroeconomics and Finance: Essays in Honor of Franco Modigliani* (Cambridge, Mass.: MIT Press).

Miles, D. K. (1989) 'Some Economic Issues in the Regulation of Financial Markets', Financial Markets Group, LSE, Special Paper 13.

Miller, M. H. and Rock, K. (1985) 'Dividend Policy under Asymmetric Information', *The Journal of Finance,* vol. 40 (Sept.), pp. 1031–51.

Miller, M. H. and Modigliani, F. (1961) 'Dividend Policy, Growth and the Valuation of Shares', *Journal of Business,* vol. 34, pp. 235–64.

Modigliani, F. and Miller, M. H. (1958) 'The Cost of Capital, Corporation Finance, and the Theory of Investment', *American Economic Review,* vol. 48, pp. 261–97.

Modigliani, F. and Miller, M. H. (1963) 'Corporate Income Taxes and the Cost of Capital', *American Economic Review,* vol. 53, pp. 433–43.

Morck, R., Shleifer, A. and Vishny, R. W. (1988) 'Characteristics of Hostile and Friendly Takeover Targets', in A. J. Auerbach (ed.), *Corporate Takeovers: Causes and Consequences* (Chicago: University of Chicago Press).

Mullins, M. (1989) 'Bursting Bubbles and Bleeding Bulls: Does the Evidence

Support the Rhetoric?', Financial Markets Group, LSE, Discussion Paper No. 56 (May).

Nickell, S. J. and Wadhwani, S. B. (1987) 'Myopia, the "Dividend Puzzle" and Share Prices', Centre for Labour Economics, LSE, Discussion Paper No. 272.

Nuti, D. M. (1987) 'Financial Innovation under Market Socialism', EUI Working Paper No. 87/285, Florence (Feb.).

Nuti, D. M. (1988) 'Competitive Valuation and Efficiency of Capital Investment in the Socialist Economy', *European Economic Review,* vol. 32, pp. 2–6.

Nuti, D. M. (1989) 'New Financial Markets: Economic Reform in Eastern Europe', Paper presented at Financial Market Group Conference (Dec.).

Okun, A. (1981) *Prices and Quantities: A Macroeconomic Analysis* (Washington: The Brookings Institution).

Pagan, A. R. and Hong, Y. S. (1988) 'Non-Parametric Estimation and the Risk Premium', unpublished manuscript, Department of Economics, University of Rochester.

Pagan, A. R. and Sabau, H. C. L. (1988) 'Consistency Tests for Hetroskedasticity and Risk Models', unpublished manuscript, Department of Economics, University of Rochester.

Pagan, A. R. and Schwert, G. W. (1989) 'Alternative Models for Conditional Stock Volatility', NBER Working Paper No. 2955 (May).

Plender, J. (1990a) 'Malaise in need of long-term remedy', *Financial Times*, July 20th, 1990; 'Throw Sand in the Takeover Machine', *Financial Times* 24 July.

Plender, J. (1990b) 'Takeovers and Short Termism: Some Policy Options', Institute for Public Policy Research, London.

Poterba, J. and Summers, L. H. (1987) 'Mean Reversion in Stock Returns: Evidence and Implications', Financial Markets Group, LSE, Discussion Paper No. 5, and *Journal of Financial Economics*, vol. 22, 1988, pp. 27–59.

Roell, A. A. (1987a) 'Regulation of Takeovers', Financial Markets Group, LSE, Discussion Paper No. 3.

Roell, A. A. (1987b) 'Rules and the Quality of Markets', Financial Markets Group, LSE, Discussion Paper No. 15.

Roell, A. A. (1987c) 'Signalling, Taxes and the Transaction Cost of Takeover', Financial Markets Group, LSE, Discussion Paper No. 18 (June).

Roell, A. A. (1988) 'Regulating Information Disclosure among Stock Exchange Market Makers', Financial Markets Group, LSE, Discussion Paper No. 51.

Roll, R. (1988) 'R^2', *Journal of Finance*, vol. XLIII, pp. 541–66.

Roll, R. (1988) 'The International Crash of October 1987', in R. Kamphuis *et al.* (eds), *Black Monday and the Future of Financial Markets* (Homewood, Ill.: Irwin).

Roll, R. (1989) 'Price Volatility, International Market Links and their Implications for Regulatory Policies', Paper presented at Conference on Regulatory Reform of Stock and Futures Markets, Columbia University.

Ross, S. A. (1976) 'The Arbitrage Theory of Capital Asset Pricing', *Journal of Economic Theory,* vol. 13, pp. 341–60.

Ross, S. A. (1977) 'The Determination of Financial Structure; the Incentive-Signalling Approach', *Bell Journal of Economics*, vol. 8, pp. 23–40.

Ross, S. A. (1989) 'Finance', *The New Palgrave: Finance* (London: Macmillan) pp. 1–34.

Sargent, T. (1972) 'Rational Expectations and the Term Structure of Interest Rates', *Journal of Money, Credit and Banking*, vol. 4.

Schmidt, H. (1989) 'Insider Regulation and Economic Theory', unpublished manuscript, Hamburg University, October.

Schwert, G. W. (1983) 'Size and Stock Returns, and Other Empirical Regularities', *Journal of Financial Economics*, vol. 12, pp. 3–12.

Schwert, G. W. (1989) 'Stock Volatility and the Crash of 1987', Paper presented at NBER Conference on 'Stock Market Volatility and the Crash', March.

Sentana, E. and Wadhwani, S. (1989) 'Semi-parametric Estimation and the Predictability of Stock Market Returns: Some Lessons from Japan', Financial Markets Group, LSE, Discussion Paper No. 62 (Sept.).

Sentana, E. and Wadhwani, S. (1990) 'Feedback Traders and Stock Return Autocorrelations: Evidence from a Century of Daily Data', Financial Markets Group, LSE, Discussion Paper No. 90 (July).

Shackle, G. L. S. (1949) *Expectations in Economics* (Cambridge: Cambridge University Press).

Shackle, G. L. S. (1955) *Uncertainty in Economics* (Cambridge: Cambridge University Press).

Sharpe, W. (1964) 'Capital Asset Prices: a Theory of Market Equilibrium under Conditions of Risk', *Journal of Finance,* vol. 18.

Shiller, R. J. (1981) 'Do Stock Prices Move Too Much to be Justified by Subsequent Changes in Dividends', *American Economic Review*, vol. 71, pp. 421–36.

Shiller, R. J. (1984) 'Stock Prices and Social Dynamics', *Brookings Papers on Economic Activity*, no. 2, pp. 457–98.

Shiller, R. J. (1987) 'Investor Behaviour in the October 1987 Stock Market Crash: Survey Evidence', NBER Working Paper No. 2446 (November).

Shiller, R. J., Campbell, J. Y. and Schoenholtz, K. L. (1983) 'Forward Rates and Future Policy: Interpreting the Term Structure of Interest Rates', *Brookings Papers on Economic Activity*, I, pp. 173–217.

Shleifer, A. and Summers, L. H. (1987) 'Hostile Takeovers as Breaches of Trust', Financial Markets Group, LSE, Discussion Paper No. 8, republished as 'Breach of Trust in Hostile Takeovers', in A. J. Auerbach (ed.), *Corporate Takeovers: Causes and Consequences* (Chicago: National Bureau of Economic Research, 1988).

Smith, R. C. and Walter, I. (1990) 'The European Market for Corporate Control: Structure, Transaction Flow, and Regulation', Paper presented at Conference organised by the Centre for Financial Economics of the Gothenburg School of Economics, Marstrand, (May).

Stiglitz, J. and Weiss, A. M. (1981) 'Credit Rationing in Markets with Imperfect Information', *American Economic Review*, vol. 71.

Stoll, H. R. (1990) 'Principles of Trading Market Structure', Paper presented at INSEAD/NYSE Conference at Fontainebleau, mimeo (May).

Summers, L. H. (1986a) 'Do We Really Know that Financial Markets are Efficient', in J. Edwards *et al.* (eds), *Recent Developments in Corporate Finance* (Cambridge: Cambridge University Press).

Summers, L. H. (1986b) 'Does the Stock Market Rationally Reflect Fundamental Values?', *Journal of Finance,* vol. XI, no. 3, pp. 591–602.

Tauchen, G. and Pitts, M. (1983) 'The Price Variability–Volume Relationship on Speculative Markets', *Econometrica*, vol. 51, pp. 485–505.

Tobin, J. (1958) 'Liquidity Preference as Behaviour Towards Risk', *Review of Economic Studies,* vol. 25.

Vassilicos, J. C. (1990) 'Are Financial Markets Chaotic? A Preliminary Study of the

Foreign Exchange Market', Financial Markets Group, LSE, Discussion Paper No. 86 (June).

Wadhwani, S. B. (1988) 'On the Inefficiency of Financial Markets', *LSE Quarterly,* vol. 2, no. 1 (Spring), pp. 1–26.

Wadhwani, S. and Mullins, M. (1988) 'The Effect of the Stock Market on Investment: a Comparative Study', Financial Markets Group, LSE, Discussion Paper No. 32 (June).

Webb, D. (1987) 'The Importance of Incomplete Information in Explaining the Existence of Costly Bankruptcy', *Econometrica*, vol. 54, pp. 279–88.

Webb, D. (1990a) 'Ownership Control Debt and Bankruptcy', Financial Markets Group, LSE, Discussion Paper, No. 76.

Webb, D. (1990b) 'An Economic Evaluation of Insolvency Procedures in the United Kingdom: Does the 1986 Insolvency Act Satisfy the Creditors' Bargain', *Oxford Economic Papers*, forthcoming.

Weil, P. (1989) 'The Equity Premium Puzzle and the Riskfree Rate Puzzle', NBER Working Paper No. 2829 (January).

West, K. D. (1988) 'Bubbles, Fads and Stock Price Volatility Tests: A Partial Evaluation', *Journal of Finance,* vol. XLIII, (1988), pp. 639–56.

West, K. D. (1988) 'Dividend Innovations and Stock Price Volatility', *Econometrica*, vol. 56, pp. 37–62.

Winiecki, J. (1989) 'The Polish Reform Programme: a Personal View', Paper presented at Financial Markets Group Conference (Dec.), reported in LSE, FMG *Review*, No. 6 (November 1989/March 1990) p.v.

Winiecki, J. (1990) 'No Capitalism minus Capitalists', *Financial Times* (20 June), p. 27.

Wyplosz, C. (1988) Comment on King and Roell, 'Insider Trading' *Economic Policy*, 6, pp. 189–90.

4 The Foreign Exchange Market and the Effect of Currency Bands

MARCUS MILLER and PAUL WELLER

INTRODUCTION

Flood and Garber (1983) argued that the expectation of Britain's return to the Gold Standard should have affected the value of the pound sterling even before the event; and they advocates the use of 'stochastic process switching' techniques to analyse such phenomena. Subsequently, it was international efforts to stabilise exchange rates (such as the Louvre Accord of 1987) which stimulated Paul Krugman (1988) to another application of these techniques – to study how currencies might behave inside wide currency bands.

In the first part of this chapter we report on the explicit solutions obtained for a simple monetary model, focusing in particular on the implications of credible currency bands. To help understand the behaviour of sterling in the period before Britain joined the European exchange rate mechanism, we also discuss how a floating rate will be affected by an expected future regime switch of this kind. Finally we consider how the credibility of a currency peg may be undermined by a shortage of reserves.

The second part of the chapter describes the solutions that have been obtained when working with a somewhat more realistic model, where real exchange rates fluctuate due to the presence of price inertia. We consider in particular how credible currency bands can affect the exchange rates, and how these effects may be reversed by prospective realignments.

All the results so far described rely on the notion that the foreign exchange market is 'rational'. The presence of market inefficiencies, and how they may be checked by currency bands, is an important issue, which we discuss in the conclusion.

MONETARY MODEL

The monetary model of exchange rate determination can summarily be expressed in the following three equations:

$$m = p + \kappa \bar{y} - \lambda E(ds)/dt - v \tag{4.1}$$

$$s = p - p^* \tag{4.2}$$

$$dv = \sigma dz \tag{4.3}$$

The first equation describes the equilibrium condition in the domestic money market. On the left-hand side is the supply of domestic money denoted m and measured in logs; on the right-hand side are the determinants of demand, where p is the log of domestic price level, $\bar{y}$ is the log of 'full employment' GNP and s is the log of the exchange rate, defined as the domestic price of foreign currency. (Note: this is the inverse of the British definition.) So $E(ds) > 0$ signifies an expected appreciation of foreign currency, which is assumed to reduce the demand for domestic money (with semi-elasticity denoted by λ). Shocks to velocity cumulate in the variable v, which is assumed, in (4.3), to follow a 'Brownian motion' process with a variance σ^2 per unit of time. (This is just the continuous time equivalent of a random walk.) Equation (4.2) states the 'purchasing power parity' always holds, where $p - p^*$ is the log of the ratio of domestic and foreign prices, the latter denoted by an asterisk.

Assuming for simplicity that both domestic output and the foreign price level are constant, so by choice of units they have log of zero, substitution yields

$$s = m + v + \lambda E(ds)/dt \tag{4.4}$$

This provides a single equation to describe the evolution of the exchange rate. Its simplicity has been achieved at the cost of assuming that the domestic economy is always at full employment, and that the real exchange rate is constant; but Krugman has shown that, as a consequence, one can obtain tractable analytical expressions to describe the path of the exchange rate.

Free Floating with a Fixed Money Supply

Note first that, with m held constant at $\bar{m}$, the solution for a freely floating rate is given by setting $E(ds) = 0$; so, from (4.4), the exchange rate tracks the velocity adjusted money stock, i.e.

$$s = \overline{m} + v \qquad (4.5)$$

shown by the 45° line labelled *FF* in Figure 4.1. As the exchange rate moves *pari passu* with fundamentals, it too follows a random walk.

A Currency Band with Infinitesimal Intervention

Suppose however that the authorities wish to contain s within some speci-fied band $[\underline{s}, \bar{s}]$. It is clear that it could be perfectly stabilised if the money stock were to be continuously adjusted so that all velocity shocks were fully 'accommodated'. But what if there is *no* accommodation so long as the exchange rate lies strictly within the band, so only when the exchange rate hits the edge of the band is m adjusted so as to neutralise the shocks to v?

It may be tempting to think that the free float solution already described applies within the band. But this is not so, as the entire path for the exchange rate must incorporate the expectations of market participants that there will be a change in monetary policy even though this only takes place at the edges. Krugman (1988) was the first to show that, for a band centred around $s = 0$, the general solution for the exchange rate is the sum of the free float value, $m + v$, and an additional term $A[e^{\rho v} - e^{-\rho v}]$, which incorporates the effect of the anticipated check to s at the edges of the band, i.e.

$$s = m + v + A[e^{p(m + v)} - e^{-p(m + v)}] \qquad (4.6)$$

where $\rho = (2/\lambda\sigma^2)^{1/2}$, and A is a constant to be determined by suitable boundary conditions. If intervention takes place only at the edge of the band, for example, the necessary boundary condition is that the solution path be tangent to the edges of the band, the so-called 'smooth pasting' condition. This gives the solution illustrated in Figure 4.1.

The intuitive justification for this tangency condition is as follows. Suppose that s has just reached its upper limit $\bar{s}$ and the path for s *cuts* the upper edge. Then if v were to jump upwards by a small amount, s would, without intervention, be expected to rise above $\bar{s}$. This expectation by construction would be the only one consistent with the equilibrium in the money market, equation (4.1). Consequently, intervention to hold s at $\bar{s}$ if v increases (but *not* to prevent a decline in s if v decreases), which reduces $E(ds)$ at that point, will violate the condition for equilibrium. Only if the exchange rate path is smoothly tangent to the edge of the band will inter-

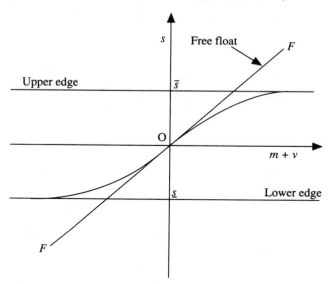

FIGURE 4.1   *Krugman's 'smooth pasting' solution*

vention to prevent s rising above $\bar{s}$ leave $E(ds)$ unchanged as is required to satisfy asset market equilibrium.

Note that the amount of time that the exchange rate is actually observed at the limits of its range will be infinitesimally 'short'. This can be shown by considering the alternative and deriving a contradiction. For suppose the exchange rate were expected to remain on the edge of the band for more than an instant. This implies that over that period of time it is expected to be stationary, or $E(ds) = 0$. But this is only true for points along the 45°, characterising a free float, so it must violate the smooth pasting condition for asset market equilibrium on the edge of the band. It also follows that the adjustment to the money stock necessary to defend the band will also be 'small', so as not to change $E(ds)$.

A Currency Band with Discrete Intervention

Subsequently, Flood and Garber (1989) have shown how 'large' or discrete interventions can be incorporated into the above analysis by allowing for intra-marginal intervention. They suppose that the authorities announce an intervention rule which specifies both the upper and lower limits (denoted U, L respectively) of the fundamental $m + v$ at which intervention will occur, and the magnitude of the intervention at each limit, and show that this will lead to an exchange rate path of the kind illustrated in Figure 4.2. The case shown has intervention points equidistant from the origin, and an intervention rule which exactly accommodates the accumulated velocity shock, thus $L = -U$. The curved path is, as before, a particular solution to (4.4). However, the boundary conditions no longer involve smooth pasting. Suppose that initially $m = 0$. Then if v hits the upper limit U, the authorities immediately tighten the money supply, setting $m = -U$. But since this intervention is fully anticipated, arbitrage imposes the requirement that there be no discontinuous jump in the exchange rate. This means that the system will jump from U to 0.

There are a number of interesting implications of this argument. First, any given currency band can be defended by any one of an infinite number of (fully credible) intervention rules. The same path, for example, would be picked out by an intervention of size $u' - U'$ promised at U' (together with its symmetric counterpart). Second, any discrete intervention will occur at a point when the exchange rate lies strictly within the *interior* of the band it is designed to support; i.e. it is intra-marginal intervention. In the special case of Figure 4.2, intervention occurs only when s lies in the centre of the band! Finally, if an intervention occurs in the Flood and Garber analysis, it

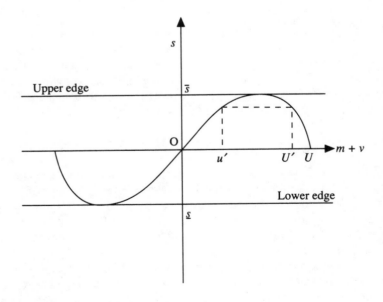

FIGURE 4.2   *Flood and Garber's discrete regulation*

will never be reversed after only a 'short' period of time. In particular, if an intervention is provoked by a positive shock to the fundamental, then an intervention of the same size but opposite sign will not occur if there is an immediately subsequent negative shock.

Anticipations of a Fixed Peg

Consider now how the exchange rate will depart from the freely floating solution *FF* under the impact of a credible announcement at time 0 that the monetary authorities are to defend a fixed exchange rate $\bar{s}$ after time *T*. This case may be of relevance for episodes like that when Britain was known to be contemplating joining the ERM, and is analysed in some detail in Ichikawa *et al.* (1990).

Given that the rate at time *T* (and after) is $\bar{s}$, the outcome between 0 and *T* may be obtained by introducing a time varying element into the relationship between the exchange rate and economic fundamentals, so

$$s = g(m + v, t) \tag{4.7}$$

and applying Ito's lemma to produce a partial differential equation of the form

$$\frac{\sigma^2}{2} g_{11}(m + v, t) + g_2(m + v, t) = \frac{1}{\lambda}(s - m - v) \tag{4.8}$$

The evolution of the exchange rate after the announcement involves finding the solution for this equation subject to the boundary condition that will hold when the band is actually implemented. This can be obtained by the separation of variables and takes the convenient form

$$g(m + v, t) = (m + v)(1 - e^{-\lambda^{-1}(T-t)}) + \bar{s}\, e^{-\lambda^{-1}(T-t)} \tag{4.9}$$

so that the exchange rate in the interval [0, *T*] is a weighted average of its value under a free float (when it is equal to the velocity adjusted money stock) and of the target value $\bar{s}$ announced by the monetary authority, with weights that vary with time (measured backwards from *T*). At time *T* the weight on the second term is unity, ensuring no jump in the exchange rate at that time.

The implication of this solution is that the credible announcement of future stabilisation has immediate effects as the rate jumps from *FF* to $g(m + v, 0)$. As shown in Figure 4.3, this means that at the time of announcement the rate will jump onto a linear solution *AA* with a slope of less that 45°; subsequently this line swivels becoming horizontal at $t = T$. Clearly the further into the future is the anticipated 'return to a fixed rate', the smaller the stabilising jump at the time of announcement, *ceteris paribus.*

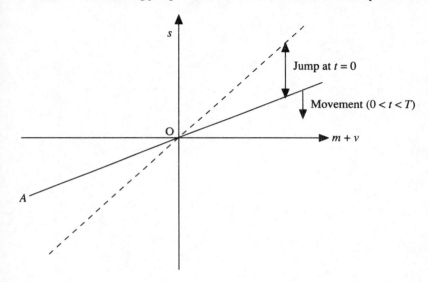

FIGURE 4.3   *Effect of preannouncing a peg, Ichikawa et al. (1990)*

Limited Reserves and Speculative Attacks

So far it has been assumed that the commitment to a currency band on an exchange rate peg is fully credible. But what if the monetary interventions required in support lead to the progressive depletion of a country's international reserves? The consequences have been studied in two recent papers, by Krugman (1989b) and Krugman and Rotemberg (1990), with results which we illustrate in Figure 4.4.

Assume specifically that the central bank is defending a fixed exchange rate $\bar{s}$, and that reductions in the demand for domestic money (increases in v) come from direct substitution into foreign currency which has to be provided by the central bank. If it is also the case that the money supply only varies when reserves do (so $M = R + C$, where M is the level of the domestic money supply and R the quantity of reserves and C is a constant), then m and v will be negatively related as shown in the top panel of Figure 4.4. When reserves are positive $m > \bar{m}$; but when they are exhausted, then $m = \bar{m} = \ln(C)$.

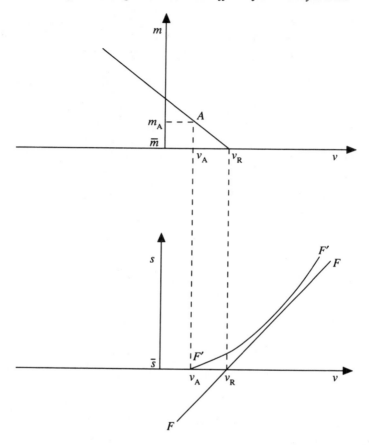

FIGURE 4.4   *Target zones with limited reserves*

Assuming that, if reserves run out, the central bank ceases all further intervention and allows a free float, then the exchange rate would switch to the free-float locus *FF*, shown in the lower panel of Figure 4.4. This is drawn to intersect the fixed parity $\bar{s}$ at the level v_R where reserves are exhausted. The lack of 'smooth pasting' at v_R reflects the irreversible nature of the policy switch.

In the second of the two papers, the authors argue that a more plausible description of policy would be the suspension of *sales* of foreign currency whenever reserves are depleted, but no change in its readiness to *buy* foreign currency at the rate $\bar{s}$. This implies that, were the velocity shocks subsequently to lower v, there would be a return to the fixed rate system. But for such a reversible regime switch, one expects smooth pasting; and the solution to the equation (4.6) where $\bar{m} = m$ and the boundary condition is tangency with $\bar{s}$ is shown as the exponential curve $F'F'$ (which asymptotically approaches to free float locus as v tends to infinity). Note that the foreign currency is 'stronger' than that it would be under a free float because the willingness of the central bank to buy it at $\bar{s}$.

It is interesting to observe that, as a result of this willingness to *return* to a fixed rate, $\bar{s}$ leaves s even before v reaches v_R. To see why this is so, note that the convexity of $F'F'$ at the point of tangency implies $E(ds) > 0$; consequently v reaches v_A there will be a sudden shift out of local money, a 'speculative attack' which uses up the remaining reserves, so m falls from A to $\bar{m}$ in the top panel of Figure 4.4. From this example we see that the smooth pasting solution for the exchange rate can be associated with *discrete* jumps in the money stock, a feature which also occurs in the sticky price model studied next.

In the paper referred to, the authors go on to analyse the operation of the gold standard using this approach.

A STOCHASTIC DORNBUSCH MODEL

In the monetary model Brownian motion processes are introduced as disturbances to a flex-price, full employment model of an economy which has no inherent dynamics of adjustment. In the absence of exogenous shocks, the economy would necessarily be at full employment with stable prices and an exchange rate that satisfies purchasing power parity. The purpose of this part of the chapter is to show how the stochastic analysis of currency bands can be applied when there are endogenous lags of adjustment.

Specifically we examine the case where prices are less than fully flexible, and the shocks are 'supply-side' disturbances to the process of wage/price setting. Formally the innovations of the Brownian motion process introduce 'noise' into the equation describing the evolution of the price level.

Though financial markets are taken to be forward-looking throughout our analysis, we focus in this chapter on the simple case where the process of price adjustment is not, as we use a stochastic version of the popular Dornbusch model (1976) where the process of price setting is a simple Phillips curve. (The procedures we use can be extended to include forward-looking labour contracts, but we do not pursue this here.)

The equations to be used in this section are as follows:

$$m - p = \kappa y - \lambda i \qquad \text{Money market} \qquad (4.10)$$

$$y = -\gamma i + \eta(s - p) \qquad \text{Goods market} \qquad (4.11)$$

$$E(\mathrm{d}s) = (i - i^*)\,\mathrm{d}t \qquad \text{Currency arbitrage} \qquad (4.12)$$

$$\mathrm{d}p = \phi\,(y - \bar{y})\,\mathrm{d}t + \sigma\mathrm{d}z \qquad \text{Price adjustment} \qquad (4.13)$$

where the variables are as defined in the last section.

Equation (4.10) is the LM curve defining equilibrium in the money market and (4.12) is the riskless arbitrage condition for the foreign exchange market. Note that disturbances to the velocity of money are omitted here, however. Instead, it is the price adjustment equation (4.13) – where prices rise if GNP is high, and vice versa – which is disturbed by 'white noise' shocks. With prices evolving in this way there is no guarantee that output will remain at any given level, nor that the exchange rate will remain at *PPP*. The log of the level of output, y, is therefore taken to be demand determined, where the level of demand depends on the real exchange rate $(s - p)$ and on the interest rate i (equation (4.11)).[1]

The dynamics of the system can be summarised in the equation below:

$$\begin{bmatrix} \mathrm{d}p \\ E(\mathrm{d}s) \end{bmatrix} = A \begin{bmatrix} p\mathrm{d}t \\ s\mathrm{d}t \end{bmatrix} + \begin{bmatrix} \sigma\mathrm{d}z \\ 0 \end{bmatrix} \qquad (4.14)$$

where p and s are now measured as deviations from long-run equilibrium, and A is a matrix of parameters (see Appendix).

The economic implications of this model are, not surprisingly, rather different from those of the monetary model already discussed. Because the fundamental in the model, namely the price level, follows an autoregressive process whose trend is endogenously determined, there are generally no closed form solutions for the function $s = f(p)$, describing how the exchange rate responds to fluctuations in the price level. However, we show how to derive the differential equation characterising $f(p)$, in the Appendix.

The absence of closed form solutions is no serious drawback in this case, as a qualitative characterisation of the solutions to be considered is available (see Miller and Weller, 1988). Some of these are illustrated in Figure 4.5. There are *two* linear solutions to the system passing through the origin, corresponding to the stable and unstable saddlepaths of the deterministic model. The stable saddlepath is assumed to be the free float solution, for the

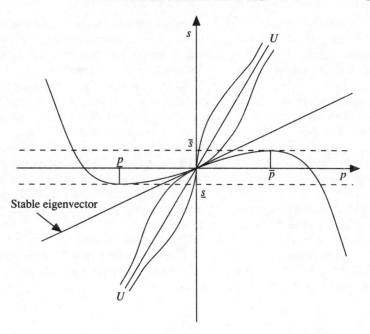

FIGURE 4.5   *Stochastic solutions through the origin*

same reasons as in the monetary model. It may have a positive slope as shown in the figure (or a negative slope, for the case of exchange rate 'overshooting').

A Nominal Currency Band

When a currency band is imposed, the appropriate solution is again identified by imposing the 'smooth pasting' condition for the monetary model, but the monetary policy to support this that we consider here is rather different. Specifically we assure that the action taken to defend the band is a 'discrete but locally reversible' change in money supply designed to equalise domestic and foreign interest rates. This implies that the exchange rate can lie for some time on the edge of the band, with any further divergent price shocks being partially accommodated in order to hold domestic interest rates constant. (The case of infinitisimal intervention to support the band is analysed in Miller and Weller (1991).)

The necessary monetary adjustment is shown in Figure 4.6 for the no-overshooting case. The equilibrium level of m and p are normalised at zero. If prices rise above their long-run equilibrium level, the economy moves into recession and the interest rate falls, so causing the currency to weaken within the band. Eventually, s will hit the top of its permitted range of variation when p has risen to $\bar{p}$, and interest rates immediately have to be raised to world levels to present further appreciation. So there is a sudden downward jump in m. If there are further positive shocks to p, they are partially accommodated, but the market is aware that when p drifts back to $\bar{p}$, the original adjustment to m will be reversed, at which point the exchange rate moves off the edge of the band. It is easy to confirm that the adjustment to m required to set $i = i^*$ will still imply that $y < \bar{y}$, so that downward pressure on prices is maintained throughout the period when the exchange rate is held on the edge of the band.

In terms of concrete policy it is probably most realistic to suppose that reversion to the original regime of floating within the band will be triggered by an index of competitiveness, which in the fixed-rate regime at the edge of the band is equivalent to the domestic price index.

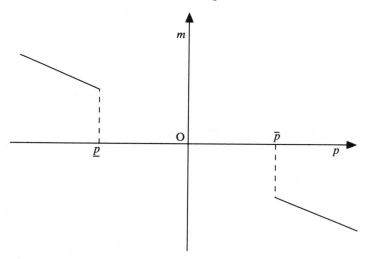

FIGURE 4.6   *Monetary policy to defend a currency band*

Realignment of the Currency Band and the Reversal of the S Shape

While a credible target zone generates the familiar S-shaped curve which is tangent to the edge of the band, we show in this section how an expected realignment can reverse the S-shape. (For further discussion see Miller and Weller (1989) and for a similar analysis in the context of the monetary model see Bertola and Caballero (1990).)

Suppose for the sake of argument that the authorities announce a rule of the following form: whenever the exchange rate hits the top of the band, the band will be realigned upwards by an amount equal to half the total width of the band: and this realignment will be validated by a change in money supply designed to shift the equilibrium exchange rate to the centre of the new band. In Figure 4.7 these equilibria will therefore lie along the 45° line labelled *PPP*. The solution for any given band is pinned down by the endpoints where this *PPP* line cuts the edges of the band; all other traject-ories will lead to predictable gains or losses when the rate reaches the edge of the band and triggers a realignment.

For the original band shown in Figure 4.7, the solution is the reverse S-shaped curve *AOA'* (cf. those trajectories near *UU* in Figure 4.5). If and when the rate hits the top edge of the band at point *A*, an upward realign-ment is triggered. By construction, *A* is now the long-run equilibrium for the realigned band, and the rate now moves on the dotted trajectory. If

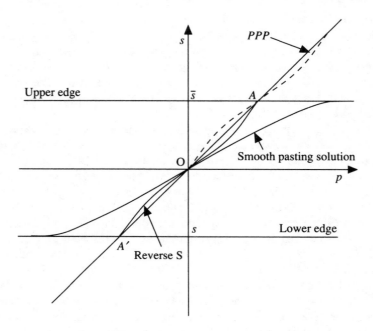

FIGURE 4.7 *Realignments and the reverse S solution*

subsequent price shocks drive the system back to point O, the realignment is reversed and the money stock is returned to its original level.

Note that there is no smooth pasting of the trajectories in adjacent bands. The reasons for this are the presence of discrete interventions; and the locally irreversible nature of the regime shift. The effect of the realignment rule has been to reverse the smooth pasting solution and replace it with a reverse S-curve.

CONCLUDING COMMENTS

The literature briefly reviewed here explores the effect of future policy 'switches' on the current value of the exchange rate. While Flood and Garber had in mind the episode of Britain's 'return to gold' in 1925, most recent research has focused on currency bands;[2] seeing how the expectation of 'intervention' at the edges affects the rate within the band, and how this can be undone by the prospect of realignment, for example. Though the techniques have been developed for the simplest monetary model, they can, it appears, be applied to more realistic models. Since they can also be used to handle other stochastic processes – with jumps, for example – one can look forward to further interesting developments along these lines.

An assumption maintained throughout this analysis, however, is that expectations in foreign exchange rate markets are rational, that they reflect the economic fundamentals involved. But are they? and, if not, how may the results be applied?

On the first point, Paul Krugman (1989a) (in his Robbins lectures on exchange rate instability) has argued p. 77 that 'the traditional fear that floating exchange rates will be subject to destabilising speculation – to speculative bubbles that do real harm – is, unfortunately, strongly supported by the evidence of the 1980s'; and his discussion of the topic contains a fascinating description of the way he 'diagnosed' the bubble in the US dollar in 1985. Certainly US exchange rate policy itself showed a decisive shift from free floating to managed rates after the mid 1980s.

If floating rates are indeed prone to instability, does this not suggest a direct role for currency bands – to combat such speculative bubbles? The sustained advocacy (since 1983) of broad 'target zones' for exchange rates by John Williamson was based on this idea; and it is explored in more detail in an essay on 'The Stabilizing Properties of Target Zones' (Miller, Weller and Williamson, 1989). Recently, however, Buiter and Pesenti

(1990) have criticised this view on the grounds that certain forms of intervention are capable of sustaining bubbles inside a target zone.

How the exact methods of stochastic analysis can best be applied in situations involving irrational behaviour is not altogether obvious. Perhaps the most promising approach is offered by models (such as those of I e Long *et al.* (1987) and Campbell and Kyle (1988)) containing two types of traders, 'smart money' and 'noise traders', where the irrationality is confined to the second group, but the promise of policy intervention has expectational effects on the behaviour of smart money.

APPENDIX: STOCHASTIC SOLUTIONS FOR THE DORNBUSCH MODEL

The evolution of the price level, p, and the exchange rates, s, determined by the equations (4.10) – (4.13) can be summarised in terms of two simultaneous stochastic differential equations (after elimination of y and i and normalising by setting $\bar{y} = 0$) as

$$
\begin{bmatrix} dp \\ E(ds) \end{bmatrix} = \frac{1}{\Delta} \begin{bmatrix} -\phi(\gamma+\lambda\eta) & \phi\lambda\eta \\ 1-\kappa\eta & \kappa\eta \end{bmatrix} \begin{bmatrix} pdt \\ sdt \end{bmatrix}
$$
$$
+ \frac{1}{\Delta} \begin{bmatrix} \phi\gamma & \phi\lambda\eta & 0 \\ -1 & \kappa\eta & -\Delta \end{bmatrix} \begin{bmatrix} mdt \\ p^*dt \\ i^*dt \end{bmatrix} + \begin{bmatrix} \sigma dz \\ 0 \end{bmatrix}
$$

(A4.1)

where $\Delta = \kappa\gamma + \lambda$. Alternatively, if we redefine variables s and p to denote deviations from long-run equilibrium, we may rewrite (A4.1) as

$$
\begin{bmatrix} dp \\ E(ds) \end{bmatrix} = A \begin{bmatrix} pdt \\ s\,dt \end{bmatrix} + \begin{bmatrix} \sigma dz \\ 0 \end{bmatrix}
$$

(A4.2)

where A is the matrix of coefficients multiplying the vector of endogenous variables on the right-hand side of (A4.1).

In order to obtain solutions to the system (A4.2), one begins by postulating a deterministic functional relationship $s = f(p)$. Following the rules for stochastic differentiation one obtains

$$
ds = f'(p)dp + \frac{\sigma^2}{2} f''(p)\, dt
$$

from which it follows that

$$E(\mathrm{d}s) = f'(p)\, E(\mathrm{d}p) + \frac{\sigma^2}{2} f''(p)\, \mathrm{d}t.$$

Substituting for $E(\mathrm{d}p)$ and $E(\mathrm{d}s)$ from (A4.2) we obtain

$$\frac{\sigma^2}{2} f''(p) + [a_{11}p + a_{12} f(p)]\, f'(p) - [a_{21}s + a_{22} f(p)] = 0$$

where a_{ij} denotes the appropriate element of the matrix A. This second order, non-linear differential equation has no closed form solutions in general, but we have argued that it is possible to characterise the qualitative features of the relevant solutions (see Miller and Weller, 1988).

Acknowledgements

This chapter is produced as part of ESRC-sponsored research on the International Monetary System and we are happy to acknowledge the expert assistance provided by Alan Sutherland in this project (funded by Grant No. R000 231417). It draws on work carried out as Visiting Scholars in the European Department of the IMF in 1989 and its completion was supported by the International Macroeconomics Programme at the Centre for Economic Policy Research (funded by grants from the Ford Foundation (No. 890-0404) and the Alfred P. Sloan Foundation (No. 88-4-23)).

NOTES

1. The choice of nominal interest rate here as the influence on output is for simplicity only. Nothing of substance in our analysis changes if we work with the real interest rate.
2. But see Froot and Obstfeld (1989) for a 'unified approach' showing that the regime switches of Flood and Garber and Krugman's smooth pasting are but two particular solutions of a general family describing exchange rate behaviour in the monetary model.

REFERENCES

Bertola, G. and Caballero, R. (1990) 'Target Zones and Realignments', CEPR Discussion Paper No. 398 (March).
Buiter, W. H. and Pesenti, P. A. (1990) 'Rational Speculative Bubbles in an Exchange Rate Target Zone', mimeo, Yale University (September).
Campbell, J. Y. and Kyle, A. S. (1988) 'Smart Money, Noise Trading and Stock Price Behaviour', NBER Technical Working Paper No. 71, Boston, MA, NBER.

De Long, J. B., Bradford, J., Schliefer, A., Summers, L. and Waldmann, R. (1987) 'The Economic Consequences of Noise Traders', NBER Working Paper No. 2715, Boston, MA, NBER.

Dornbusch, R. (1976) 'Expectations and Exchange Rate Dynamics', *Journal of Political Economy*, vol. 84, no. 6 (December), pp. 1116–76.

Flood, R. P. and Garber, P. (1983) 'A Model of Stochastic Process Switching', *Econometrica*, vol. 51, pp. 537–52.

Flood, R. P. and Garber, P. (1989) 'The Linkage Between Speculative Attack and Target Zone Models of Exchange Rates', NBER Working Paper No. 2918 in Krugman and Miller (1991).

Froot, K. and Obstfeld, M. (1989) 'Exchange Rate Dynamics Under Stochastic Regime Shifts: A Unified Approach' (Washington: International Monetary Fund), Working Paper (June).

Ichikawa, M., Miller, M. and Sutherland, A. (1990) 'Entering a Pre-announced Currency Band', *Economic Letters*, vol. 34, no. 4, pp. 363–8.

Krugman, P. R. (1988) 'Target Zones and Exchange Rate Dynamics', NBER Working Paper No. 2481 (January).

Krugman, P. R. (1989a) *Exchange Rate Instability* (Cambridge, MA: MIT).

Krugman, P. R. (1989b) 'Target Zones with Limited Reserves', mimeo, MIT (August).

Krugman, P. R. and Miller, M. (1991), eds., *Exchange Rate Targets and Currency Bands* (Cambridge: Cambridge University Press).

Krugman, P. R. and Rotemberg, R. (1990) 'Target Zones with Limited Reserves' (revised), mimeo, MIT (July), in Krugman and Miller (1991).

Miller, M. and Weller, P. A. (1988) 'Solving Stochastic Saddlepoint Systems: a Qualitative Treatment with Economic Applications', Warwick Economic Research Paper No. 309 (December). Also available as CEPR Paper No. 308 (April 1989).

Miller, M. and Weller, P. A. (1989) 'Exchange Rate Bands and Realignments in a Stationary Stochastic Setting', in M. Miller, B. Eichengreen and R. Portes (eds), *Blueprints for Exchange Rate Management* (New York: Academic Press) pp. 161–73.

Miller, M. and Weller, P. A. (1991) 'Currency Bonds with Price Inflation', *Economic Journal*, vol. 101, no. 409.

Miller, M., Weller, P. and Williamson, J. (1989) 'The Stabilizing Properties of Target Zones', in R. C. Bryant *et al.* (eds), *Macroeconomic Policies in an Interdependent World* (Washington: International Monetary Fund) pp. 248–71.

5 Externalities from Education

MARTIN WEALE

1 INTRODUCTION

A wide range of economic benefits is often thought to flow from education. In advanced societies it is clear that a reasonable level of literacy and numeracy is necessary if one is not to be at a severe disadvantage in day-to-day life. Advanced countries typically regard it as important that the population should be educated to some minimum level, and as a consequence impose compulsory education typically without charge. That education is of benefit to the individual is of little doubt. The conventional view is that, by undergoing education an individual raises his human capital and is thus able to command a higher rate of pay in the labour market (Schultz, 1961).

However, the question then arises whether the social benefit of education is fully reflected through the market in the increased rate of pay of the individual, or whether there is an economic externality from the provision of education. This chapter takes a fresh look at the issue,[1] assessing some of the ways in which the social benefit might differ from the private benefit of education. Section 2 illustrates the effects of university education on the incomes of individuals, and notes that the evidence offered by this conflicts with views which are commonly held about scarce subjects. Section 3 discusses various other aspects of education, and points out that these could have non-market economic importance.

Section 4 develops the idea that an educated workforce may raise everyone's productivity in a way which means that the benefits of education are not reflected in salaries, and looks at evidence for this, by means of a comparison of regional labour income in the United Kingdom. Sections 5 and 6 assess the idea that there may be a link between education and economic growth, and Section 7 examines this with reference to the economic performance of the OECD countries from 1973 to 1985. Section 8 summarises the main conclusions.

112

2 PRIVATE AND SOCIAL RETURNS FROM HIGHER EDUCATION

The notion that higher education leads to higher salaries would conform to everyone's expectations, and is well supported by the data. Clark, Rees and Meadows (1988), in a survey of 1980 graduates, found that, in 1986, the average 1980 graduate earned £12 346 p.a. Non-graduates of similar age (26–29) earned only around £10 000 p.a. The earnings prospects of graduates are in fact better than this suggests, because graduate income tends to rise during their working life, while the incomes of many non-graduates tend to peak in their twenties, and the comparison with the national average rate of pay per person employed, which was around £8 700 p.a. is perhaps more instructive. As might be expected some areas of study are more helpful than others. Engineers are reasonably well paid, as are economists. Science graduates, except for biologists do quite well. Graduates in arts and humanities do less well, with the least-remunerated subject being education, with an income of £9 960 p.a.

This does not, on its own, demonstrate that individuals benefit from education. Against the higher salaries must be offset the fact that three years' salary is forgone during the period of study. But we should note, at this point, that it is by no means clear that all forms of education necessarily lead to a higher salary, even before any account is taken of income forgone during the period of education.

Rudd (1990) describes in detail the results of a survey looking at the value of a social science PhD. He found that, for a male social scientist with a first-class degree and a PhD who graduated between 1972 and 1977, the median salary was, in early 1987, £13 100. For a social scientist who failed to complete his PhD or took a master's degree which comprised mainly research, the median salary was £18 100, while for those who had taken a taught master's degree the median salary was £18 000. For those with no university level postgraduate qualification the median was £20 900. A similar pattern was found for women and for both men and women with upper second degrees.

The explanation of this is twofold. First of all, the salary pattern probably emerges simply because employers regard on-the-job experience as being more useful than research training in universities. And secondly, that doctors of philosophy tend, disproportionately to take badly-paid jobs in universities. Rudd also found that many doctors of philosophy tended not to regard their period of postgraduate study as helpful to their jobs. He suggests that the case for the provision of grants for doctoral study must rest on the contributions to knowledge which are made. Any analysis of postgradu-

ate education based on purely financial measures would lead to the twin
conclusions that (i) incomplete PhDs should be encouraged rather than
discouraged and (ii) public funding of PhD students in the social sciences
should cease.[2] Moreover, these conclusions are not new, but have been
known since at least the early 1980s (Advisory Board for the Research
Councils, 1982).

However these figures do nothing more than illustrate the return to the
private individual from education. In practice we should distinguish the
private return which accrues to the individual from the social return which
accrues to the country at large. These will differ for at least two reasons.
First of all, the cost of 'free' education must be taken account of in
assessing the social return. And secondly, a correction must be made for the
fact that, while the individual receives income net of tax, the benefit to
society accrues on a gross basis. But finally, of course, there is the possibility that the benefits of education accrue to society in ways which are not
measured by market data. This is examined in Sections 4 to 7.

The government's view is that the social benefit of higher education is
normally smaller than the private benefit accruing to those individuals who
undertake higher education. The argument presented by the recent White
Paper on student loans (HMSO, 1988) is that the student receives education
substantially at the cost of the state (although he does forgo three years'
salary), and then goes on to earn a higher salary as a consequence of
training. The return to education obviously depends on the extent to which
that higher salary is regarded as a consequence of training rather than as a
consequence of innate ability, but studies typically assume that between 60
and 100 per cent of the increased pay is a consequence of training.

On this basis we can calculate both private and social rates of return as
the rates of interest which discount the financial benefits to be equal to the
costs. Table 5.1 shows the Government's estimates of these rates of return
by subject group.

This table suggests that the private rates are higher than the social rates
of return. It should also be noted that, with the exception of the arts subjects,
the social rates of return are all positive. Broadly similar figures will be
found for other countries, although, as our example of social science PhDs
demonstrates, education can have a clear negative return. The government
has used the argument that private rates of return are above social rates in
order to justify policies which reduce the element of state subsidy to higher
education. The introduction of student loans reflects this. But the most
interesting issue is the policy implication of the gap between social science
and science rates of return.

TABLE 5.1 *Private and social rates of return in higher education HMG estimates*

Subject	Private rate of return (% p.a.)	Social rate of return (% p.a.)
Social Sciences	26.0	8.0
Engineering	25.5	4.5
Sciences	19.5	3.0
Arts	8.5	< 0
All subjects	22.0	5.0

From *Top-up Loans for Students*, Cmnd 520 (HMSO, 1988). It presents the annual rates of return for male students, compared with those who have at least two A-levels and do not take degrees. The calculations assume that 60 per cent of increased earnings are explained by higher education.

A Shortage of Scientists?

It is frequently argued that the country suffers from a shortage of scientists.[3] In fact, the Minister of Education has recently issued a decree to the universities (or at least to my own university) telling us to raise our intake of natural scientists at the expense of the social scientists and arts' students. How clear is the evidence that there is a shortage of scientists? It will come as not surprise to find, drawing again on the results of Clark, Rees and Meadows (1988), that the best paid graduates by occupation in the 1986 survey were 'investment analysts' who made an average of £27 133 p.a. Advocates and barristers come next on £21 748 p.a. The highest-earning category of scientists is electronic engineers on £15 484 p.a. These market rates of pay seem to be symptomatic of a shortage of lawyers and investment analysts rather than of a shortage of scientists.

The same sort of result can be reached by looking at what science graduates do with their degrees. In 1981–2 33.7 per cent of full-time undergraduates were studying science or engineering. By 1987–8 this fraction had risen to 34.4 per cent. But of those graduating with science degrees in 1981, 7.8 per cent joined private practice accountancy, banking, insurance and other commerce. By 1988 the fraction of science graduates entering accountancy etc. had risen to 12.8 per cent. This is symptomatic of an excess rather than of a shortage of scientists.

A similar conclusion can be deduced from the data on rates of return (Table 5.1). For the social and private rates of return are highest in the social sciences, and lower in the 'real' sciences and in engineering. If graduates faced diminishing marginal productivity, so that one science graduate could command a large salary, but as the number increases and their scarcity declines, so the salary each can command declines, then the implication of these figures is, once again, that we have too many natural scientists relative to social scientists. The government should encourage the production of social scientists, so as to bring down the social rate of return from a social sciences degree in line with that earned on the natural sciences. Unless there is something very wrong with the free market, this must be expected to depress the return on natural sciences and to raise the return on social sciences. On the basis of the White Paper figures, the allocation of national resources in the production of qualified personnel will be worsened rather than improved.

These observations are not meant to deny the absence of a shortage of scientists, and, in any case I would be highly embarrassed at making such a claim to the British Association for the Advancement of Science. I am, however, pleased to see that a government which has, in so many areas place its faith in market forces, being prepared to pursue a policy which finds relatively little justification in the market data.

Social Returns to Education?

Are the estimates of social rates of return incorrect? Is the government misplaced in its policy of encouraging natural rather than social sciences? The first question can be addressed more simply than the second. I propose to look at whether the benefit of education is fully reflected in the salaries of the educated, or whether there is evidence for some diffuse benefit which accrues to society at large without being reflected in the incomes of those who have been educated. If such a diffuse benefit can be identified, then any society which attempted to justify higher education in the market place would be making a grave error, and would be condemning itself to a standard of living lower than would be achieved by an interventionist government.

My investigation into this takes two forms. First of all, I look for evidence for whether the presence of people with tertiary training in regions of the United Kingdom tends to raise income more than in proportion to the extra remuneration of the graduates. Secondly I look for evidence of whether education raises growth rates in OECD countries, thereby conferring a benefit on society which cannot be picked up in the calculations of Table 5.1. However, before looking at this, it is worth mentioning other ways in which education can benefit individuals and affect societies.

3 EDUCATION AND SCREENING

The bulk of this chapter focuses on the link between education and productive capacity, with the underlying assumption that this will be directly visible one way or another. However, education may well raise people's level of welfare independently of any effect on productive capacity. Educating people in developing countries about the importance of public health may have an important effect on welfare even if none on economic growth. And in developed countries there can be little doubt that education helps people to enjoy their leisure.

But I should mention the argument[4] that education works as a screening device. Employers are able to identify better workers as a consequence of the fact that they have passed exams, and therefore that the higher rates of pay reflect innate ability rather than the benefit of education. An extension of this argument is that education trains people to fit into their social roles rather than developing their mental abilities, with the implication that it is important mainly as a force for maintaining the social status quo. However, as I shall demonstrate, in some circumstances at least, screening on its own can provide a justification for provision of education at public expense.

I noted, in Section 2, the dreadful handicap imposed by having a PhD, and the fact that those with PhDs did not generally regard them as helpful in their jobs. This suggests that the near-requirement of a PhD for an academic job in the social sciences is a way of controlling entry into a profession which is seen as attractive *per se*, rather in the way in which commissions in cavalry regiments commanded high prices in the nineteenth century. But one could imagine that, at the same time it is a rather efficient filter, in that it identifies those who are likely to be good at working in academic posts. To be a lively teacher one needs to be developing and explaining new ideas. At least it seems reasonable that the two should go together.

Why should the state bear some of the cost of the screening process? The argument could hinge on a failure in the market to recognise the true value of tertiary training. If education, particularly at an undergraduate level, makes a contribution to economic and social welfare over and above anything recognised in graduate rates of remuneration, then it makes considerable sense to keep a filtering device in place and to support PhD students out of public funds. Only if the benefits of tertiary education were reflected in the market place, could it reasonably be argued that the cost of the screening device should be split between universities as employers and their prospective employees.

This observation reflects the general proposition that, where an industry has benefits which are not reflected in the price of its output, it makes sense to subsidise the industry one way or another. In this case a public subsidy to the screening process represents, in effect a subsidy to the cost of production. Even if screening is the dominant aspect of some types of education, this does not necessarily remove the case for a public contribution to its costs.

4   A SPATIAL EXTERNALITY

Lucas (1988) suggests that there may be general benefits, in terms of productive capacity, arising simply from the fact that educated people live near each other. In much the same way as a telephone set is no use unless there are other people with telephone sets, so too, education may be more useful if there are other educated people around. Business will work better. The fact that an educated individual may raise the marginal productivity of other people as well as his own, is not something for which his salary is likely to remunerate him.

Let us set out the idea formally; there are two types of individual, and two different levels of education. L_1 agents are educated for less than L_2 agents. I do not propose to look at the factors influencing the education investment decision (which would require analysis in terms of a population of heterogeneous individuals) but simply at its consequences. There is assumed to be, from the point of view of employers, unit elasticity of substitution between the two types of labour in the production of aggregate labour power, Λ, so that

$$\Lambda = L_1{}^{\alpha}L_2{}^{(1-\alpha)} \tag{5.1}$$

where α is the fraction of the total wage bill which accrues to the untrained labour force. The presence of an externality would be suggested if, after the effective labour force is calculated, there seems to be some positive link between the income per unit of effective labour and the fraction of the population which is trained. Of course it may be objected that any identifiable relationship arises simply from the fact that equation (5.1) misrepresents the way in which the trained and the untrained combine their labour, and I discuss the question of sensitivity after presenting some numerical results.

This type of externality is capable of investigation, by means of a cross-sectional study. There are suitable regional data for Great Britain; these can be used to see whether there is evidence for any external benefit of higher education. The advantages of a regional study over an international study are clear. Standards of education are likely to be much more uniform within Great Britain than they could be expected to be in an international comparison. And it is much more likely that Great Britain forms a single capital market than that a group of diverse countries should. Against this there are a number of problems. A high level of training in the South-East is much more likely to have external benefits for East Anglia than it is for Picardy even though the physical separation is not very different. And regional income statistics are normally regarded as being less reliable than national statistics.

Data on regional output and employment are provided by *Regional Trends*. The 1981 Census provides data on the tertiary-trained economically active population as a fraction of the total. Recent editions of *Regional Trends* also provide data on the fraction of the economically active population, allow me to examine the evidence for a link between training and productivity in the regions in 1988 as well as in 1981. The data are shown in Table 5.2. I can also observe that, taking the two years together, an average of 14 per cent of the population was trained at a tertiary level. In addition, I assume that a trained person is paid 1.3 times the salary of an untrained person, a figure which is lower than the ratio of 1.5 suggested by

TABLE 5.2   *Trained population in Great Britain by region and labour income per person employed*

	1981			1988		
	a	*b*	*c*	*a*	*b*	*c*
North	97.79	11.8	159.89	99.35	12.3	161.97
Yorks & Humberside	94.68	12	154.62	96.84	13.2	157.17
East Midlands	101.73	11.9	166.23	96.18	13.4	155.97
East Anglia	102.20	12.3	166.61	96.27	13.4	156.13
South-East	106.60	15.6	171.74	106.18	17.6	170.67
South-West	101.50	13.2	164.74	100.01	14.3	161.66
West Midlands	89.76	11.8	146.76	91.31	13.7	147.91
North-West	93.99	12.9	152.76	96.60	13.9	156.35
Wales	96.86	12.8	157.50	94.17	13.6	152.60
Scotland	98.93	13.8	160.19	99.73	14.1	161.31

a   Labour income per person employed, with the average for Great Britain = 100.
b   The percentage of the workforce trained at a tertiary (but not necessarily degree) level.
c   Labour income per unit of effective labour. Only relative values are of interest.
Data are taken from the 1981 Census and *Regional Trends*, 1983 and 1990.

the observations of Section 2 because I am including training to below degree level, then my assumption about the way in which tertiary-trained and untrained labour combine, implies a value of $\alpha = 1 - 1.3 \times 0.14 = 0.818$. Using this I can calculate values of Λ for each region, from the data of Table 5.2, and investigate whether the values of labour income per unit of effective labour are related to the fraction of tertiary-trained people in the labour force. If we have corrected the size of the labour force for the presence of tertiary-trained labour they should not be. I discuss the question of sensitivity of the results to the assumptions which have been made subsequently.

The obvious way to test this would be to examine the correlation between the two variables. If I do this, I find that it is, in statistical terms, highly significant. However, closer inspection of the data reveals that the South-East is an outlier. It has a high value of labour income per unit of effective labour employed, and it also has a high fraction of tertiary-trained people. One might say that this supports our case, and in some sense it does, but if the South-East is omitted from the sample, the correlation loses its significance.

A compromise between including and neglecting the South-East is to look at a rank correlation. This avoids giving excessive weight to extreme values, but ensures that they are not neglected. A positive rank relationship does not, of course, prove that there is some extra benefit which is not reflected in the labour income per unit of effective labour, but it does provide some evidence in support of the view.

If we look at the rankings of labour income per unit of effective labour, where the latter is the value of Λ and calculated using our value of $\alpha = 0.818$, then we find a ranking which is significant at a 15 per cent level in 1981 but not even at a 25 per cent in 1988. On their own these would not be seen to be very convincing evidence.

However, if we combine the two pieces of information, by pooling the two rankings, then the margin of uncertainty, arising from the small size of the sample will be reduced. Furthermore, because the rankings of regional labour income per unit of effective labour in 1981 and 1988 are not highly correlated ($R^2 = 0.27$), it could not be said that the 1988 data are little more than a replication of the 1981 data. Pooling yields a positive link between income per unit of effective labour and the fraction of the workforce with tertiary training. The pooled value of $R^2 = 0.14$ which is statistically significant at a 10 per cent level given the larger number of observations (18 degrees of freedom).

The conclusions are not very sensitive to a number of changes. First of all, any correction for hours worked does not seem alter our conclusions. Secondly, they are not changed if the mark-up of trained/untrained remuneration is assumed to be 1.5 rather than 1.3. And thirdly, if the elasticity of substitution between trained and untrained workers is assumed to be greater than that implied in equation (5.1), the correlation is improved.

Since we are forced to use rank correlation methods, it does not prove possible to quantify the benefits. And the value of R^2 of 0.14 is not very high. But there does seem to be some evidence to support the view that employment income in each region is more influenced by tertiary training than the market remuneration of those trained at a tertiary level would suggest.

5 EDUCATION AND ECONOMIC GROWTH

In Section 4 we discussed a static situation and looked for evidence about the benefits of a labour force with tertiary training. Any static link has direct implications for economic growth. An expansion of economic output is possible either because productive inputs are increased or because of 'technical progress'. The early studies of the contribution of education to economic activity found their origins in growth accounting (see Denison, 1967; Maddison, 1987). This is an attempt to explain growth in national income by means of growth in inputs (labour and capital) and other factors. Technical progress is then needed as a residual to equate the growth in inputs to the growth in output. In a simple study one might treat all types of labour as equivalent, but it is not difficult to see objections to this. Educated people are typically paid more than uneducated people, and an increase in the fraction of education people ought therefore to be regarded as an increased labour input. If we assume that the value of the input is measured by the rate of remuneration in the market, then it is possible to calculate the extent to which economic growth is attributable to an increase in the effective labour input, not as a consequence of any change in man-hours worked, but simply because extra education leads to a more efficient labour force.

Such studies typically show that the role of education is important. For example, Matthews, Feinstein and Odling-Smee (1982) note that the effective labour force in the United Kingdom increased by about 1.2 per cent between 1856 and 1973, and suggest that almost half of this can be attributed to an increase in the average level of education of the workforce. Nevertheless, these studies value education on the basis of the incomes that the market place gives to the educated. If this were the end of the story, we would accept the figures of Table 5.1, and conclude that society was earning an unreasonably low return from the typical Arts/Humanities student and *a fortiori* from the PhD student who makes the mistake (both in private terms and social terms) of completing his dissertation. These studies cannot, on their own, show up any other role for education. The calculation is mechanical. One observes the growth in outputs, deducts the growth in inputs on the basis of market valuations, and the residual is technical progress.

Other authors have, however, given education a much more positive role, arguing that realised technical progress is linked in some way to education. Easterlin (1981) addressing the Economic History Association argued that, in the nineteenth century, 'the more schooling of appropriate content that a nation's population had, the easier it was to master the new technological knowledge becoming available'. In other words education was important not merely because one educated man or woman had a productivity larger than that of the uneducated, but because education actually raised the extent to which the economy was able to exploit new techniques and thus raised its growth rate. As a consequence an increase in the *corps* of educated people would be expected to raise the rate of growth of the output of the uneducated as well as increasing the amount of product as a direct consequence of education. Someone who has been educated to a level no higher than that usual in Queen Victoria's days may nevertheless be much more productive because, as a consequence of the education of others, they are able to use their labour time much more effectively.

Easterlin argued that a precursor to economic takeoff was the development of the wide availability of primary school education. In the UK, the USA, France and Germany, there were more than 400 children in primary education per 10 000 of population in the early nineteenth century. Italy did not reach the same level until 1850 and Yugoslavia only made it in 1900. In South America, the early economic success story, Argentina had reached this level when the first figures appear, in 1880, while Brazil, a late starter, did not educate its children to this extent until 1920. There is the obvious risk of muddling cause and consequence, but Easterlin notes that the increase in education precedes the onset of modern economic growth. This makes obvious sense in the light of the above argument. New techniques and methods are not exploited and understood by primary school children, but the training which they receive allows them to apply such techniques in later life.

Similar conclusions are reached by Hicks (1980) and Wheeler (1980) who see a link between literacy and economic growth among today's backward countries. I must, however, report results found by Dasgupta and Weale (1992). We compared growth in national income per head with increases in literacy rates among 42 of the poorest developing countries for the period 1970–80 and did not find a significant rank correlation! I am not able to offer any explanation of this except that, in the modern world, literacy drives have been particularly powerful in socialist developing countries, and that these have therefore been found in countries which adopt economic policies which inhibit growth.[5]

There is a close analogy with the case which we have already studied. The regional comparison was intended to look at whether there was any evidence for the view that tertiary training had an effect on regional incomes which was not reflected in rates of pay, and our tenuous conclusion was that there seemed to be. That effect was purely static. Any dynamic effect on growth rates is likely to be much more important, and might be expected to provide a more powerful case for intervention in the education sector, particularly if, as with the sort of phenomenon we are discussing now, economic growth depends on the level and not the extension of education.[6] The reason for this is very simple. If our overall goal is the present discounted value of national income[7] then a small change in the growth rate will have a powerful effect on the discounted total of present and future national income.

There is, however, one important point which must be borne in mind in interpreting any effect of education on economic growth. Studies often show that there is a tendency among the advanced countries at least, for the low-income countries to 'catch up' the high income ones. Dowrick and Nguyen (1989) in a study to which I shall return later, estimate that 2.5 per cent of the gap in income between low income and high income countries is closed by this process in every year.[8] This catch-up process might happen because, for example, once methods have been tested out and demonstrated, they can be taken on board even in countries where the level of educational attainment is not sufficient to allow them to be exploited immediately.

If the situation is indeed one in which economies tend to catch up with the economic leader, then the economic importance of education is likely to be much reduced. The reason is that, as a consequence of the catch-up process, then eventually all countries will tend to the same growth rates. Absolute income levels will differ, but this is much less important for any analysis of the present discounted value of education than a permanent difference in growth rates.

Setting the point out formally, suppose that there is a notional maximum rate of growth, g_m, made possible by the development of new ideas in the most advanced country and elsewhere. A less advanced country may then face growth from two sources. As a consequence of a lower level of education, it is able to grow directly at a rate of only αg_m, but it also grows from the diffusion of ideas which have been made to work in the advanced country. The percentage rate of growth, independently of any changes in inputs, is then given as

$$\frac{\dot{Y}}{Y} = \alpha g_m + \frac{\beta(Y^* e^{tg_m} - Y)}{Y} \tag{5.2}$$

The solution to this differential equation is

$$Y = \beta Y^* e^{tg_m} / (g_m - \alpha g_m + \beta) + \{Y_0 - \beta Y^* / (g_m - \alpha g_m + \beta)\} \; e^{(\alpha g_m - \beta)t} \tag{5.3}$$

It can be seen that there are two elements of external growth. The first component, $\beta Y^* e^{tg_m} / (g_m - \alpha g_m + \beta)$ shows growth at the maximum long-term rate. This comes from the tendency from the economy to catch up with the most advanced country. The second component, $\{Y_0 - \beta Y^* / (g - \alpha g_m + \beta)\} \; e^{(\alpha g_m - \beta)t}$, shows the influence of domestic growth and the direct benefits of catching up. Since $\alpha \leq 1$ and $\beta \geq 0$, this second exponential term must be lower than the first, and so the economy will, at the end of the day, have a lower income as a consequence of its low level of education, but, unless $\beta = 0$, it will not grow more slowly.

The present discounted value of the future income of this economy is given as

$$\text{PDV} = \frac{\beta Y^*}{(g_m - \alpha g_m + \beta)(r - g_m)} + \frac{(g_m - \alpha g_m + \beta)Y_0 - \beta Y^*}{(g_m - \alpha g_m + \beta)(r - \alpha g_m + \beta)} \tag{5.4}$$

and the effect of any increase in α will be much smaller if β, the catch-up coefficient, is very close to zero than if it is a reasonably powerful effect. However, we must note that this is a steady-state formula. It does not say what will happen if there is a gradual increase in α, because of, for example, an increase in the school-leaving age which takes many years to influence the educational attainment of the whole working population. This issue is investigated numerically, in Section 7, working from equation (5.2).

This analysis, in principle, offers one reason why education should not be left to the market place. The models suggest that there may be a classic externality present. We have stressed the fact that the education of some may lead to economic growth, or at least a higher level of income which would benefit everyone.

The implication of this is that it is worth uneducated people contributing to the cost of education, by means of tax payments. The reason for this is that the uneducated earn higher incomes as a consequence of education. A failure to contribute to the cost of education would reduce the incomes of the uneducated as well as the educated. However, the growth model which we have looked at so far identifies the role of education as a means of assimilating ideas. Not only does it create a situation in which the market cannot reward the educated with the full benefits of their education, but it raises two other particular problems.

An International Externality

The first problem is that the model has assumed that there are ideas generated in the advanced country which can be taken on board by other countries. It is, in essence, a model of the take-up of ideas in a multi-country world, and, in a later section we will assess it empirically in this way. However, the advanced country faces the particular problem that it is actually the source of the ideas which benefit everyone else. Now, we know that the position is in fact more complicated than this. Relatively less advanced countries may be a source for ideas, even if their general level of education and training means that they do not explain them to the full. But those countries which generate the ideas which support the income growth of the most advanced country are helping their neighbours and are not rewarded for this economically. Perhaps this does not matter too much. Countries derive prestige from recognition through other means, such as the receipt of Nobel prizes. We do not hear the United States and the United Kingdom arguing that they should tax other advanced countries for having produced a disproportionate number of the ideas which have made modern economic growth possible, although this may well be true. It is, on the other hand, sometimes argued that Britain should (as it now has) switch away from pure research because we have derived relatively little direct economic benefit from it.

An Intertemporal Externality and the National Debt

The second problem, which applies both to the countries producing the bulk of the ideas leading to technical progress and to those educating their populations so that they can absorb this progress, is that of an intertemporal externality. In a growing economy, a higher rate of growth, or indeed even a higher level of income, benefits future generations as well as the current generation, provided, at least that some of the skills learned by one generation are passed on to their successors. This is self-evidently true. There are many areas where it is easy to do something once it is explained, but where the task would be impossible if one were confronted simply by the task and the necessary equipment. The idea underlying the model is that education leads to the development and application of new ideas which raise the level of human capital above the level already existing; at the same time the existing body of human capital would only depreciate slowly and does not disappear with the generation which created it.

A consequence of this is that a population which is concerned only about its own welfare would provide a lower level of education than one which is also concerned about the welfare of future generations. Or, conversely, some mechanism which allows parents to charge their children for the benefits of the parents' education, would provide some means of offsetting this intertemporal externality.

The issue can be explored formally by means of a model such as Meade's (1966) description of overlapping generations, but here I restrict myself to a few basic points about the issue. First of all, the problem arises not merely with investment in education, but also with other types of investment. Investors who face the prospect of death will want an enhanced return to offset the fact that they may die before all the benefits of their investment are realised (Blanchard, 1985). Secondly, there is a well-tried method of imposing a burden on a future generation, and that is for the government to finance the excess of the socially desirable level of education over the privately desirable level by means of borrowing. The maintenance of a national debt at an appropriate level will impose on future generations a burden equal to the benefit they gain from the education of the current generation. I mention this because we have become used to hearing (or at least we used to hear, when the government had a large budget surplus) that fiscal policy should be managed with the aim of clearing the national debt. Yet here we have a case where it is socially desirable for the government to be in debt, not merely at some stages of the economic cycle, but on a permanent basis, and even though there is no offsetting capital asset by any conventional measure.

6   INCREASING OR DECREASING RETURNS?

The analysis of Section 5 might be taken to suggest that, by devoting more time to education, a country is able to raise its growth rate without limit (or at least subject only to the constraints imposed by the need for raw materials and the requirement to preserve the environment). Rosen (1976) indeed argues that the rate of cumulation of human capital for an individual being educated is linearly dependent on the duration of education, and this model is used by Lucas (1988). If each generation passes on a constant fraction of its human capital to its children, then such a model implies a linear relationship between the duration of education and the rate of growth. With a constant rate of discount, such a society would have an incentive to extend education to the point where the rate of growth of output equalled the rate of interest, making the discounted value of future income infinite. This creates an obvious logical problem.

Denison (1967, p. 85), relying once more on earnings data, suggests an element of increasing returns, a position more extreme than Rosen's. He argues that earnings increase by about 5 per cent p.a. for each year of schooling up to eight years, and by about 8 per cent p.a. for each year beyond that. This point does not, of course, necessarily relate to the sort of effect which we are considering because we do not expect the social benefits of more rapid technical progress to be reflected in rates of pay. But we should note, in any case, that not all the market evidence supports the Denison/Rosen view. Perlman (1988) argues that there may be overeducation in the United States, and in the United Kingdom, as I mentioned in Section 2, there does appear to be diminishing returns to postgraduate education. This can only be reconciled with Denison's data if returns are increasing at some points before decreasing returns set in. Observations about rates of pay, even though they look at something different from the sort of benefit from education in which we are interested, do seem to be consistent with diminishing and even negative returns from prolonged periods of study.

In Section 6 we assumed that the country could only grow at fraction α of the maximum rate of growth, unless it was helped out by catch-up, but we did not discuss how α was related to the duration of education. Our supposition was that economic growth comes partly from the development and adoption of new ideas. The production of new ideas may or may not be dependent on the general level of education, but for the time being we shall take it to be exogenous. The maximum possible rate of growth depends on the development of new ideas, and therefore implicitly on the cumulation of human capital in the most advanced country. However the ability to implement new technology in any particular country depends on the level of education of the population. The notion of an upper bound to the rate of growth makes a linear relationship between education and growth impossible and, incidentally, avoids the problem of an infinite present discounted value of future income posed by Rosen's assumption.

If g_m is the maximum rate of growth, then the concept of diminishing returns could be represented by the relationship

$$\alpha g_m = g_0 + (g_m - g_0)kE/(1 + E)$$

where E is the number of years of education, so that, without any education, the growth rate would be g_0 and, as the amount of education rises, it would approach g_m asymptotically. We are thus able to investigate any empirical evidence for diminishing returns to education, by comparing the fit of this relationship with that of a linear relationship, and we proceed to do this in the next section.

7   INTERNATIONAL COMPARISONS OF EDUCATION AND GROWTH

The analysis of Sections 5 and 6 suggested that the rate of growth in an economy might be dependent on the length of the education of its population, among other factors. White (1988) argues that this is particularly likely to be true of the 1970s and 1980s, because technical progress over this period has been dependent on the application of techniques by means of skilled labour, rather than on their embodiment through capital investment.[9] We now look at the empirical evidence for any link between educational attainment and economic growth in this period.

Statistics are available on the average number of years of education received by the population aged 25–64 in each country (OECD, 1974). These data are calculated from Census results of around 1970, and projections are also made to 1980. Such data include the education of the inactive population as well as the active population, and they include education undergone by people who failed to qualify at the end of it. Furthermore, despite the best efforts of the OECD statisticians, there must be significant differences in the meaning of the various categories of education.

We now attempt to use these data to investigate whether there is any empirical basis for a link between education and economic growth, with the main aim of quantifying any sensitivity of the growth rate of an economy to the length of education of its workforce. An implication of the model of Sections 4 and 5, and of the growth accounting exercises discussed at the start of Section 6, is that we would expect to see the growth rate depending on both the average level of education of the working population and on its increase. There are, of course, other factors which are likely to influence growth. In addition to the catch-up phenomenon, which we have already discussed, increases in capital and labour inputs would be expected to lead to growth in output.

Ideally one would build a model which would reflect these effects, but fortunately Dowrick and Nguyen (1989) study growth in the OECD countries and break down their growth rates over the period 1973–85 into components arising from cyclical factors, growth in employment, growth in the capital stock, 'catch-up' with more advanced countries and a residual. We can approach the problem much more simply by studying whether educational attainment has any link with residual growth. The results will not be exactly the same as would be found from the building of a complex model, but there is no reason to think, in the circumstances of these data, that they give a misleading view of the magnitude of the effects involved. The basic data are shown in Table 5.3 and are plotted in Figure 5.1.

With the relatively small number of observations, it seems sensible to look for a relation between total average years of education, extension of education and residual economic growth, rather than try to distinguish the effects of the different components. I was unable to find a significant effect of the extension of education on residual economic growth, and therefore only report in detail the regressions with these terms restricted to zero.[10]

TABLE 5.3 *Educational attainment and economic growth*

Country	Educational attainment			Growth in attainment (%)			Economic growth (% p.a.)	
	1	2	3	1	2	3	Unexplained	Total
Belgium	6.0	3.4	0.49	0.0	1.6	4.8	0.29	−0.19
Canada	5.8	3.8	0.31	0.1	1.8	5.5	0.28	−0.03
Denmark	5.0	4.1	0.36	0.0	0.8	4.9	−0.01	0.06
France	5.0	3.8	0.35	0.0	1.6	6.1	0.40	−0.08
West Germany	4.0	5.1	0.18	0.0	0.1	4.1	0.64	0.36
Greece	4.5	1.2	0.21	1.1	4.9	0.0	−0.36	−0.07
Italy	4.3	1.9	0.19	0.5	3.6	3.6	−0.87	0.06
Japan	6.0	3.6	0.35	0.0	1.7	3.8	0.21	1.24
Netherlands	6.0	2.3	0.35	0.0	2.7	3.7	−0.46	−0.73
Norway	7.0	1.4	0.29	0.0	4.4	8.2	0.58	1.93
Portugal	2.5	1.0	0.15	1.6	5.2	10.3	−0.86	−0.13
Spain	3.4	1.5	0.16	0.4	4.7	9.3	0.56	−0.31
Sweden	6.0	2.0	0.31	0.0	3.3	6.8	−0.25	0.03
UK	6.0	3.9	0.23	0.0	1.1	4.9	−0.02	−0.42
USA	5.8	4.5	0.76	0.0	0.9	5.6	0.66	−0.28

The first three columns show the average number of years of primary, secondary and tertiary education of those aged 25–64 in 1970. The second group of three columns shows the rate of increase of the average number of years of each type of education of those in the 25–64 age group expected during the period 1970–80. The last two columns show the unexplained and total annual average growth rates of the economies during the period 1973–85. These growth rates are measured relative to the OECD mean.

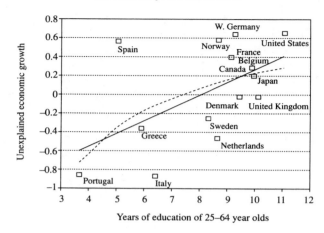

FIGURE 5.1   *Unexplained growth and educational attainment*

TABLE 5.4   *The effect of educational attainment on economic growth*

(i)	Constant returns to education	
	UXG = 0.138ED – 1.11	$R^2 = 0.32$
	(2.48) (2.30)	
(ii)	Diminishing returns to education	
	UXG = 8.65ED/(1 + ED) – 7.64	$R^2 = 0.29$
	(2.49) (2.48)	

UXG, unexplained economic growth; ED, educational attainment of the workforce.

Table 5.4 shows the results of two regression equations. These are carried out using the 1970 level of educational attainment to explain residual economic growth over the period 1973–85. However, no differences of any importance arise if one uses the OECD figures for the growth in educational attainment to construct an estimate of attainment in 1979 and relates this to residual growth over the same period. The first describes a straight line while the second implies diminishing returns to education. The results of this exercise confirm what can be seen in Figure 5.1. There is no evidence of diminishing returns in these data, in that the function with diminishing returns fits slightly worse than that with constant returns.

Nevertheless, as I have argued, one would expect diminishing returns to set in at some point, and therefore be cautious about drawing conclusions excessively dependent on their absence.

The Benefits of an Extension of Education

The results of the regression analysis may be used, together with the formula for the present discounted value, to try to assess the benefits which would be won by a country such as the United Kingdom if it extended the level of education of its workforce by one year. The calculation should, however, be interpreted as indicative of the plausible magnitude of the numbers involved rather than a precise calculation. It should also be noted, however, that these benefits are lower than the present discounted value shown by the formula in Section 6, simply because it takes nearly 50 years for the effect of an increase of one year in the education of the young to be fully reflected in the educational attainment of the workforce. Not only does this reduce the present value of the overall benefit, but it also shifts the benefit disproportionately away from the current generation, making the intertemporal externality all the more important.

As we observed in Section 5.6, the result is likely to depend on the value of the catch-up parameter as well as on the value of the basic growth rate relative to the rate of interest. In order to illustrate this, one can use equation (5.11) for the growth in income to calculate the benefits of an extension of education for different values of these parameters. Table 5.5 shows the effect arising from the increase in the rate of growth only. The value of g_m is assumed to be 3 per cent p.a., and the increase in education is assumed to raise the actual rate of growth from 2 per cent p.a. to 2.138 per cent p.a. The linear regression in Table 5.4 implies that this is the effect of one extra year of education.[11] The calculations are carried out for a country which is assumed to have an initial income level of 60 per cent of the maximum. The present discounted values of the private and social benefits are shown in Table 5.5. Calculations are presented in the case where there is no catch-up and with the value of the catch-up parameter as estimated by Dowrick and Nguyen (1989) at 0.025. The calculations are shown for discount rates of 3.5 per cent p.a., 5 per cent p.a. and 7 per cent p.a.

In the calculation it is assumed that the extra year of education raises the labour income of the educated by 8 per cent, and therefore, if one quarter of national income is assumed to accrue to capital owned by the average individual, his total income is increased by 6 per cent. The cost of the extra education is assumed to be 110 per cent of the year's earnings forgone, with the extra 10 per cent representing the cost of tuition.

TABLE 5.5   *The effect of an extension of education on discounted income*

	Percentage increase in private discounted income	Percentage increase in social discounted income
No catch-up		
$r = 3.5\%$ p.a.	3.2	10.2
$r = 5\%$ p.a.	2.4	4.2
$r = 7\%$ p.a.	1.1	1.6
Catch-up ($\beta = 2.5$ per cent p.a.)		
$r = 3.5\%$ p.a.	0.8	1.6
$r = 5\%$ p.a.	0.4	0.6
$r = 7\%$ p.a.	−0.4	−0.2

The private benefit of education reflects the gain to an individual who is assumed to be the only person to undertake extra education at the margin. It therefore reflects the increase in income arising from the direct effect reported by Denison (1967), but not the benefits of faster economic growth. These latter benefits only accrue with a general increase in education. The social benefit, on the other hand takes into account the fact that the growth rate is changed, and cumulates the effect of this into what is effectively the infinite future.[12]

The results show, as they are intended to, the sensitivity to the underlying assumptions. An extension of education would be a marked benefit in the absence of 'catch-up' ($\beta = 0$) and $r = 3.5$ per cent p.a. In the presence of catch-up and with a discount rate of $r = 7$ per cent p.a., it becomes a bad thing. But, except in this case where an extension of education is a bad idea, it becomes quite clear that the long-term social benefits of education are likely to be at least 40 per cent above the private benefits. Once the duration of education influences economic growth, then it becomes clear that a considerable part of the benefit accrues to future generations. It is reasonable to expect them to contribute towards the cost.

9   CONCLUSIONS

This chapter has first of all demonstrated that policy-makers do not behave as though they believe the returns from education are measured by rates of private remuneration. Otherwise we would be aiming to cut back on scientists and to raise the number of economists in the universities.[13]

Once one accepts that there may be external benefits which do accrue to education which are not measured in the market place, then the case for government intervention in the market for education becomes overwhelming, and may extend to subsidising the methods by which the education industry selects those who join it, as well as making sure that those who are educated do not have to bear the full cost.

Externalities can arise in a number of ways, and this chapter has illustrated two of them. The first was a static externality. The idea was simply that a relatively large trained population might raise labour productivity by more than would be reflected in their pay differentials. The second idea was dynamic. The nature of technical progress may be such that a society's ability to take up new production techniques depends on its level of educational attainment. Unless economic growth is also influenced by extent to which output is below that of the most advanced country, this means that the rate of growth will depend on the duration of education. Because ideas are not lost once they are implemented, such a situation means that benefit from education accrues not only to those currently alive who are not educated, but also to future generations. As such, it suggests that part of the burden of current education should be borne by future generations. One way of doing this is to maintain a national debt.

Both aspects were investigated empirically, and there seemed to be some evidence to support the proposed externalities. The implication of this is that one should be nervous of any educational policy which is pursued with reference to the benefits measured as they accrue to private individuals. Attention should shift to the social returns.

Acknowledgements

Many useful comments were made on an earlier draft by participants in a seminar at Churchill College, Cambridge. Paul Dunne was particularly helpful in drawing my attention to areas of importance.

NOTES

1. For a survey of the work done on this in the 1960s see Blaug (1970).
2. Rudd (1986) reaches a similar conclusion for the 'hard' sciences.
3. Arrow and Capron (1959) remind us that this is not a new issue.
4. Arguments about screening and the social role of education are helpfully summarised by OECD *Employment Outlook*, July 1989.

5. The same point could be made about parts of the developed world. Czechoslovakia and the eastern part of Germany have undoubtedly underperformed given the level of education of their populations; it is not unreasonable to attribute this to the economic structures which were imposed on them.
6. This is set out clearly by Lucas (1988).
7. Discounting means that national income is aggregated from now into the distant future. The aggregate would be infinite if the foreseen values of future income are simply added up. Discounting reflects the view that jam today is more desirable than jam tomorrow. Provided that the rate of interest used in discounting is higher than the rate at which the economy is expected to grow the present discounted sum of future income will be finite. If current income is Y and it is expected to grow at a rate g, then the present discounted value of future income is $Y/(r-g)$.
8. This may be contrasted with the view of Stiglitz (1988) who argues, without any reference to the evidence, that differences in growth rates persist, and then develops a model which 'explains' this 'stylised fact'. Stiglitz's view is, however, supported by Baumol and Wolff (1988).
9. This may explain why Smith, Hitchens and Davies (1982) scarcely discuss the issue, while Steedman and Wagner (1987) give it considerable prominence. Begg (1990) warns of the extent to which excessive emphasis on training can lead to the neglect of other important issues.
10. As noted, one should ideally integrate the estimation of these effects with the calculation of the explained growth rates. But as a check that our much simpler approach has not been too far off the mark, one can regress the explained growth rate along with the duration of education on the unexplained growth rate. This 'overfitted' regression gives a value for the sensitivity of unexplained growth to education of 0.1, instead of 0.138. The statistical significance of the regression is, however, less marked, with a t statistic of 1.72.
11. The diminishing returns function implies an increase in the growth rate of only 0.08 per cent p.a. for a country like the United Kingdom.
12. In fact the calculation is performed by adding up for 1000 years. Because future income is discounted, this is in effect an infinite summation.
13. Apparently in the United States, where student demand is more sensitive to market forces, one third of all undergraduates study either economics or business studies.

REFERENCES

Advisory Board for the Research Councils (1982), *Report of the Working Party on Postgraduate Education,* Cmnd. 8537, HMSO.

Arrow, K. J. and Capron, W. M. (1959) 'Dynamic Shortages and Price Rises: the Engineer-Scientist Case,' *Quarterly Journal of Economics*, vol. 73, pp. 292–308.

Baumol, W. J. and Wolff, E. N. (1988) 'Productivity Growth, Convergence and Welfare: What the Long-run Data Show', *American Economic Review*, vol. 78, pp. 1155–59.

Begg, I. G. (1990) 'Training as an Instrument of Regional Policy: the New Panacea?', *Regional Studies*, vol. 24, pp. 357–62.

Blanchard, O. J. (1985) 'Debt, Deficits and Finite Horizons', *Journal of Political Economy*.

Blaug, M. (1970) *Economics of Education*. Penguin Books.

Clarke, J., Rees, A. and Meadows, P. (1988) '1980 Graduates – where are they now?', *Department of Employment Gazette*, vol. 96, pp. 495–506.

Dasgupta, P. and Weale, M. R. (1992) 'On the Measurement of Well-being', *World Development*, forthcoming.

Denison, E. F. (1967) *Why Growth Rates Differ* (Brookings Institute).

Dowrick, S. and Nguyen, D. (1989) 'OECD Comparative Economic Growth: 1950–85; *American Economic Review*, vol. 79, pp. 1010–30.

Easterlin, R. A. (1981) 'Why Isn't the Whole World Developed', *Journal of Economic History*, vol. 41, pp. 1–20.

Hicks, N. (1980) 'Economic Growth and Human Resources', Working Paper 408. (Washington: World Bank).

HMSO (1988) *Top-up Loans for Students*, Cmnd. 520.

Lucas, R. E. (1988) 'On the Mechanics of Economic Development', *Journal of Monetary Economics*, vol. 22, pp. 3–42.

Maddison, A. (1987) 'Growth and Slowdown in Advanced Capitalist Economies: Techniques of Quantitative Assessment', *Journal of Economic Literature*, vol. 25, pp. 649–98.

Matthews, R. C. O., Feinstein, C. H., and Odling-Smee, J. (1982) *British Economic Growth: 1856–1973* (Oxford: Clarendon Press).

Meade, J. E. (1966) 'Life-cycle Savings, Inheritance and Economic Growth', *Review of Economic Studies*, vol. 33, pp. 61–78.

OECD (1979) *Education Statistics Yearbook*.

OECD (1989) *Employment Outlook*, July, pp. 49–50.

Perlman, R. (1988) 'Education and Training: an American Perspective', *Oxford Review of Economic Policy*, vol. 4, 82–93.

Rosen, S. (1976) 'A Theory of Life Earnings', *Journal of Political Economy, Supplement*, vol. 84, pp. 545–68.

Rudd, E. (1986) 'The Value of a PhD in Science or Technology in Britain', *European Journal of Education*, vol. 21, pp. 223–50.

Rudd, E. (1990) 'The Early Careers of Social Science Graduates and the Value of a PhD', *Journal of the Royal Statistical Society. Series A*, vol. 153, pp. 203–32.

Schultz, T. W. (1961) 'Investment in Human Capital', *American Economic Review*, vol. 51, pp. 1–17.

Smith, A. D., Hitchens, D. M. W. N. and Davies, S. W. (1982) *International Industrial Productivity: A Comparison of Britain, America and Germany*. National Institute of Economic and Social Research Occasional Paper.

Steedman, H. and Wagner, K. (1987) 'A Second Look at Productivity, Machinery and Skills in Britain and Germany', *National Institute Economic Review*, no. 122, pp. 84–96.

Stiglitz, J. E. (1987) 'Learning to Learn, Localised Learning and Technological Progress', in *Economic Policy and Technological Performance* Dasgupta, P. and Stoneman, P. (Cambridge: Cambridge University Press).

Wheeler, D. (1980) 'Human Resource Development and Economic Growth in Developing Countries: a Simultaneous Model', Working Paper 407 (Washington: World Bank).

White, M. (1988) 'Educational Policy and Economic Goals', *Oxford Review of Economic Policy*, vol. 4, pp. 1–20.

6 Health and Markets

GRAHAM LOOMES

The subject of 'Health and Markets' could hardly be more topical. Britain has just introduced – in April 1991 – a range of reforms that have been portrayed as bringing a number of more business-like, market-type mechanisms into the operation of the National Health Service and the provision of health and community care more generally.

Most households in the UK have received through the post a small booklet called *The NHS Reforms and You* which set out to provide some information about what the reforms originally elaborated in the document *Working for Patients* of 1990 might mean to Britain, and to reassure us (with the aid of lots of friendly little cartoon characters and a number of carefully phrased questions and answers) that the proposed changes 'are designed to give you a more efficient and an even better service – above all, a service that puts you, the patient, first. They are intended to reinforce the main aim of the National Health Service – to help people live longer and enjoy a better quality of life.' (HSR6, p. 2). A little further down the page, printed in blue ink for extra emphasis, the booklet promises: 'As now, the NHS will continue to be open to all, regardless of income, and paid for mainly out of general taxation. NHS services will continue to be largely free at the point of use.'

Given the controversial nature of (some of) the new reforms, and the interests and concerns that surround them, it would be rather strange if I were to talk about 'Health and Markets' without spending at least some time looking at various of the proposals in more detail; and in due course this is precisely what I intend to do.

For example, there was the announcement in mid-July 1990 that the community care reforms, which had been closely associated with the NHS reforms and which were also scheduled to come into effect in April 1991, would now be phased in over three years. Then at the beginning of August, the NHS Chief Executive, Mr Duncan Nichol, announced that the reduction of waiting lists would be given a top priority, and indicated that the performance-linked element in health service managers' salaries might well be substantially affected by their success or failure in shortening these waiting lists. Later, Secretary of State Kenneth Clarke announced that 65 organisations had applied for the status of NHS Trusts and that he expected to make decisions on these applications before the end of November 1990: subsequently he has done so, approving almost all of the applications for self-governing status.

In due course I shall return to these issues. But first I want to set my remarks about current health care policy in the context of a (necessarily brief) review of the key issues arising from an economic analysis of the scope and limitations of markets in the field of health.

THE COMMODITY IN QUESTION

When discussing the way any particular market operates – or fails to operate – it is often helpful to begin by considering the nature of the commodity being produced and consumed. In the present case, it is not merely helpful, but essential.

The first point to note is that although the title of this chapter is 'Health and Markets', there is really no question of a market for health *per se*. You cannot buy and sell good health itself any more than you can buy and sell a clear conscience or a sense of humour. What *can* be produced and consumed is health *care*, by which I mean a range of goods and services whose *main* purpose is to try to improve people's mental and/or physical health. The question then is to what extent *market* mechanisms are the most appropriate means of organising the production, distribution and consumption of the very broad spectrum of health care goods and services.

However, before tackling that question, there is another important point to be made. Although most industrialised societies devote a substantial part of their human and technological resources to health care, and although many people have great faith in (or at least, high hopes for) what the health care sector can do to improve the length and quality of their lives, the evidence suggests that health care is only one of the factors that affects people's health – and is not necessarily the most important. The quantity and quality of what people eat and drink, the level of public and private hygiene, housing conditions, working conditions, and other aspects of what might sweepingly be called 'lifestyle' may all play a greater or lesser role in determining people's states of health.

As if to illustrate this point, on the day after Mr Nichol's statement about waiting lists, the *Daily Telegraph* (2 August 1990, p. 6) not only published details of the waiting list figures, but also reported some data from the latest of a long catalogue of studies showing continuing differences in life expectancy between different sections of the population of Britain today which are attributable to *social* and *economic* disparities of one kind or another. These inequalities have little to do with the existence or non-existence of health care markets, but have much more to do with the functioning – or malfunctioning – of markets for junk food, tobacco, alcohol, housing and employment, combined with serious shortcomings in education and training, working conditions and the control of pollution. One theme which could easily be developed at much greater length under the heading 'Health and Markets' is the way in which the operation of some markets and the failures of other markets may positively damage many people's health to an extent which can only be partially patched up by health care expenditure. However, in the space available to me I do not believe I could do full justice to that very important theme. Instead I must restrict myself here to a discussion of the extent to which markets or market-like mechanisms are the most appropriate means of organising the production and delivery of *health care* goods and services, with particular reference to Britain in the 1990s.

MARKETS IN GENERAL AND THE HEALTH CARE MARKET IN PARTICULAR

In general, most economists think that markets work best when the following conditions are met:

A: Consumers have adequate experience of, or information about, the product and its value or usefulness to them, compared with the value/usefulness of alternative products.
B. Consumers can obtain the same or very similar products equally well from a variety of independent suppliers who are for their part knowledgeable about alternative methods and costs of production.
C: Production and consumption of the product has little effect on people other than the producers and consumers concerned – there are no substantial benefits from which other people cannot be excluded, nor any substantial costs or damage inflicted upon other people, nor any breaches of fundamental values or rights.

Under these textbook conditions, markets are thought to be highly efficient mechanisms for matching up consumers' desires and purchasing power with the technology and resources available. However, this is a theoretical ideal: in practice, it is really quite hard to think of many actual markets which meet *all* of those conditions. And in the case of health care, there are many important instances where *hardly any* of the conditions outlined above are even remotely satisfied.

Of course, there are *some* health care goods where markets can and do operate more or less straightforwardly – for example, goods such as sticking plasters, antiseptic ointments, and a whole range of medicines that can be purchased without prescription to relieve headaches, sore throats, upset stomachs and the symptoms of colds or mild influenza. By and large, these are examples of cases where conditions A, B and C *generally* hold *reasonably* well – although even here one needs to inject a note of caution, since consumers are still quite heavily dependent on the producers and/or government regulators to assure the overall quality of the product, and in particular to do what no individual consumer can be expected to do, namely to keep an eye on the nature and frequency of any adverse side-effects, especially those arising from long-term or repeated consumption. But given that these risks are thought to be really quite small, the fact that consumers can acquire sufficient experience to judge the short-term usefulness of these products, the fact that the products are generally being used to treat fairly minor health problems, the fact that there is a sufficient range of available alternatives, and that these goods are generally priced within most people's ability to pay – all these factors come together to allow markets in these products to operate tolerably well.

However, for many other important cases, the picture is very different, and is characterised by imperfect information and considerable uncertainty. For example, most of us have very little idea about which mild or serious or life-threatening conditions we will suffer during our lifetimes, or when we will suffer them. We often do not know that health problems are developing, because in the early stages of development many conditions do not manifest obvious symptoms; and even when we do experience symptoms, most lay people may be uncertain about how to interpret their significance. Once a condition is suspected, we may be uncertain about what treatments are available, what they involve, how much they will cost and how effective they are likely to be. Moreover, many of these uncertainties cannot simply be resolved by consulting a health care professional. For while (it is to be hoped that) they are much more knowledgeable about these matters than the average member of the public, they also operate in an uncertain world: diagnosis is an imperfect science (or art); many diagnostic tests or screening procedures involve a degree of fallibility (and may even involve some additional element of risk); different experts may genuinely disagree about the relative merits of different treatments; and ostensibly the same treatment may produce quite variable results with different patients in ways that are difficult to predict.

So uncertainty is an important and pervasive characteristic of health and health care. But of course uncertainty is not unique to this area of life.

Indeed, it is a feature of almost every sphere of human activity; and one common response to it is to develop some system of insurance.

Private markets exist to handle insurance against risks of losses due to theft, or fire, or car accidents. Why not leave it to a private market in health insurance to take care of the uncertainties in *this* area of life?

Well, of course some societies *do* try to use private health insurance markets for this purpose; but there are serious difficulties and shortcomings. Two major areas of difficulty can be identified under the headings of *adverse selection* and *moral hazard*. Let us consider each of these in turn. In another section of the ideal textbook world, each person seeking any kind of insurance would be rated on the basis of the 'true' risk that they will suffer a loss, and their premium would be set accordingly. Attempts by insurance companies to do something along those lines can be seen in the case of motor insurance: young and/or inexperienced drivers will generally be charged a higher premium because it is known that *on average* these groups are more likely to have accidents than older, more experienced drivers. Of course, this is hard on certain individual young people who may be particularly competent or careful drivers: they might (rightly) feel that a premium based on the average for their group is too high for them person-ally, and if they could not find a company or policy that would somehow take account of their particular lower-than-average riskiness, they might wish to choose not to buy any insurance at all (although by law they are required to have at least third party cover). This illustrates adverse selec-tion, where the below-average risks might wish to opt out of the insurance market, leaving the insurance companies with only the higher-risk cus-tomers, leading to higher premiums which result in some members of the next-lowest risk groups opting out; and so on.

In practice, adverse selection in motor insurance can be combated partly by the law requiring all drivers to have at least third party cover, partly by a more sophisticated type of policy involving deductibles, no-claims bonuses, etc., and partly by individuals actually having only a rather impre-cise idea of their own 'true' risk status. The result is a market which functions imperfectly, but more or less acceptably. Some policyholders may be rather hard-done-by, but it can be argued that for the most part they *chose* to run a car rather than use alternative forms of public or private transport, and were able to anticipate the insurance costs at the time of making their choice, so that no very grave social injustice is involved.

The same view will frequently *not* be taken towards health insurance, however. Maintaining your health is not seen as a 'luxury' good like maintaining a private car; and if a society were entirely dependent upon a private health insurance market where companies discriminated against bad health-risk groups in the same way that they discriminate against bad driver-risk groups, then it is the old, the sick and the poor who would have to pay the high premiums (which they are least able to afford), while the low-risk young, fit, rich people would get off most lightly – or perhaps wish to opt out altogether if average premiums were charged across the board. Typically, then, private health insurance markets fail to provide anything like adequate cover to all members of society at prices they can afford, and this is felt by many people – including many of those who *can* afford adequate cover – to be an undesirable or unacceptable situation requiring intervention. One possibility – as in the United States, for example – is for the government to let private insurance markets operate for those who can be covered tolerably well, and try to plug the worst gaps with schemes like Medicare and Medicaid, using public money to provide some kind of 'safety net' for the elderly and the poor. The alternative adopted in Britain under the National Health Service as presently conceived is, in effect, to operate a system of compulsory insurance funded out of tax revenues, with a private health insurance market and a number of private hospitals operating in a relatively limited 'luxury goods' capacity. As the earlier quotation from the Department of Health's booklet indicated, the government's stated intention is, apparently, to continue on this basis – although there is also a clear intention (*not* made explicit in that booklet) to encourage more purchase of private health insurance and more use of private hospitals and to privatise other ancillary services.

However, whether funding for health care comes principally from private health insurance, or from public taxation, or from some combination of the two, problems still remain, and the problem of *moral hazard* is a convenient place to start. The basic idea here is that when people have some form of health insurance and no longer need to meet the full costs of any treatment on a 'pay-as-you-go' basis, their behaviour may change. It is not so much that we behave less cautiously and therefore incur more injuries and illnesses (although this may be part of the story); what is perceived to be a more serious problem is that once we fall ill, we are likely to take maximum advantage of the fact that the insurance company or the taxpayer is footing part or all of the bill and we may therefore consume health care resources well beyond the point where the benefits justify the costs. The notion is that if we were ourselves paying for every additional item of service, we would only go on purchasing further items of care so long as the perceived extra benefits exceeded the extra cost to us. Whereas if private insurance or public funding effectively makes additional consumption free (or almost free) to us, we have an incentive to demand more and more health care so long as it generates *any* (or almost any) personal benefit. But the fact that the additional care is (almost) free to me as an individual does not mean that it is *really* free, but only that the costs have been shifted onto others. Moreover, since these costs are greater than can be justified by the benefits accruing to me, this represents a wasteful use of scarce social resources. Put another way: if, instead of being used to produce relatively small additional benefits to me, these resources could be redirected to uses which produce much greater benefits to other people, the population *as a whole* would be better off.

In the context of health care markets – in the United States, for example – this problem is liable to be aggravated by another aspect of the failure of conditions A, B and C set out earlier.

Recall the fact that although health care professionals are certainly not perfectly knowledgeable, they are nevertheless much more knowledgeable about diagnosis and treatment than most of the rest of us, and we often rely heavily on them to tell us not only what is wrong with us but also what to do about it. In other words, we are not sovereign consumers forming our health care demands on the basis of our own preferences combined with adequate independent information about the available health care alternatives. On the contrary, many of our demands are heavily influenced by the health care professionals we consult – that is, by the very people who supply the goods and services which, on their advice, we consume. The independence between demand and supply, which plays such an important role in the textbook story of efficient markets, is often seriously compromised in the real world of health care. And when this happens within a market framework, it provides the conditions for the phenomenon known as 'supplier-induced demand'. In conventional textbook markets, an increase in the supply of a commodity is generally expected to lead to a greater volume of trade at a lower market price (all other things being equal); but it has often been observed in the United States that an increase in the supply of physicians in a population may actually be associated with *no* fall, and possibly even a *rise*, in the price of physician services, and this may be explained in terms of supplier-induced demand: that is, when the increase in the number of physicians leads to a reduction in the average physician's standard workload (and income), he may encourage patients to take fuller advantage of their insurance cover and his greater availability to consume more expensive (although not correspondingly more beneficial) health care.

In an extreme form, the asymmetry of information between patient and doctor (or dentist, optician etc.) and the special position of the health care professional may lead to overtreatment to the point of positively damaging the patient's health. More often, perhaps, there is some (small) marginal benefit to the patient and some (greater?) benefit to the physician, at the expense of the insurer and/or society more generally. The important thing to note, however, is that with the uncertainty inherent in the health care field and the scope for 'judgement' that this allows, combined with the inter-dependence of demand and supply due to the asymmetry of knowledge between patients and professionals, free markets have no automatic inbuilt mechanism for correcting the problem and eradicating the inefficiencies that result. Indeed, the 'natural' incentives work in the opposite direction, and it is often other things, such as personal ethics, professional codes of conduct, external monitoring by insurance companies and, in cases of damage to the patient, the fear of litigation that may inhibit the extent of the waste of scarce social resources.

In the context of the British National Health Service, the asymmetry of information and power between professionals and patients, combined with the fact that many NHS services are substantially subsidised or free (in money terms, anyway) at the point of use has resulted in a range of different problems.

As things stand at present, hospital staff are salaried employees of the National Health Service with no strong *financial* incentives to induce more demand for care. But they may be motivated instead by other considerations, not all of which are *necessarily* conducive to the efficient provision of health care. For example, it has been suggested that some clinicians substitute the pursuit of status and prestige for the pursuit of financial profit. Instead of accumulating personal wealth, they may look to build a reputation and an 'empire'. Instead of working in the less glamorous but much-needed specialties, undertaking the (possibly rather repetitive) tasks which would meet patients' priorities, it may be that a number of health care professionals wish to devote more of their energies to cases that *they* find more interesting, and are drawn to areas of medicine that offer greater variety and stimulation, characterised perhaps by the opportunities to use new technology and to practice innovative rather than routine procedures.

The danger is that under these circumstances resource allocation may be unduly influenced by the interests of the practitioners rather than the wel-fare of the patients. This worry is not restricted to the high profile areas of 'heroic' medicine: in the absence of what may be thought of as 'the discipline of the market', it is not unnatural for health care professionals to take the view that they are trained to practice medicine not book-keeping, and to subscribe to the maxim of doing the best they can for their patients without being particularly concerned about the resource implications of such behaviour. The wide variations in practices, procedures – and lengths of waiting lists – between different hospitals (or even between different consultants in the same hospital department) may be seen as evidence of the lack of coherent incentives and the potential for wasting resources.

Much the same could be said of general practice. Most GPs are independent contractors rather than salaried employees, and the main component of their income is based on the number of people registered with their practice, irrespective of the treatment (if any) that they receive. Once again, this has the advantage that there is no strong incentive to induce extra health care demand. Indeed, there is a danger that it may cause behaviour to err in the opposite direction: that is, GPs may be tempted to play a passive role, waiting for patients to come to the surgery (and perhaps hoping that not too many actually come, or even effectively discouraging them by limiting surgery hours) rather than actively promoting health. And with GPs being remunerated principally on the basis of the number of patients on their books rather than the time actually spent with them, there is clearly an incentive for GPs to reduce the demands upon their time by, for example, substituting prescriptions for counselling, and by referring patients to the hospital sector for tests and/or 'specialist opinion', rather than undertaking time-consuming investigations themselves. Like their hospital counterparts, GPs have in the past typically had little information about the resource implications of such behaviour and/or little incentive to be concerned about such things, compared with their more immediate combination of concerns with the pressures on their own resources and the welfare of the patient in front of them. And as in the hospital sector, wide variations have been observed in such things as surgery hours, prescription patterns, referral rates, and the uptake of screening and immunisation services which, at best, can only be partly accounted for by variations in the composition of different GPs lists. One obvious implication is that at least some of this behaviour is using scarce resources less well than they could and should be used.

Now I do not want what I have said above to be interpreted as a general attack on the competence or the morals of the great majority of health care professionals. Of course there are *some* who are incompetent, and there are *some* others who put earnings before ethics – for example, dentists who drill and fill healthy teeth, or surgeons who allow long NHS waiting lists to persist so as to maintain the demand for the private operations at the local private hospital which give that same surgeon a useful supplementary income. Such people are *not* representative of the mainstream of professionals who are strongly committed to trying to improve the health and welfare of their fellow human beings. I believe that the majority of these professionals would wish, if they could, to play their part in a system which allocates scarce health care resources so as to produce the greatest possible benefits for the population as a whole. So, for example, if they became aware that some scarce resources used in one way give smaller benefits than they could produce if switched to an alternative use, I dare say that most would see the force of the argument for switching those resources rather than depriving some people of greater benefits in order to provide smaller benefits to some others.

However, we have seen that free markets cannot be relied upon to produce the kind of desirable allocation described above. On the other hand, even those most strongly committed to a National Health Service will acknowledge that the present system also has a number of deficiencies and still falls well short of allocating resources so as to produce the maximum health benefits.

So will the proposed NHS reforms, with their emphasis on the introduction of more businesslike, market-type features into the system, achieve the stated objective of 'a more efficient and an even better service . . . to help people live longer and enjoy a better quality of life'?

Let us now examine the main proposals in the light of the analysis outlined above. For convenience, I shall discuss them more or less in the order they appear in the public relations booklet, which I shall quote from time to time.

We begin with general practice. GPs contracts will be restructured so as to encourage them to provide a wider range of services, including a more active programme of prevention and health promotion. The idea is that this will be achieved partly by financial incentives linking some of a practice's income to performance – e.g. the achievement of immunisation or screening targets. But since a substantial part of a practice's income will still be related to the numbers of patients registered, another element of the strategy is to provide people with better information about the services offered by the different practices in an area and make it easier for patients to switch to practices providing more attractive services, thereby increasing the income of those practices at the expense of the 'less competitive' practices.

In principle, this sounds fine: more services, more information, more choice – surely this must be a good thing. And yet there are still grounds for caution – and for carefully monitoring what actually happens. For example, it is not obvious that switching from one doctor to another is necessarily a good thing – the nature of *primary* care, and *family* practice means that there may be quite a lot to be said for *continuity* of the relationship between patients and the practice team. Unless, of course, the doctor is not terribly good at his job. But unfortunately *this* information – which is what many patients may be most concerned about, but least able to judge in advance – is *not* what the local Family Health Services Authority will provide.

Moreover, in a system where the main cost of consulting your GP is the time and inconvenience of travelling to and from the surgery, the people most able to exercise the freedom of switching to the best practice (supposing that judgement really can be made) are those who are most mobile – which typically means those who are better off. They are also the ones most likely to acquire the information and make what judgements can be made. So the net effect may be that it is the more affluent, more educated people who get the better services, while the poorer, less mobile members of the community have less choice and a greater chance of having to put up with fewer services – even though their needs may be more pressing.

On the other side, how will GPs respond to the new structure of incentives? Consider the immunisation and screening targets. It is widely accepted that the groups who stand to benefit most from such programmes – those on low incomes, in poor housing, with more children – are the ones with the lowest levels of voluntary uptake. So GPs with a large proportion of such people on their list will have to spend more time, effort and resources to achieve the higher thresholds in the incentive scheme. If they were really acting like dispassionate suppliers in a textbook market, many of them would not embark on such a programme because it would not be sufficiently profitable to them – in which case the people who *should* stand to benefit most would be the ones actually least likely to receive the services. So there is a danger here that the incentives will have a perverse effect. Ironically, what will probably help to offset such perversities will be the fact that many GPs will choose *not* to behave as profit maximising suppliers, but will instead bear some of the extra costs themselves in the interests of the patients on their lists.

There is clearly concern too about the proposal whereby 'larger practices will be able to choose to take control of some NHS funds to finance a range of local services for their own patients – including certain hospital treatments, and the costs to the NHS of prescriptions and some staff needed for the practice' (p. 12). To the extent that this proposal encourages greater awareness of the fact that health care resources are really not free, and to the extent that it provides GPs with the information needed to make better decisions about how to allocate those costly resources, such a proposal may have much to recommend it. Once again, however, there is another side to this coin: there is no point in introducing budgets unless they bite: but when individual budgets begin to bite, they may induce responses which are socially wasteful or undesirable. For instance, budget-holders may try to shift certain costs onto other people. We have already seen evidence of this in the NHS: for example, hospitals under financial pressure are liable to discharge patients earlier (and perhaps with a minimal supply of medicines etc.) so that the cost of further care is borne by friends, relatives, GPs and/ or local community services in a way that may not be in the interests of the individual patient nor society as a whole. Despite the reassurances in the booklet, some doubts remain. Practices might not strike 'costly' patients off their lists: but might they refuse to accept new ones who they perceive to be 'high-cost risks'? After all, this would be a perfectly sensible *market* strategy for any individual practice to adopt. And since health care professionals are an intelligent and enterprising lot, no doubt many other strategies will also be developed, not all of which will necessarily work in the direction of making the best use of scarce health care resources.

There are other aspects of the primary care reforms that might also be discussed, but since I too face a budget constraint in the space allocated to this chapter, let me move on to consider some of the proposed reforms at the hospital and health authority level.

A key feature here is the proposed separation between *purchasers* and *providers*. The purchasers will now be the local Health Authority managers, funded according to the size of the population in their area, with adjustments to take account of different local conditions (such as the age profile of the population). Armed with these funds, each Health Authority 'will make agreements with a range of hospitals and other units . . . . These agreements will match a specified level and quality of service with a specified amount of money' (p. 16).

It is envisaged that the providers – the 'range of hospitals and other units', which includes private hospitals and the new NHS Trusts – will then compete with each other to supply those services, the idea being that the competition between providers, and the separation between providers and purchasers will simulate a market-like environment – sometimes referred to as an 'internal market' – and produce efficient contracts for a comprehensive range of services.

Once again, this all sounds very fine in principle. But a number of observers have articulated some serious concerns. First, in order to enter into a sensible agreement to deliver particular services for a specified amount of money, providers need reasonably good information about the costs involved – and there are grave doubts about whether many NHS hospitals yet have information of sufficient quality to meet the task. Secondly, it is one thing to write a contract about the *quantity* of services, but it is a great deal more difficult to specify, monitor and enforce contracts about the *quality* of a commodity such as health care. Experiences of contracting out apparently rather less complex services such as laundry and cleaning have drawn attention to some of the difficulties of quality control.

Moreover, this is a problem which markets may not only fail to solve, but may actually exacerbate, as a recent tragic episode demonstrates. At present, there is no market in blood in Britain, and according to the booklet there is no intention of introducing such a market: 'The National Blood Transfusion Services is entirely dependent on voluntary blood donors . . . . No patient and no hospital will be asked to pay for the blood you donate' (p. 26). However, in some other countries there *is* a market in blood, and one of the effects of paying people for their blood is that it gives people who know that they are unhealthy, *but who are not easily observed to be sick*, an incentive to conceal the fact (because if they admitted it, they would not get paid). In short, the creation of a market in blood also creates an incentive to cheat on quality, which results either in a greater risk to those receiving the blood, or else requires costly monitoring, or possibly entails both of those things.

Unfortunately, although Britain has no *internal* market in blood, the NHS did purchase blood products from countries which do operate such markets; and the result of cheating on quality, combined with inadequate monitoring, was that more than a thousand British haemophiliacs were infected with HIV. More than two hundred have already died.

That should be a sobering lesson to all those who get too easily intoxicated by the idea of the white magic of the marketplace. It is to be hoped that no such dreadful consequences will arise from quality cheating in contracts between NHS purchasers and providers operating under the proposed new system. But it would be foolish to ignore the incentive to cheat; and if some providers enter into contracts on the basis of insufficiently good cost information, they may well find themselves under pressure to be 'economical with the quality'.

A further set of issues arise from the role of the purchaser under the new arrangements. We saw earlier that many individuals may not have the necessary knowledge, experience or information to demand the appropriate quantity and type of health care, and may therefore rely to a significant extent on more knowledgeable professionals to determine their consumption of health care. Under the new arrangements, however, it is Health Authority managers who will act on our behalf. For those who consider that it is already difficult enough for many patients to communicate their values and preferences to their family doctor, it is natural to wonder how consumers' preferences will be better represented under the new system. The answer given in the booklet is a little vague: 'Health Authorities will do this by asking local people what they think of the services on offer, and by discussion with local GPs' (p. 17). This sounds like a very weak and imperfect means of representing consumers' preferences – and all the more so since Health Authorities no longer include members drawn from among elected local representatives, but instead have members selected by the Regional Health Authority. Moreover, as the announcement by Mr Duncan Nichol about waiting lists indicated, managers are liable to receive their instructions not from local people but from central government via the NHS hierarchy.

Of course, the build up of waiting lists undoubtedly reflects unsatisfied consumer demands; and there are undoubtedly steps that managers can take to improve the situation, including the apparently elementary step of check-ing existing lists and removing patients who have died or been treated elsewhere – a measure which may reduce lists by about 16 per cent, according to published evidence (see, for example, *the Guardian*, 2 August 1990, p. 2).

But it must be remembered that while waiting lists are undoubtedly in part the result of inefficiency, they also reflect the fact that with insufficient resources to treat *all* patients that enter the hospital sector, some medical conditions are given less priority than others. It is perfectly reasonable to ask whether the current system of prioritisation accords with the wishes and best interests of the population. But it is also reasonable to ask on what basis the change in priorities announced by Mr Nichol was decided – for it is not *simply* a matter of using existing resources more effectively: if managers' performance-linked pay is to be related to their success in reducing waiting lists, there will be a substantial incentive to divert funds away from other services and use them, under the new arrangements, to buy in more elective surgery, much of which will no doubt be provided by the private hospitals who have excess capacity for such operations. In other words, there is at least the possibility that, far from reflecting local health priorities, the purchasing role of the Health Authorities may be used to achieve the objectives of central government, which at least some observers suspect may include an ideological commitment to boost the private sector by shifting NHS funds in its direction.

If it is claimed that the diktats about new priorities better reflect consum-ers' preferences, it is surely reasonable to expect policy makers to be open and explicit about the way in which those preferences were ascertained. Further opportunities along these lines will come in the course of evaluating applications for NHS Trust status.

At present, anyone relying on the booklet may be unclear about the nature and status of the proposed trusts. On page 20 it states: 'They will have a range of powers and freedoms not available to other units. These will include the ability to own their assets, employ their own staff and set their rates of pay, and borrow money to develop their services.' But on page 21 it states that NHS Trusts are going to remain completely within the NHS: 'They will continue to be run by NHS staff on NHS property.' No doubt it will become clearer during the next few months how far Trust property is 'their own' and how far it remains NHS property, and how far their staff are NHS staff and how far they are 'their own staff'. Presumably it will also become clear exactly how consumers' preferences will enter into the decisions about granting Trust status. The booklet says:

> Before an NHS Trust is established, all those with an interest – staff, GPs, health authorities, community health councils and above all, the local public – will be *asked their views* about an application to set up a Trust and will have an opportunity to *express an opinion*. These views will be taken into account *when a decision is made* on the application. (p. 21).

The emphasis is mine, intended to draw attention to the apparent vagueness – and potential inadequacy – of the consultation process. In the case of NHS Trusts, will the Secretary of State assume that all those who fail to make themselves heard will be regarded as being in favour of whatever he decides? It will be interesting to see.

It will also be interesting to see just how freely the market for hospital staff will be allowed to operate. We know that there are already shortages of nurses and other trained staff, and that the demographic trends – with fewer school-leavers coming onto the labour market – will tend to make the shortages more acute. If the result of allowing providers to compete with each other for staff is to bid up salaries, while the total public funding does not increase correspondingly, the result of competition will not be more and better services, but fewer services, with an incentive to substitute young, inexperienced and/or untrained staff for qualified and experienced staff – with the dangers to the quality of care and the welfare of patients that this might entail. How will consumers' interests and preferences make themselves felt under these circumstances?

One final point on the subject of competition between providers. There may be at least three kinds of hospitals competing to provide services, namely hospitals still under direct Health Authority control, NHS Trusts, and private hospitals. As the booklet makes explicit, Trusts 'will have a range of powers and freedoms not available to other units' (p. 20). And it seems that private hospitals may have further advantages relative to the other two types of provider: for example, unlike Trusts, they cannot be obliged to provide services that they would otherwise not choose to provide; and it seems they will not be subject to the same restrictions about pricing policy – e.g. they appear to have more freedom to cross-subsidise certain services if they consider it to be a desirable move as part of their broader market strategy. In some earlier policy discussion documents there was repeated mention of 'level playing fields'; but at present there is at least the suspicion that the ground is really quite uneven – conditions which are not conducive to a genuinely competitive game.

If I seem to be taking a rather pessimistic view of the prospects for these reforms, you must remember that I am an economist – and economics has long been known as 'the dismal science'. But I will give one further example of the kind of development which has influenced my attitude, namely the recent decision to reschedule the implementation of the community care reforms.

When the announcement was first made, there was an attempt to suggest that the delay was necessary because the local social services were not ready to implement the change; but this was flatly contradicted by a survey of 96 Directors of Social Services, 95 of whom said that they *were* ready, with their staff having devoted considerable time, energy and resources in order to become ready.

In fact, it turned out that the main reason for the late decision to reschedule implementation was government ministers' desires to delay the financial impact of the reforms – estimated to be likely to raise the level of community charge, or poll tax, by perhaps a further £15 per head – until after the next General Election. I must say that it does seem hard to reconcile such behaviour with a genuine desire to give you and me – the actual or potential consumers of health and community care services – greater opportunities to make our preferences felt. Recall that a primary argument for the community charge was that everybody would pay at least something towards the provision of local services, which would give them a greater stake in the way those services were organised, and which would therefore make the elected councillors more directly accountable and more sensitive to their electors, with the 'discipline of democracy' encouraging greater efficiency and a better match between consumers' preferences and the pattern of local services. In principle, one candidate might offer a more restricted set of services entailing a lower community charge, while another candidate might offer electors the chance to vote to pay more for a higher level of service. Yet instead of allowing the very mechanism they had introduced to run its natural course, central government intervened to over-rule elected local councils and 'cap' their spending powers. And now, instead of allowing the mechanism to give electors the chance to have a more direct stake in the level of community care provision, the government has again intervened, apparently motivated more by its own electoral interests than the efficient provision of care to the more vulnerable members of the community.

Altogether, then, it is far from clear that the separation of purchasers from providers will give consumers' interests greater weight and at the same time stimulate fair and effective competition between providers. On the evidence so far, it is not possible to reject the interpretation that, far from decentralising purchasing power and production decisions in a way that will enhance the match between resources and preferences, the reforms may be designed to increase the power of central government to control costs and restrain public expenditure, while creating conditions favourable to the operation and expansion of the private sector.

Unfortunately it is difficult to reach a firmer judgement at present because the health reforms outlined in *Working for Patients* only came into effect in April 1991, and there are still many uncertainties. There are widespread concerns that despite all the frenetic activity in recent months, the quality of information available to both purchasers and providers is not up to the task. There has also been a great asymmetry in the focus of that effort, with most of the activity being directed to the measurement of *costs* and relatively little attention paid to the measurement of *outcomes* and *benefits* – and we cannot seriously hope to bring about a good match between costs and benefits if we have only imperfect measures of costs and hardly any measures at all of most benefits.

Before any new pharmaceutical product is allowed to be prescribed, it will have undergone extensive clinical trials and evaluation. Yet a set of fairly radical new 'treatments' are to be practised on health services in Britain without anything remotely resembling careful clinical trials and evaluation. What we know about 'Health and Markets ' tells us that there are many problems with markets in health care, including the possibility of a number of undesirable and potentially serious side-effects: so at the very least, there must now be an extensive programme of monitoring and evaluating the impact of these reforms as they come into effect – and the results of such a programme must be published for all to see. This is a poor second best to a proper controlled study, but major changes to the way we organise our health care system can have far greater potential for good or ill than the introduction of some new drug or surgical procedure, and we must monitor them no less closely.

7 Inflation and the UK Labour Market

STEPHEN NICKELL

INTRODUCTION

Inflation is endemic in Britain. Aside from the odd year, inflation in Britain has been higher than the average of the OECD countries for the last forty years. This is as true for the anti-inflationary 1980s as for the inflationary 1970s and the 'libertarian' 1960s. In the light of this fact, we look at the problem of inflation both in general terms and in the British context. Furthermore, we shall consider inflation from a particular point of view, namely that of the labour market, although it would perhaps be more apt to describe the viewpoint as the supply side.

In much previous work on inflation, it has been thought convenient to distinguish between demand-pull inflation and cost-push inflation. This is, in a sense, an unfortunate distinction because it gives the impression that there are two competing theories of inflation underlying these two expressions. This is not the case. So, although our viewpoint is from the supply side, we do not present a model of inflation which is, in any sense, inconsistent with demand-side theories such as 'monetarism', for example. All we do is demonstrate where the supply side, in general, and the labour market, in particular, fit into the story.

At the outset, therefore, it is worth emphasising that inflation is a demand-side phenomenon in the sense that, by appropriate demand-side (monetary and fiscal) policies, inflation can *always* be controlled. Of course, there may be serious technical problems in exercising control, relating to such matters as the operation of financial markets and the like. Nevertheless, in principle, the statement is correct. If so, where does the labour market enter the story? Surely, as Peter Wiles argued so passionately nearly twenty years ago in the *Economic Journal* (Wiles, 1973), it is obvious that if union leaders press strongly for higher pay rises, higher inflation will result. Despite the fact that it is apparently obvious, it is fundamentally wrong. With an appropriately tough monetary and fiscal stance, this rise in inflation can be strangled, if not at birth, at a very tender age. What is the story? Clearly higher pay demands generate inflationary pressure. But when this meets the tough policy stance, then one of two things can happen. Either union leaders will note the tough policy stance and modify their demands at the outset or, and this is more likely, unemployment will rise rapidly and, very soon, union members, fearing for their jobs, will ensure that their leaders change their position. The potential inflationary pressure leads, not to higher inflation, but to higher unemployment.

Suppose, however, that the inflationary pressure comes from a source which cannot be modified. A sharp rise in imported commodity prices, for example. How do things work in this case? A rise in imported commodity prices makes the country poorer. This is an inescapable fact. Since wages make up by far the largest part of National Income, it is more or less inevitable that they must decline in real terms. In the light of this, there are three possible outcomes following the rise in commodity prices. First, wage demands are modified to offset the commodity price rise, overall cost pressures remain unchanged and inflation is contained. This tends to happen if the labour market is highly competitive or, interestingly enough, if wage bargaining is highly centralised, as in Scandinavia. In this latter case, all the parties to the centralised wage bargain can see what is happening from their economy-wide perspective, and wages tend to be modified accordingly. The second possibility is that wage demands are not immediately modified but the government takes a tough policy stance. Unemployment rises rapidly and this forces the appropriate adjustment. The third possibility is that wage demands are not modified and the government takes an accommodating policy stance. Inflation then starts to rise. The tough stance and consequent unemployment then typically follows at a later date in order to prevent the inflation getting out of control.

These scenarios reveal the fundamental picture. Inflationary pressure may arise from the supply side and may thus quite sensibly be described as 'cost-push'. But whether or not such pressure actually turns into rising inflation depends on the policy response on the demand side. In the simple framework sketched above, the supply side of the economy determines the position of the tradeoff, in this case between rising inflation and unemployment. The demand side, which includes the macroeconomic policy stance of the government, then determines the precise mix of inflation increase (or decrease) and unemployment which comes about. Notice that the tradeoff we have here is not one between particular *levels* of inflation and unemployment but is one between *rates of change* of inflation and *levels* of unemployment. While the former kind of tradeoff was thought to exist in the early 1960s, following the work of Phillips (1958), this rather rapidly proved not to be the case.

Finally, it is worth remarking that while our stories have referred solely to inflationary pressure arising from the supply side, this is not always the case. Clearly inflationary pressure and rising inflation can appear directly from the demand side simply by having a more expansionary policy stance. Thus we might describe demand-pull inflation as a situation where inflation rises via a demand expansion in the face of a fixed supply-side tradeoff. Cost-push inflation, on the other hand, arises when the tradeoff between the rate of change of inflation and unemployment 'worsens' and the resulting inflationary pressure is turned into rising inflation by an accommodating policy stance on the demand side. There is only one theory here. The rate of change of inflation is always determined by the demand-side stance *relative* to the position of the supply-side tradeoff.

In what follows, we shall focus on the supply-side tradeoff. In an open economy such as Britain's, this tradeoff is rather more complicated than that described above, since it contains a third element in addition to inflation and unemployment, namely the trade deficit. So we shall first set out a simple model to demonstrate how the tradeoff arises and then present some numbers which illustrate how this tradeoff has moved in Britain over the last thirty years. We can then see how the position on the demand side has determined the actual outcomes in terms of inflation, unemployment and the trade deficit. We shall, also, briefly look at the current position.

A MODEL OF INFLATION

The Demand side

In this section, we construct a simple model of the economy starting with the demand side. The idea here is to demonstrate that, in a world where prices are sticky, the demand side can be thought of as determining the level of real demand in the economy and the level of international competitiveness. Furthermore, we suppose that real demand is always satisfied and is, therefore, the same as real output (GNP).

In log-linear form, the demand side consists of the following equations.

Money demand: $m - p = y_d$. (7.1)

Goods demand: $y_d = \sigma_1 x - \sigma_2 r + \sigma_3 c$. (7.2)

Competitiveness (definition): $c = e + p^* - p$. (7.3)

Uncovered interest parity: $i = i^* + \Delta e^e$.   (7.4)

Expected depreciation: $\Delta e^e = \Delta p^e - \Delta p^{*e} - \delta(c - \bar{c})$.   (7.5)

m = real money stock, p = price level (GDP deflator), y_d = real demand = real GDP, x = exogenous real demand factors including fiscal policy stance, world economic activity, autonomous expenditure (e.g. autonomous shifts in consumption), r = domestic real interest rate, c = competitiveness, e = exchange rate measured as the domestic currency value of one unit of foreign currency, so a rise in e represents a depreciation of the domestic currency, p^* = world price of output in foreign currency, i = domestic nominal interest rate, i^* = foreign nominal interest rate, Δp^e = expected domestic inflation, Δp^{*e} = expected foreign inflation, $\bar{c}$ = expected long-run equilibrium competitiveness and Δ represents the time difference.

This is more or less the simplest open economy model which can be constructed, and any number of complications can be incorporated without changing anything which is important for our purposes. Equation (7.1) is a standard quantity theory demand for money function equation (7.2) is a simple IS curve. Equation (7.3) defines competitiveness and (7.4) is an arbitrage condition which holds if investors are risk neutral and there are no impediments in the currency market. That is, the return from investing in domestic securities is the same as that from investing in foreign securities correcting for expected movements in the exchange rate. Finally equation (7.5) says that expected currency depreciation reflects the inflation differential modified by a tendency for the exchange rate to help competitiveness towards its long-run expected level.

These equations solve out to yield

$$y_d = m - p \tag{7.6}$$

$$c = c_1(m - p) - c_2 x + c_3 r^* + c_4 \bar{c} \tag{7.7}$$

where $r^* = i^* - \Delta p^{*e}$, the foreign real interest rate, and $c_1 = 1/\Omega$, $c_2 = \sigma_1/\Omega$, $c_3 = \sigma_2/\Omega$, $c_4 = \sigma_2\delta/\Omega$, $\Omega = \sigma_2\delta + \sigma_3$. If prices are sticky in the short run, then (7.6) and (7.7) illustrate how exogenous demand side shifts will influence real demand (output) and competitiveness. The key variables here are exogenous demand factors, x, and monetary policy, m. Different combinations of these will produce different combinations of real demand and competitiveness. In particular, competitiveness depends crucially on the tightness of monetary policy relative to exogenous demand factors. If money is tight relative to exogenous demand, then competitiveness will be low, essentially because interest rates and hence the exchange rate are high. So, for example, if monetary policy is reasonably expansionary but tight relative to exogenous demand factors (which are, therefore, very expansionary), then we have high real demand and low competitiveness (a high exchange rate). This kind of policy was pursued by the US in the period 1983–4. If, on the other hand, monetary policy is very expansionary and hence loose relative to reasonably expansionary exogenous demand factors, then real demand is high and competitiveness is high. This reflects the UK situation in the period after the stock market crash. The opposite of this, with very tight money and contractionary demand factors, yields low demand and low competitiveness, as in the UK in 1980–81.

We have now set the demand-side scene and we can turn to the supply side. This will tell us the consequences of demand-side shifts in real demand and competitiveness on our key variables, namely unemployment, the trade deficit and inflation.

The Supply Side

The supply side of our model has the following simple log-linear form.

Production function: $y_d - \bar{y} = -u$ (7.8)

Price setting: $p - w = \beta_0 + \beta_1 [y_d - \bar{y}] + \beta_{12}c - \beta_2\Delta^2 p$ (7.9)

Wage bargaining: $w - p = \gamma_0 - \gamma_1 u + \gamma_{12}c - \gamma_2\Delta^2 p + z_w$ (7.10)

Trade deficit: $c = \delta_0 + \delta_1[y_d - \bar{y}] - \delta_2 td - z_c$ (7.11)

y = potential output, w = wage, $\Delta^2 p$ = the rate of change of inflation, u = unemployment rate, z_w = exogenous factors raising wages, td = trade deficit as a proportion of potential output, z_c = exogenous factors tending to improve the trade deficit.

Again we have a very simple framework which omits long-run growth factors and any unemployment dynamics or hysteresis effects. (A more detailed analysis may be found in Carlin and Soskice (1990) for example.) The production function (equation (7.8)) simply relates unemployment to deviations of demand (output) from its (exogenously given) potential level, $\bar{y}$. The price setting model (equation (7.9)) expresses the mark-up of (GDP) prices on wages as a function of three variables. Prices are increasing in demand, for obvious reasons. The price mark-up is also increasing in competitiveness because it seems likely that, as firms become more competitive in world markets, demand becomes less elastic and higher mark-ups can be sustained (i.e. world sales become more profitable). The role of changes in inflation $[\Delta^2 p]$ is very important. As we have already noted, prices are sticky in the short run. If inflation is rising, firms find that costs are rising more rapidly than expected and, to the extent that prices are sticky and tend to lag behind costs, this tends to squeeze profits and reduces the mark-up of prices on wages. The period 1974–5 in Britain provides a classic example of this process in action.

The wage bargaining equation (7.10), expresses the wage outcome as a mark-up on (GDP) prices although the actual bargaining procedure concerns nominal wages. The real wage outcome is decreasing in the level of unemployment which is, of course, an inverse measure of labour market tightness. The role of competitiveness here is very important. A rise in competitiveness generates upward pressure on wages via real wage resistance. As competitiveness increases, imports become more expensive and the cost of living rises (note that the cost of living is a weighted average of GDP prices and import prices). In so far as workers resist the consequent fall in living standards, this will exert upward pressure on wages relative to GDP prices. The role of increases in inflation $[\Delta^2 p]$ is similar here to that in price setting. If inflation is rising, prices typically turn out higher than was expected when the wage bargain was struck and, as a consequence, wages turn out lower relative to GDP prices. Rising inflation tends to squeeze real (product) wages, *ceteris paribus*.[1]

Finally we have a whole group of variables represented by z_w which reflect autonomous sources of wage pressure. These can be grouped conveniently under three headings. First, union effects. These capture any changes in the level of pressure exerted on wages by trade union militancy. Second, real wage resistance effects. As we have already noted with competitiveness, any factors which tend to produce autonomous falls in living standards will lead to upward pressure on wages. Such factors will include taxes on labour (e.g. income tax) and goods (e.g. VAT), and adverse changes in the international terms of trade (e.g. a rise in the world relative price of commodities). Finally we have reductions in the effective supply of labour at given unemployment. Such reductions can arise via increases in the generosity of the unemployment benefit system or increases in the degree of occupational or regional mismatch between the unemployed and available vacancies. Both of these will tend to reduce the effective availability of labour.

The last equation (7.11) determines the trade deficit although it has been written with competitiveness on the left-hand side for future expositional convenience. This simple equation says that the trade deficit is increasing in demand and decreasing in competitiveness. The final term, z_c, captures any exogenous factors which tend to improve the trade balance, the most notable of which, in the British context, is North Sea oil.

By manipulating these equations, we can now determine the impact of demand and competitiveness, which appear from the demand side, on unemployment, the trade deficit and changes in inflation. More specifically we have

$$u = - [y_d - \bar{y}] \quad \text{(from (7.8))}. \tag{7.12}$$

$$td = \frac{1}{\delta_2} [\delta_0 + \delta_1 [y_d - \bar{y}] - c] - z_c \quad \text{(from 7.11))} \tag{7.13}$$

$$\Delta^2 p = \frac{1}{\alpha_2} [\alpha_0 + \alpha_1 [y_d - \bar{y}] + \alpha_{12} c + z_w] \quad \text{(from (7.8), (7.9), (7.10))}. \tag{7.14}$$

where $\alpha_0 = \beta_0 + \gamma_0$, $\alpha_1 = \beta_1 + \gamma_1$, $\alpha_{12} = \beta_{12} + \gamma_{12}$, $\alpha_2 = \beta_2 + \gamma_2$. These equations tell us first that demand directly determines unemployment, so when demand is low, unemployment is high and vice versa. Second, they reveal that the trade deficit is increasing in demand and decreasing in competitiveness. Third, we see that inflation rises with both demand and competitiveness. The latter effect is worth some comment. When competitiveness is high, imported goods are more expensive and this enables firms which produce goods in competition with imports to raise their prices and also exerts upward pressure on wages as workers attempt to compensate for increases in the cost of living.

We can now see the implications of various demand-side scenarios. If demand and competitiveness are both high, we have low unemployment and rising inflation with the trade deficit being small or even negative. If demand is high but competitiveness is low, we have low unemployment, a large trade deficit and more or less stable inflation. These two possibilities immediately reveal a tradeoff between inflation and the trade deficit in the sense that, with low unemployment, one can have more of one and less of the other with different demand-side scenarios.

The Fundamental Supply Constraint

In order to examine such tradeoffs in more detail we need to do some manipulation on our three equations (7.12), (7.13), (7.14). Let us simply eliminate demand, $[y_d - \bar{y}]$ and competitiveness, c. This yields the fundamental tradeoff equation

$$[\alpha_1 + \delta_1\alpha_{12}]\, u + \alpha_2\Delta^2 p + \alpha_{12}\delta_2 td = \alpha_0 + z_w - \alpha_{12}z_c \qquad (7.15)$$

How should we interpret this rather complex looking expression? What it does is to tell us those combinations of unemployment, u, rates of change of inflation, $\Delta^2 p$, and trade deficit, td, which are available. Shifts on the demand side can move the economy around on this constraint but they cannot get the economy off it. However, the constraint can and does move. Any rise in autonomous wage pressure, z_w, will worsen the tradeoff in the sense that at least one of u, $\Delta^2 p$ and td must be higher. On the other hand an increase in any exogenous factor which improves the trade balance, z_c, will improve the tradeoff.

The existence of this constraint has very important implications. For example, for some time now in Britain we have had a trade deficit and rising inflation ($td > 0$, $\Delta^2 p > 0$). The constraint tells us that however subtle are the demand-side manipulations of interest rates, exchange rates, taxes, government expenditures, savings incentives, joining the ERM etc., we cannot stabilise inflation and reduce the trade deficit without a substantial increase in unemployment, unless either z_w goes down or z_c goes up. Since it is hard to shift these in the short run, the constraint tells us we simply have to lump it. If we want stable inflation and a lower trade deficit, we must have higher unemployment. If we want to bring inflation down [$\Delta^2 p < 0$] we must have even higher unemployment.

It is clear from this discussion that the role of the wage pressure and trade balance factors, z_w, z_c is absolutely crucial since these are the only things which can move the constraint around. When we come on to our discussion of the British economy we shall consider them in some detail. In the mean time, however, their effect can usefully be summarised by the notion of the equilibrium level of unemployment, $\hat{u}$ (sometimes known rather misleadingly as the 'natural rate', although an object which is less embedded in nature is hard to imagine). This equilibrium level may be defined as that unemployment rate which is consistent with constant inflation [$\Delta^2 p = 0$] and balanced trade ($td = 0$). From (7.15) we thus have

$$[\alpha_1 + \delta_1\alpha_{12}]\hat{u} = \alpha_0 + z_w - \alpha_{12}z_c \qquad (7.16)$$

and we see that $\hat{u}$ summarises the impact of z_w and z_c on the fundamental tradeoff. Indeed (7.15) can now be rewritten as

$$[\alpha_1 + \delta_1\alpha_{12}]u + \alpha_2\Delta^2 p + \alpha_{12}\delta_2 td = [\alpha_1 + \delta_1\alpha_{12}]\hat{u} \qquad (7.17)$$

So as $\hat{u}$ rises, the fundamental tradeoff gets worse and the economy is more beset by problems. We now have a framework within which to analyse the British economy and in the next section we shall attach some actual numbers to our equations.

BRITAIN'S INFLATION PROBLEM

In order to apply this framework to the British economy we must have some parameter values. The ones we present here are derived partly from equations presented in Layard and Nickell (1986) and partly from new estimates. Full details may be found in chapter 9 of a recent book on unemployment (Jackman, Layard and Nickell, 1991). It is important to recognise that the numbers which are presented are subject to considerable error. They are based on averages of the past behaviour of the economy and on models which are clearly a gross simplification of reality. Nevertheless, they provide a useful flavour of what is actually going on. The equation which corresponds to (7.17) above has the form

$$0.091 \log u + 0.05u + 1.07\Delta^2 p + 1.25td$$
$$= 0.091 \log \hat{u} + 0.054\hat{u} - 1.27\Delta u \qquad (7.17)$$

where u is the unemployment rate (OECD standardised measure, which is currently slightly above the UK published rate), $\Delta^2 p$ is the rate of change of annual inflation, td is the trade deficit as a proportion of potential GDP, and Δu is the annual change in the unemployment rate.

This equation differs significantly from its theoretical counterpart in two respects. First, it is not linear in the unemployment rate. This is simply an inevitable consequence of our attempts to fit the data. Second, the change in the unemployment rate also appears in such a way that if unemployment is rising (falling), the fundamental tradeoff improves (worsens). This is known as a hysteresis effect. Why does it happen? The main reason is that when unemployment is actually going up, pressure on wages is significantly reduced whatever the level of unemployment. This is hardly surprising, for when workers actually see job losses taking place all around them, this leads naturally to their modifying wage demands. So when unemployment is actually going up, the tradeoff temporarily improves.

What are the tradeoffs implicit in (7.17)? At constant unemployment, a rise in the trade deficit of 1 per cent of potential GDP is worth just over one percentage point per annum off the rise in the inflation rate. In this sense, therefore, the trade deficit can be thought of as suppressed inflation. Alternatively, at constant inflation, a one point rise in the trade deficit as a percentage of potential GDP is worth around three quarters of a percentage point off unemployment (from a baseline level of 6 per cent, which is around the current rate). Finally, at constant trade deficit, a one point rise in unemployment from the 6 per cent baseline will reduce the rise in inflation by around 1.3 percentage points per annum.

We can also use equation (7.17) to produce estimates of the equilibrium rate of unemployment and so, in Table 7.1, we present some results for the past 35 years. During the first two periods we consider, the economy was rather close to equilibrium on average with a low level of unemployment, but by the early 1970s the equilibrium rate of unemployment was starting to creep up. During this period, this produced higher unemployment and increasing inflation which was offset by a significant trade surplus. After the first oil shock, in 1974, equilibrium unemployment moved up very sharply and with actual unemployment lagging significantly behind, there was a rapid increase in inflation and a sharp movement into deficit on the trade front. This was a key period for the British economy, for the fundamental tradeoff worsened dramatically and the attempt to avoid a very sharp increase in unemployment had severe consequences for inflation and the trade deficit. In the early 1980s, there was then a very rapid reversal of this process. Unemployment was allowed to rise to unprecedented heights and, as a consequence, inflation fell rapidly and the economy moved into a large surplus on the current account. Since that time, the situation has moved rapidly again in the other direction. Unemployment has come down to well below the equilibrium rate, inflation is rising and we have a huge current account deficit. Current estimates reveal that unemployment will have to rise by at least 2 percentage points in order to stabilise inflation and bring down the deficit. We are now heading slowly in this direction.

TABLE 7.1   *Estimates of equilibrium unemployment in Britain based on equation (7.17)*

	1956–9	1960–68	1969–73	1974–80	1981–87	1988–90
$u(\%)$	2.24	2.62	3.39	5.23	11.11	7.27
$\Delta u(\%)$	−0.06	0.035	0.43	0.30	0.76	−0.90
$\Delta^2 p(\%)$	0.58	−0.11	1.00	1.51	−1.45	1.03
$td(\%)$	−0.57	−0.22	−0.81	1.06	−1.39	1.44
$\hat{u}(\%)$	2.2	2.5	3.6	7.3	8.7	8.7

The values of Δu, td are lagged two years and that of $\Delta^2 p$ is lagged one year to take account of the time it takes for these factors to feed through the model into unemployment.

It is clear from this analysis that the problems of the economy since the first oil shock arise essentially from the large rise in the equilibrium rate of unemployment. This has made the policy choices very much tougher in the sense that, while it is still possible to control inflation by appropriate demand-side policies, the costs of doing so on the unemployment or trade front are politically very much harder to bear. In the light of these remarks, we must attempt to shed some light on why equilibrium unemployment has risen, particularly the dramatic change in the 1970s. So, in Table 7.2, we set out some rough estimates of the contribution of various factors. Recall that these reflect autonomous shifts either in wage pressure variables or in factors influencing the trade balance. The actual numbers in Table 7.2 refer to the contribution of each factor to the change in equilibrium unemployment since the late 1950s.

Considering each factor in turn, the first reflects the beneficial impact of North Sea oil on the trade balance. This has produced a dramatic improvement in the tradeoff in the most recent period considered. Mismatch refers to a measure of the labour market mismatch between the skills of the unemployed and those required by employers. By adding to pressure on wages at given levels of unemployment, this has made a significant contri-

TABLE 7.2   *The contribution of various factors to equilibrium unemployment in Britain*
(percentage points)

	1956–59	1960–68	1969–73	1974–80	1980–87
$\hat{u}$(%)	2.2	2.5	3.6	7.3	8.7
Rise in $\hat{u}$ from 1956–9	–	0.3	1.4	5.1	6.3
Contributing factors					
North Sea oil	–	0	0	−0.28	−2.86
Mismatch	–	0.09	0.44	0.99	2.53
Terms of trade effects	–	−0.41	−0.50	0.99	2.26
Benefit system	–	0.34	0.93	0.64	1.12
Unions	–	0.34	0.60	1.42	1.50
Taxation	–	0.09	0.09	0.12	−0.20
Unmeasured	–	−0.15	−0.16	1.22	1.95

The contributions of the various factors to the rise in $\hat{u}$ assume that there is a two-year lag before they impact on unemployment because of the time taken for them to feed through the system. Furthermore, because of the non-linearity in the unemployment effect in equation (7.7), any specific change in a contributory factor has a bigger effect on equilibrium unemployment if the baseline level of unemployment is higher. This accounts for the larger numbers in the right-hand columns.

bution in recent years. Terms of trade effects are another important factor arising essentially from the behaviour of commodity prices. Their impact comes about via real wage resistance and in earlier years it was favourable, with real commodity prices declining secularly from the Korean war to the first oil shock. Their dramatic rise in 1974 and again in 1979–80 generated significant upward pressure on wages and this was enough to offset the favourable effects of North Sea oil. The increasing generosity of the unemployment benefit system has had a relatively small impact but that of increased union militancy has been fairly substantial. There appears to have been no reduction in this latter effect in the 1980s, which is quite surprising given the pressure on unions over this period. There are two points worth noting here. First, the lags in the system mean that the impact of unions on equilibrium unemployment in 1980–87 is caused by their activities at least two years earlier (i.e. 1978–85) because of lags in the system. Given that the defeat of the miners in 1985 was the key symbol of the reduction in union power, the effects of this had yet to show through to any great extent. Second, it has frequently been noted that while unions have been much more cooperative in achieving productivity improvements in the 1980s, the anti-union legislation appears to have had little effect on wage bargaining activities, once account is taken of the general labour market situation (see Matthews and Minford, 1987). So, for example, now that the labour market is buoyant, we see the traditional union sectors again leading the way in wage demands, as they did in the early 1970s.

The contribution of changes in taxation, via real wage resistance, has had a relatively minor impact but there remains a considerable residual contribution arising from factors which we are unable to measure and about which we can only speculate. In this regard, there are several points worth bearing in mind. First, the breakdown in Table 7.2 is very rough and ready. The number of factors which influence real wage resistance and the effective supply of labour are simply enormous and most of them are more or less impossible to measure. For example, obtaining accurate measures of labour market mismatch is very difficult, particularly since the consequence of various efficiency drives in the Government Statistical Service meant that detailed figures on the occupational breakdown of unemployment and vacancies were no longer produced after the early 1980s. There is some evidence from the CBI surveys that skill mismatch is considerably worse now than it was in the late 1970s and much worse than in the early 1970s,[2] but accurate quantitative information is very hard to come by.

The second point concerns the inadequacy of the measures used. Thus the benefit effect, for example, is based on the benefit replacement ratio, that is the ratio of unemployment benefits to post-tax earnings. But this is not, in fact, the key feature of the benefit system for our purpose. Far more important is the pressure exerted on the unemployed to take up jobs, which is difficult to measure, although there is some evidence that it was reduced with the separation of Benefit Offices and Job Centres in the 1970s and significantly increased again with tougher rules in the late 1980s. For example, international comparisons reveal that benefit systems which are structured to avoid the build up of long-term unemployment, are very effective in reducing equilibrium unemployment. This does not mean that the system has to be one in which the unemployed are simply starved back to work after a certain period. Thus in Sweden, a country not noted for any absence of generosity in its welfare system, the benefit replacement ratio is far higher than in Britain but after a certain time (around 14 months) unemployed individuals are offered either reasonable jobs at the going rate or retraining, which they more or less have to take up. Consequently there are hardly any long-term unemployed in Sweden, which has favourable consequences both for the individuals concerned and for the workings of the macroeconomy.

Finally, with regard to Table 7.2, it is worth speculating on the current position. Since the mid 1980s, the favourable impact of North Sea oil has been much reduced but this has been offset by the improvements in the terms of trade effects via the fall in real commodity prices, and the increase in the severity of the benefit system which we have already mentioned. However, the weakness of the training system ensures that we have persistent skill mismatch problems and, overall, we should not be surprised if the equilibrium unemployment rate remains around 8 per cent. So we are still facing the same unpleasant tradeoff which has been with us for some fifteen years now. Furthermore, unless we can organise the labour market so as to reduce the upward pressure on wages which remains with us despite apparent labour market slack (as measured by unemployment),[3] then this same unpleasant tradeoff will be with us for a good few years yet.

SUMMARY AND CONCLUSIONS

In the preceding analysis we have demonstrated the existence of a fundamental supply-side constraint in the economy which takes the form of a three-way tradeoff between unemployment, the trade deficit and increases in inflation. The mix of monetary policy and exogenous real demand factors then determines which combination of these three outcomes actually occurs. Demand factors cannot, however, shift the underlying tradeoff in any simple way.[4]

In the British context, we have demonstrated that the fundamental constraint has shifted adversely, particularly over the last two decades. As a consequence policy makers have been confronted with ever more difficult choices and this has resulted in a persistent problem of high unemployment and relatively high inflation. We have enumerated some of the factors underlying this adverse shift, although we have by no means obtained a complete picture.

Finally, it is worth correcting an impression which may have been gained by the reader, namely that given the existence of the fundamental supply-side constraint, the government's task is very simple. In the short run, it chooses monetary and fiscal policies to select the desired point on the constraint, and in the long run, it undertakes appropriate supply-side policies to move the constraint in a favourable direction. Unfortunately the former is very difficult because we do not know precisely where the constraint is, and given the other shocks on the demand side, the actual consequence of any particular monetary and fiscal policy mix cannot be predicted with any great accuracy. The latter is even harder because most of the relevant factors are outside the direct control of government.

NOTES

This chapter was prepared for the *Oxford Review of Economic Policy* and, also, for presentation at the meeting of the British Association in Swansea, August 1990.

1. One point is worth clarifying here. We have just noted that rising inflation tends to squeeze real wages. But when we were discussing pricing, we found that rising inflation tends to squeeze profits and reduce the mark-up of prices on wages. But this is tantamount to raising real wages! How can rising inflation do both things at once? The answer is simple. Real wages and changes in inflation are both determined within the system along with many other things. Inflation cannot change unless something else changes as well. An exact analogy is provided in a simple supply and demand system. On the supply curve, quantity is increasing in price and on the demand curve it is decreasing. This ensures that price cannot change unless something else shifts.
2. Thus, the CBI Industrial Trends Surveys report the following numbers for manufacturing.

	Percentage of firms reporting shortages of skilled labour (1)	Percentage of firms reporting shortages of unskilled labour (2)	(1) ÷ (2)
1969–73	24.4	9.0	2.71
1974–80	19.3	5.1	3.78
1988–89	22.4	4.0	5.60

3. It is worth emphasising that the upward pressure on wages which we currently observe, despite 6 per cent unemployment, is not simply a matter of militant unions and feeble managers. In large parts of the labour market firms are forced to pay substantial wage increases simply to retain and recruit workers, which suggests that mismatch problems of various kinds must be severe.

4. In the longer term, demand factors may influence the position of the fundamental constraint by their impact on capital accumulation and hence on the available level of capacity. Any effects arising from this source are, however, likely to be short-lived.

REFERENCES

Carlin, W. and Soskice, D. (1990) *Macroeconomics and the Wage Bargain* (Oxford: Oxford University Press).

Jackman, R., Layard, R. and Nickell, S. (1991) *Unemployment* (Oxford: Oxford University Press).

Layard, R. and Nickell, S. (1986) 'Unemployment in Britain', *Economica* (special issue on unemployment) vol. 53 (August) S121–170.

Matthews, K. and Minford, P. (1987) 'Mrs. Thatcher's Economic Policies 1979–87', *Economic Policy*, vol. 5 (October) pp. 57–102.

Phillips, A. W. (1958) 'The Relation between Unemployment and the Rate of Change of Money Wage Rates in the United Kingdom 1861–1957', *Economica*, vol. 25, pp. 238–99.

Wiles, P. (1973) 'Cost Inflation and the State of Economic Theory', *Economic Journal*, vol. 83, pp. 377–98.

Index

accountants 54
adjustment processes
  and expectations 11
  and order 12–13, 14
Admati, A.R. 72
agents 7
  and co-ordination 12
  and externalities 9
  forecasting by 7–8
Ahmed, S. 53
airports *see* British Airports
  Authority
Albon, R. 32
Ali, M. 53
Amersham International 25
Amihud, Y. 80
antitrust policy 21
arbitrage pricing theory 65
ARCH models 70, 71, 73
Argentina 122
Arrow, K.J. 133n
asset markets, volatility and higher
  moments 69–74
asset pricing 57–62, 74
  arbitrage pricing theory 65
  consumption risk 64–5, 66, 67
  and current dividends 76
  day of the week effect 59
  discount rate 74, 80
  and information 58, 59–60, 74,
    75–7
  mean reversion 61, 62
  and takeovers 79
  volatility 50
  see also financial markets; risk
AT & T 22, 27, 30, 32
Attanasio, O. 59, 66, 71
Auerbach, A.J. 57
Ausubel, L.M. 81
Averch, H. 38

Baillie, R.T. 73
bankruptcy 53, 54, 56
banks 52
  in command economies 56

and equity participation 52–3
  Islamic 53
  lending 52–4
  see also central bank; financial
    markets
Barclay, M.J. 72
BAT takeover 78
Baumol, W.J. 30, 134n
Beesley, M.E. 30, 31, 34
Begg, I.G. 134n
Belgium 129, 130
Bell companies 40
Beltratti, A. 59
Bertola, G. 107
Bhagat, S. 80
Bibolini, D. 67
BIS capital adequacy requirements 69
Bishop, M. 34
Blanchard, O. 56, 126
Blaug, M. 133n
blood market 148
Bobinski, C. 56
Bollerslev, T. 65, 66, 70, 71, 72, 73
Bradley, M. 78
Brazil 122
Breeden, D.T. 64
brewing industry 22
British Airports Authority 27, 28, 29
British Airways 25
British Gas 24, 25
  allocative inefficiency 35–6
  regulation of 33
British Leyland 25
British Rail 25, 26
British Steel 25, 26
British Telecom
  investment 40
  performance 34–5
  regulation of 33
  service quality 36
Britoil 25
bubbles 62, 108
building societies 52
Buiter, W.H. 108
Bulkley, G. 61

169